ASCENT

ASCENT

THE MOUNTAINEERING EXPERIENCE IN WORD AND IMAGE

Edited by Steve Roper and Allen Steck

Sierra Club Books   San Francisco

ASCENT

THE MOUNTAINEERING EXPERIENCE IN WORD AND IMAGE

ASCENT, *Volume IV*

The following previous editions of *Ascent* are available from Sierra Club Books:

Volume III (1980)
Volume II, No. 6 (1975–76)

The Sierra Club, founded in 1892 by John Muir, has devoted itself to the study and protection of the earth's scenic and ecological resources—mountains, wetlands, woodlands, wild shores and rivers, deserts and plains. The publishing program of the Sierra Club offers books to the public as a nonprofit educational service in the hope that they may enlarge the public's understanding of the Club's basic concerns. The point of view expressed in each book, however, does not necessarily represent that of the Club. The Sierra Club has some fifty chapters coast to coast, in Canada, Hawaii, and Alaska. For information about how you may participate in its programs to preserve wilderness and the quality of life, please address inquiries to Sierra Club, 530 Bush Street, San Francisco, CA 94108.

Jacket design: BONNIE SMETTS
Book design: JON GOODCHILD/TRIAD

Illustration Credits

Front jacket: Climber on the Central Tower of Paine, Patagonia. ALAN KEARNEY.
Back jacket: Los Cuernos del Paine from Lago Pehoe, Patagonia. OLAF SÖÖT.
Frontispiece: Lenticular clouds above the Kahiltna Glacier, near Mt. McKinley. OLAF SÖÖT.
Page v: Drawing by Vinessa Nevala.
Page vi: Atop the Père Éternel, reputed to be the smallest summit in the Alps. JOHN CLEARE.
Page viii: East from Mont Blanc. JOHN CLEARE.
Pages 79, 80, 82: Caricatures by J. L. Benoit courtesy of Yves Ballu, first published in the magazine *Montagnes*.
Page 136: Drawing by John Svenson.
Page 175: Grand Capucin, Chamonix. STEVE MILLER.

Library of Congress Cataloging in Publication Data
Main entry under title:
Ascent, the mountaineering experience in word and image.
    1. Mountaineering—Addresses, essays, lectures.
2. Mountaineering—Fiction. I. Roper, Steve.
II. Steck, Allen.
GV200.A83 1984   796.5'22   84–5379
ISBN 0–87156–826–8

Published simultaneously in Great Britain by Diadem Books Ltd.
ISBN 0–906371–66–x

Printed and bound in the United States of America by The Kingsport Press, an Arcata Graphics company. Color photo sections printed by Dai Nippon Printing Company, Ltd., Tokyo, Japan.
10 9 8 7 6 5 4 3 2 1

Contents

Introduction

SINCE ITS INCEPTION IN 1967, *Ascent* has undergone numerous changes. Originally conceived by Allen Steck to fill the gap left when the *Sierra Club Bulletin* became primarily a conservation magazine, the first issue reflected a California bias as well as financial naiveté—the 48-page magazine's price was set at a mere dollar. During the next few years the annual magazine became thicker, less provincial, and more realistically priced.

By the mid-1970s the editors—an unpaid and rotating collection of climbers who appreciated good writing and diverse graphics—decided that the project was not only time-consuming but in danger of stagnating. After *Ascent 1975/76* arrived (the double year in the title was a pretense, for 1975 was simply skipped), publication became even more erratic, and it was not until 1980 that a new volume appeared. This hiatus seemed worthwhile to the editors, however, for the finished project—expanded greatly from the original concept—was packed with articles, fiction, graphics, and color photographs: it was no longer a magazine but rather a 272-page softcover book dedicated to portraying "the mountaineering experience in word and image."

With the current volume—the first to appear in hardcover—*Ascent* has completed its metamorphosis from annual journal to full-fledged book. We hope it will be the first of a series of hardcover books that will incorporate the best available work on a four-year cycle. (And, to this end, we will begin actively soliciting new material in the spring of 1986; write us at that time—335 Vermont, Berkeley, CA 94707—for further information.)

As we began gathering material for this volume, we reflected on the ever-changing nature of mountaineering and how these changes affect the sport's literature. With the variety of options now available—expeditions to exotic ranges, alpine-style Himalayan dashes, free soloing, winter ascents—one might think that today's climbers so single-mindedly pursue the year-round possibilities of their sport that they have no time to read or write anything beyond factual, "for the record" climbing accounts. So many of these tedious accounts find their way into magazines and journals that we sometimes wonder if the literate mountaineer has been supplanted by an invasion of inarticulate superclimbers. While slightly credible, this narrow view of present-day climbers is an oversimplification, as evidenced by the excellent articles these same magazines and journals occasionally publish. The collection at hand—largely the product of young, active climbers—offers further proof that literate mountaineers are not in short supply.

Continuing our recent emphasis on fiction, this

Ascent contains several stories that portray facets of mountaineering never found in journal articles or expedition books. Our longest piece of fiction, Jeff Long's "Angels of Light," is partly based on a true incident: a plane carrying a load of marijuana crashed into a Sierra Nevada lake not too long ago, and climbers recovered some of the cargo. And a person connected with this event died in somewhat mysterious circumstances a short time later. Using these skeletal facts and his fertile imagination, Long weaves a story full of big-wall climbing and sinister intrigue. The present piece—which we feel stands on its own—is the first third of a novel that Long hopes to publish soon. Interested readers may write to the author in care of *Ascent*.

Another ambitious work of fiction is Geoff Childs's "Leviathan." Set in Kathmandu and the high Himalaya, the story describes the fate of an expedition led by a man obsessed with a forbidding and beautiful peak.

Joe Kelsey, a long-time *Ascent* contributor, checks in with a retelling of the Faust legend, confronting the age-old question: What price does one pay to tarry with an obsession?

Not all of our fiction deals with such weighty matters: first-time contributors Talbot Bielefeldt, David Gancher, and Charles Hood offer the reader short pieces that exhibit the dark and mordant humor beloved by mountaineers.

Chris Noble, another author new to *Ascent*, relates a chilling tale of a strange occurrence in the Far North: this incident belongs to the realm of mythology—or does it?

Readers who become sated with make-believe can turn to ten nonfiction articles. Three of our authors, David Grimes, Eric Sanford, and Paul Willis, describe the current scene on the most sought-after big mountain in North America, Mount McKinley—or Denali, as most climbers call it nowadays. The reader will quickly learn why one mountaineer calls the ascent of Denali "the greatest social climbing experience on earth." The color and black-and-white photos accompanying this Denali overview portray the mountain in its various aspects, from crowded camps to pristine cornices and mile-high buttresses.

Three essays deal with issues that concern and often provoke controversy among today's climbers. David Roberts discusses the implications of climbing "publicly," that is, starting out on a climb with the idea that a film, a book, or at least a lecture lies in the immediate future. Roberts questions whether this fairly recent development is good for mountaineering. Tom Higgins deals with a rather esoteric subject, but one that has the potential for changing rockclimbing: should a route be done using newfangled "tricks?" We hope his essay will stimulate campfire discussions and further articles. In a lighter vein, Joe Kelsey describes the multitudinous tribulations he encountered while working on his guidebook to the Wind River Mountains.

Two of our pieces explore new ground for *Ascent*. Rick Slone's "Mrs. Robertson Is Climbing Again" is not the story of a "hard man" or a hard climb. Norah Robertson has climbed neither the Eiger nor the Grandes Jorasses; indeed, her name is hardly known beyond the mountaineering community in Scotland. But we think the reader will agree that Norah's accomplishments are in a class by themselves. Ron Matous, in his colorful account of a Karakoram expedition, also eschews technical climbing for the most part, concentrating instead on the matchless and unpredictable experience of trekking in remote Baltistan.

The Black Canyon of the Gunnison River, in Colorado, is one of the finest places in the country to practice pure rockclimbing, yet it remains relatively unknown. Ed Webster, veteran of many trips to this narrow slash in the earth, relates the history of the gorge and vividly describes a few of his own climbs.

Mountaineers who lust after the famous Patagonian towers might think twice after reading Bobby Knight's article about the Central Tower of Paine. Screaming winds, nightmarish bivouacs, and restless days in camp highlight this account of a six-week epic. Olaf Sööt's black-and-white photo essay, portraying the varied aspects of the Patagonian landscape, also evokes the mystery and loneliness of this distant land.

We are especially pleased with the work of our other artists and photographers—Jamichael Henterly, Hank Levine, Margaret Berrier-Petranoff, and Debra Smith—whose drawings and photos appear throughout the book.

THE EDITORS

It is impossible of course to provide an entirely satisfactory explanation for any recreation. The predominant motive in any human activity varies according to the temperament of the individual. Mountaineering provides good exercise in pleasant surroundings, a sense of satisfaction in overcoming difficulties, the joy, akin to dancing, of controlled rhythmic movement, a stimulating contact with danger, a wealth of beautiful scenery and a release from the tiresome restrictions of modern life. The expert likes to practise or display his skill. Some confess to having been drawn to climbing by a physical inferiority complex engendered by their failure at school to hit a ball straight and far. These motives are probably sufficient in themselves, and they certainly form the basis of many other sports. But in the deep devotion to any form of active endeavour there is generally something else we seek. In the case of mountaineering it is a kind of personal identification with the hills themselves, which comes of intimate understanding and strenuous contest and which brings with it a wealth of philosophical content. Above all, in my view, the attraction lies in the memory of those rare moments of intellectual ecstasy which occur perhaps on a mountain summit, perhaps on a glacier at dawn or in a lonely moonlit bivouac, and which appear to be the result of a happy coincidence in the rhythm of mind and scene.

Eric Shipton
From *Upon That Mountain*

Joe Kelsey

ILLUSTRATIONS BY DEBRA SMITH

The Man Who Climbed Too Well

FAUST ATTACKED THE BOULDER AGAIN. He had already failed several times but told himself that if he was ever to do the climbs he wanted to, he must master this problem. So he kept trying.

He stepped onto the first footholds, stretched for high handholds, raised his right foot to a knee-level nubbin, began to mantel . . . and again fell, landing on his back.

"Goddamned rock!" He knew better than to climb in anger, but nothing else had worked. As he began to mantel yet again, a voice behind him said, "If you reach your left hand a little higher, you'll find a good hold."

Faust had heard no one approaching but could not look down since he was about to fall. In desperation he lunged up the face, grabbing blindly, and found the hold, a sharp little flake. Leaning out against it, he easily completed the move and reached the top of the boulder.

Faust caught his breath and turned to see who had advised him. It was a scrawny, scraggly haired, black-bearded fellow Faust had seen in the company of many of the outstanding climbers—though Faust had never seen him actually climb. No one knew much about this shadowy character, not even his real name. The climbers knew him as Mephisto, ap-

parently a nickname inspired by the cynical gleam in his dark eyes.

After Faust descended the back side of the boulder, wondering why a companion of renowned alpinists was visiting an obscure practice rock, Mephisto asked how long he had been climbing. "About a year. Only on weekends. I'm in school." Faust felt awkward explaining himself to a man who knew the world's best climbers.

Mephisto pointed out other difficult boulder problems, and with his advice Faust made several moves he had never dared try.

Mephisto suggested they climb together some time. Faust was so pleased to have impressed one of the elite that he agreed quickly. He had been throwing himself at the boulders for months, hoping for such an opportunity.

Faust asked what type of climbing shoes to wear, but Mephisto told him it made no difference. "No pair of shoes has ever been the determinant. The secret is not shoes but attitude. It is commitment: not looking back, not considering the consequences of falling. You must decide you won't fall. More climbers have fallen from lack of confidence than from improper footwear. You must believe you should be on *that* rock at *that* moment. If you ever doubt, if you ever ask, 'What the hell am I doing here?'—then you are in trouble."

I

Faust was eager to tell Gretchen of his lucky meeting. She was silent, though, when he said Mephisto had invited him to climb, and conversation was awkward during the evening. In the weeks afterward they drifted apart, and soon they stopped seeing one another, though they had been together for years. Faust did not care; his mind was on climbing and on getting into shape for harder routes.

Faust usually climbed with his friend Tom. Tom was an easy-going fellow who rarely bouldered during the week, but he and Faust climbed at the same level and complemented each other, one providing drive and the other a good-natured perspective. Tom, little caring whether a route was easy or difficult, always enjoyed the climb.

Faust, eager to show Tom his new ability and to lead his first 5.9, persuaded Tom to try Embryonic Journey the following weekend.

Faust climbed to a small ledge below a leaning crack, overhanging and obviously the crux. Placing a nut carefully, he tried the first move once, lost his nerve, and retreated. He jerked on the nut to be sure he trusted it, then inserted another above it. As he hesitated, the words of Mephisto came to him. Commitment. Don't look back. Don't doubt yourself.

Faust jammed his fingers into the crack, moved his feet up, then his fingers, and did not stop until he reached the top of the crack. He had done it! He had needed only to think positively and commit himself. He felt better about climbing, and himself, than ever before.

Tom's turn came; he tried the first move in the crack but said he couldn't do it, that he needed tension. Faust told him to try again. "If I can't do it this time," Tom shouted, "I'll need pull from the rope." He stepped into the crack once more but again could not move higher. "Tension!" he cried. Faust pulled the rope. "More tension," Tom yelled. "Pull harder!"

As Faust leaned back on the rope to help his friend, a tight smile crossed his face. Tom had failed, but Faust had found the secret of climbing: ignore the thought of failure. He did not climb with Tom again.

The climbers drank their beer in Auerbach's Cellar. Mephisto was there that evening and came over to ask Faust about his day's climbing. Faust told him, and he was impressed. "As I always say," Mephisto said, "if you commit yourself and control your emotions, you can climb anything. You are assured of success."

"But I don't want to be assured of success," Faust answered. "I want adventure. I want to feel emotion, whether it be hope, fear, joy, hurt, or surprise. By finishing school I could be a success: a secure job, a loving wife, a comfortable home. But that's not what I want."

"Well said!" Mephisto was pleased. "Then you must commit more than just your body to the rock. You must commit your soul to the idea of climbing. You must make the mountains your home, become an outsider in civilization. But then you risk more than breaking your body; you risk losing your soul. If once you look back to see what might have been and regret the life you've chosen, you are doomed."

Faust understood. "It is what I want. I will do it." He decided to leave school to have more time to climb.

Mephisto introduced Faust to Valentine, one of an elite few who climbed the most difficult routes. This superclimber was eager to tell Mephisto about his accomplishments for the day: "Three pitches of 5.10 and two of 5.11."

"Well done," said Mephisto. "Sounds like you're really into climbing this year."

Valentine had paid no attention to Faust until he happened to see his new acquaintance on Embryonic Journey; then he asked Faust to climb the next day.

"How about Sympathy for the Devil?" Faust asked. "I've heard it's one of the best climbs."

"One of the best?" Valentine sounded perplexed. "It's only 5.9. I'd like to do Not for Everyone. Two 5.10 pitches."

The next morning Valentine, belayed by Faust, led the difficult first pitch of Not for Everyone. Faust realized that this was a special opportunity to climb at a higher level; he concentrated on the rock and climbed well.

He reached the belay ledge expecting to be congratulated, but Valentine merely handed him the hardware and said, "Your lead, man." Faust slowly reracked the nuts he had collected and looked up uncertainly, wondering if he was prepared to lead such an intimidating pitch. He had expected Valentine to lead, but now he could not refuse his turn. "How is this pitch?" he asked.

"Not as bad as it looks," was the reply.

Having no choice, Faust began the pitch. It *was* as bad as it looked, but Faust—despite occasional quivering and a few nervous requests to "Watch me!"—was equal to the difficulties and soon reached a large ledge near the top.

When Valentine reached the ledge, there were no comments such as "nice lead." He just scrambled to the top, untied, coiled the rope, and started down the trail.

When Faust saw Valentine the next weekend, the veteran barely acknowledged him. Faust wondered if he had not climbed well enough, for Valentine had another climbing partner and did not need Faust.

Mephisto took Faust to meet another important climber. This was Wagner, perhaps the best-known climber in the country because of the writing he did. Every issue of every climbing journal carried an article by Wagner. He reported scores of first ascents and also discussed techniques, ethics, and aesthetics.

Faust wanted to try Möbius Strip, but Wagner asked what the point would be. "It's been done too often for another ascent to matter."

Instead, they went to try a new route. Wagner proved to be a good partner, competent and ambitious. His only faults were a tendency for his mind to wander while belaying and the inscrutability, to Faust, of his motivation. Wagner led the first pitch showing no emotion: no complaining, but no elation either.

When Faust's turn came to lead, he was not sure where to start, and he wondered whether he would be able to place adequate protection on the steep face. He made one move at a time where it seemed easiest, placing a nut at every opportunity. Eventually, he reached a stance where the holds became smaller. He could see no crack suitable for a nut in the next section; he gave up the idea of protection and studied the next moves.

Had Faust known, from a guidebook rating, that the next move was within his ability, that after one thin step he could reach a useful handhold, he would not have hesitated. But he had to decide which way was easiest, whether he was capable of the moves, and whether he could place protection soon enough. He would have to commit himself to his own decision, not to a written description. His last protection was far below; a mistake would mean a long fall.

Faust could have considered climbing down and giving up the route, but he did not. He banished all thoughts of falling, took a deliberate breath, and delicately stepped up. Standing on small holds, he could not afford the luxury of admiring his situation or indulging in emotions. Concentrating on maintaining his balance, he stretched slowly upward, found a hold, and stepped up to better holds. He finally relaxed as he placed an overdue nut.

The pitch had proved to be excellent. Faust had been skeptical of first ascents—exercises in egotism, he had thought—but as he belayed, he realized the pleasure of such pure adventure.

A photograph of Faust leading the crux pitch appeared in the next issue of *Ascent*. Wagner wrote that the route was as aesthetic as could be, that their ethics were of the highest, and that the climb was a meaningful experience. He named the route Wrath of God. Faust read the article and, while he could not disagree with anything that Wagner had written, found the words a hollow, sterile facsimile of his own experience.

Faust spent the next year climbing, working only enough to survive. He did progressively more difficult routes, including longer climbs in the mountains, and made several first ascents. He even followed Valentine on a route rated 5.12.

One Saturday evening, when Faust walked into the Cellar, he was surprised to see Gretchen at a table with a group of weekend climbers. They were in good spirits, glad to be out of their academic prisons and free for two days, and proud of their accomplishments that day.

Gretchen introduced Faust to her friends, and he hesitantly pulled up a chair, uneasy because his presence took the edge off the others' spirits. Perhaps the superior climbing he did put their own modest achievements in a different perspective, but more likely it was the serious look in his eyes and his inability to laugh that placed their frivolity in a different context.

Faust nevertheless tried to participate; seeing Gretchen reminded him of what he had given up to climb. He tried to tell her what he had been doing since he had last seen her but found it difficult to explain. Gretchen seemed more interested in the 5.6 routes discussed by her tablemates. As Faust drank more beer, he became more frustrated. Finally he could not restrain himself and asked Gretchen, "Would you like to make love to someone who has climbed a 5.12 off-width?"

"Not particularly," was her answer.

Faust had a prolific climbing career during the ensuing years. Of the many superb routes he ascended, the most noteworthy was the first ascent of the Walpurgisnacht Wall. Several attempts had been made on the 2,500-foot face, but some teams were turned back by technical difficulties, others by weather or stonefall.

During the winter before this climb, Faust discussed the route with Wagner and Valentine. Wagner was excited at the prospect of climbing—and writing about—the most difficult route yet done, while Valentine talked of the terrific free climbing they would encounter. They disagreed about aid slings. Wagner felt that not having such slings would jeopardize their chances of success. Valentine, not wishing to be tempted into using them, argued against them as extra weight. Faust did not care.

The three climbers made an unusual discovery on the approach to the wall: a bottomless bergschrund. They knew that crevasses in the midst of large glaciers often appear infinitely deep, but bergschrunds, where the glacier has pulled away from a rock wall, are invariably shallow.

The first day of climbing went smoothly, though Valentine led a very difficult crack and a lightning storm enlivened the afternoon. They bivouacked on a small ledge. Wagner and Valentine talked into the night, rating the pitches and speculating about the remaining 1,000 feet. Faust stared at the stars. He was where he wanted to be and savored each moment, content not to know what lay ahead. Faust was the first to be ready in the morning.

Several pitches, free but difficult, took the climbers to a large ledge below an ominous crack. It was Faust's turn to lead.

As he wedged his left arm and leg into the crack and began inching upward, stones falling from above crashed onto the belay ledge. Faust was aware of the need for haste but could climb no faster. The crack was smooth, and protection was difficult to place.

Valentine, who had insisted on free climbing, was persuaded otherwise by a large rock that barely missed him. "Hurry up!" he screamed. "Use aid if you have to. It doesn't matter. Let's get the hell out of here!"

"I'd nail it if I could," Faust shouted, "but it's too wide. We'd need a dozen five-inch bongs." He continued struggling up the crack.

Stones continued to fall. As Faust reached a ledge at the top of the crack, he heard Valentine wail, "I'm sorry we came on this damned wall." Suddenly an immense boulder, loosened by melting snow, came crashing down, hitting Valentine directly, severing his rope, and knocking him into space. The wall was steep; Faust and Wagner knew he had fallen to the base. They heard no sound of impact, though, nor could they see a body on the glacier. The only explanation for Valentine's disappearance occurred to Wagner. "He must have fallen into that 'schrund," he said, his voice trembling.

Faust led the remaining pitches. His concentration more acute than ever, he seemed oblivious to

stonefall, difficulty, lightning, and the recent tragedy. Since the final pitch—a low-angled slab—looked easy, he carried only a few nuts. But a violent hailstorm began to pelt the climbers and rock, and Faust, feet slipping, had to grip small holds while futilely trying to place protection. Feeling his fingers losing strength, he eventually had no choice but to forget about falling and move up quickly.

Clouds had piled up to the east when Faust stepped onto the narrow summit ridge. The sun, low in the west, cast his shadow onto the cloudbank—the Specter of the Brocken. He paused to contemplate this ghostly phenomenon and in that moment knew all the relief, pain, triumph, and sorrow a man can know. Then he screamed, "Off belay!" and anchored his rope to a solid block.

Only a few climbers were in the Cellar when Faust entered. He had been climbing now for twenty years. Earning enough money to support himself, he had found no work that had given him satisfaction. He had slept with many women but loved none. While loving the mountains as few have, he was beginning to wonder about the other, missing facets of his life.

The cocktail waitress was an old friend named Lilith. She had seldom climbed but had been around climbers as long as Faust could remember.

Lilith sensed Faust's depression and asked why. He confessed his doubts about the narrowness of his life and his worries about growing old.

"Then why don't you find something new?" she asked.

"This is the best life I can imagine," Faust answered. "I can't ask for more. And I am committed: I couldn't quit."

"Then you have sold your soul to the devil."

"What do you mean?"

"Who got you started climbing?"

"Well," Faust replied, "I climbed some before I met Mephisto, but it was he who convinced me to give my whole self to the mountains."

"Just as I guessed. You have sold your soul, just as I have."

"You have? For what? To whom?"

"Mephisto. I was working in a restaurant in the city and hating life. He took me climbing once. I didn't care about the climb, but I liked climbers. I didn't stay with Meph, but there have been many others since. I've been a waitress at every bar with a view of mountains in this country. I've waited for someone to finish every climb. Still, it's been a good life; I wouldn't change it."

"You speak of Mephisto as though he actually were the devil," Faust said.

"He's not?" Lilith asked. "What about his name?"

"It's a nickname." Suddenly Faust was not so sure. "Isn't it? His beard, those eyes: he *looks* like a devil."

"Didn't he make you a great climber?" Lilith was enjoying Faust's discomfort. "Better than you ever dreamed of being?"

"I became good by working hard," Faust protested, "by struggling and suffering. Mephisto only advised me. You say I've sold my soul," he continued. "Doesn't that involve a formal agreement with the terms specified?"

"With lawyers, perhaps. But Meph can be informal with climbers. Did he say nothing about a deal?"

Faust thought. "He said that to experience the ecstasy of climbing I'd have to commit myself, never considering alternatives, and know that climbing was what I should be doing. He also said that if I ever looked back or wished to be out of the mountains, I was doomed."

"Then those are your terms," Lilith said. "Look down, back, or anywhere else, and it's hell for you, baby."

"You don't believe in hell, do you?"

"I can't think about it. I've got to enjoy my life serving beer to climbers."

"Is that all you got for your soul?"

"It's enough. I look back at the past fifteen years fondly. I've been close to many fine people; I've liked the climbers I made love with. Selling my soul saved me from being a suburban housewife. But I can't look ahead. If I ever wonder where I'll be at sixty-five, I'm a goner."

Mephisto happened to be in the Cellar and joined Faust while Lilith waited on other drinkers. Faust asked, as directly as he dared, "Is it true I've sold my soul to climb?"

"As I told you," Mephisto answered evasively, "if you ever doubt you should climb, you are doomed."

"Does a person have to sell his soul to climb well?"

"No. Saints also make good climbers. Have you seen your old friend Tom lately?"

"No," Faust replied. "What's he been up to?"

"He's become a fine climber. I've seen him do 5.9 smoothly, with no hesitation. He did Deliverance last Sunday."

"Then why isn't he trying 5.10?" Faust wanted to know.

"Because he's content doing 5.9. Tom is a happy man. He loves his wife and kids. He enjoys his work—and climbing 5.9 competently. Not the fierce pleasure you've gotten from climbing beyond your limit, but he is content."

"How can I tell which climbers have bargained away their souls?" Faust asked.

write also. Anyone who substitutes photography for living in the present, who thinks ahead to his winter slide show, has sold his soul—sold it for very little. Yet some creative spirits use photography to live intensely in the present."

"The doomed get so little for their souls," said Faust. "Money, fame, a gratified ego. But I have gotten less."

"Nonsense," Mephisto snorted. "You have gotten the most; you've loved climbing. Compare yourself to Valentine and Wagner. Valentine got up difficult routes he didn't enjoy. Wagner has the regard of armchair mountaineers and little more. But you, Faust, have known joys few have known. You have looked out from many a ledge and known you were where you wanted to be, doing what you wanted to be doing. For you it has been worth it."

Faust thought before responding. "Perhaps, Meph, but I'm getting old. It's time to repent, to start in a new direction, to find meaning beyond climbing."

Mephisto laughed. "What makes you think it is possible? When you've known the ecstasy you have, life as an ordinary citizen is difficult. The ecstasy has set you apart. The gap between you and others will make their lives appear to you to be meaningless. You will see them enjoying Christmas, cheering for a football team, taking pride in a child's report card, and they will seem empty to you. No, Faust, for you it is too late—too late to repent."

"Maybe," Faust said, "but I want to try. I've decided."

"Then we should climb together first," Mephisto declared, grinning. "We never have, though we agreed to long ago. I have in mind a desert pinnacle in a canyon that was named the Gates of Hell by the U.S. Cavalry. They pursued an Indian shaman—a madman who proclaimed himself a messiah—into the canyon. He was not seen again."

"Has the pinnacle been climbed?" Faust asked.

"No ascent has been reported," was the reply.

Mephisto moved to another table, and Faust was rejoined by Lilith.

"What price do you suppose I will pay for repenting?" Faust asked her.

"Perhaps you've already paid," she replied, "by being oblivious to life and also to death—your own or another's."

"Not true," said Faust. "I've just never talked about Valentine's fall."

"But you climbed again as soon as your cut hands healed. The day after Robert Kennedy's assassination you led your hardest climb yet. You heard on your way to another climb that Kent State students had been shot by the National Guard, but once your hands touched rock, it didn't matter to you."

"Those with no regard for ethics," Mephisto began, "those who place success above the means to success—they have fallen from grace."

"Then the advocates of clean climbing are saints?"

"On the contrary. Climbers overly concerned with ethics are suspect. Every time you read 'We had a good time because we climbed clean,' not only do you know they didn't have a good time; you can recognize another lost soul.

"However," Mephisto continued, "the distinctions between the saved and the damned are so subtle that it's not easy to tell who's which. People who make money from climbing are often damned—and the money's not that good. But some of the purest souls guide because they love to teach, or run shops to earn an honest dollar serving their friends. Most writers will roast in hell—so to speak—but saints

"That's the only way to climb," Faust protested. "If I didn't keep going at such times, I couldn't have done the climbing I've done."

"My point exactly," Lilith countered.

Faust and Lilith left the Cellar together. As they were leaving, Mephisto was talking to a young man Faust had seen bouldering. Faust had noticed his determination and recklessness, how he fell often but refused to give up. Mephisto was evidently arranging a climb for the fellow.

Faust wanted to say something, to tell the young climber what he was getting into. But what could he say? He didn't know whether to recommend a deal with the devil or not; he didn't know if his own deal had been worthwhile.

But he couldn't turn down Mephisto's offer of an adventure. So it was that Faust followed his old mentor along game trails past the entrance to the Gates of Hell and through large talus to the base of the pinnacle. The climb itself was a typical desert climb: sheer red sandstone, straight-in cracks, occasional loose blocks.

The climb was well within Faust's capabilities, it turned out. But the descent was not.

A single overhanging rappel took them to a notch, from which a gully led down behind the pinnacle. The notch was so desolate that Faust was painfully conscious of the irreversibility of pulling down the rappel rope.

The gully, choked with loose rocks, was steep enough that constant care was required. Sand covered all the holds. Water seeping from cracks made the rock slippery and nourished a variety of thorny plants. Often the two climbers started down one way only to be stopped by a steep step; they had to climb back up and seek an easier way. Their frequent slips sent stones tumbling down; the sound of bouncing rock continued indefinitely, as though the gully went on forever.

Faust became worried. He was hot and thirsty, but the trickling water tasted too foul to drink. The gully twisted, and the walls overhung in such a manner that he could not see his position relative to the canyon floor; but he imagined he and Mephisto had already descended more than the vertical distance they had earlier climbed. But the gully continued, and still they encountered short cliffs, loose stones, and prickly vegetation.

At one drop-off Faust leaned out, spewing sand into the abyss, and peered down. Through a bluish haze of the kind that tints distant views of endless mountains, he could see, in the depths below, jagged arêtes lit by fiery shades of crimson and magenta, as if burned with alpenglow.

Finally he asked, only partly in jest, "Doesn't this gully ever end?"

Mephisto looked back at Faust with his usual enigmatic smile and answered, "No, it doesn't."

Ron Matous

Masherbrum, and Back Again

JUNE 30, 7:00 P.M. We have entered the eighth hour of what we are told is a twenty-hour drive. Dusk gives the landscape a mystical quality and my reflections a wistful note. So does the hashish that Renny Jackson and I, sharing the back seat of this careening van, smoke almost continuously in an effort to either sleep through the marathon journey or make it so entertaining that sleep is irrelevant. Up front, Chas and Anne Macquarie have already fallen asleep with their legs stretched across Eric Reynolds, who hasn't woken up to notice. Rick Wyatt turns around to join us in our decadence. Five hundred miles of twisting, rutted road, with its dizzying drops into the churning Indus River, go much more quickly when one can't remember more than two minutes of it at a time.

Our driver asks us to pass him the pipe, but we refuse. "You have to drive," we say. "Eat your Dexedrine and get us to Rawalpindi." Captain Zia Niazi of the Pakistani army translates for us and hands over another of the heart-shaped pills. It is he who will have to endure the driver's drug-driven jabbering all night long; none of the rest of us can understand a word he's saying.

A monstrous avalanche sweeps down the north flank of Masherbrum. RON MATOUS.

We lurch around corner after hairpin corner, skidding slightly on the slide debris that seems to constitute most of the road surface. My head slams against the window as we detour around a gap in the pavement that frames a segment of the river, a thousand feet below. The hash keeps bouncing out of the pipe, and a draft blows out the matches. Conditions are difficult.

The road drops more steeply for a bit, so we go faster. In this overloaded and underpowered Toyota minibus, the driver has to take what opportunities he can to practice for the upcoming Le Mans. Dear Allah, don't kill us now. I'd thought my relief at getting out of the Karakoram alive was justified, but that danger pales beside this ride.

Only as it gets dark can my thoughts unrivet themselves from the road and turn back to the expedition just ending. It is pleasant to think of it now as a whole that, despite the notable lack of mountaineering success, is comprised of some of the finest experiences of my life, all drawing to a conclusion, all unique, all my own.

I arrived in Pakistan quite alone; the other six members of the expedition had all missed a connection somewhere. With 180 pounds of gear I stood, perplexed, in the middle of what looked to me like a huge, restless pajama party until one of the loosely

9

clad figures carried my bags to a little black taxi and threw them in. I gave the driver the name of a hotel I vaguely remembered Chas mentioning as a place we might stay. The only word the driver understood was "hotel," and so ensued a frantic ride around the tourist district of Rawalpindi as he took me to the most expensive hotels in turn. Each time, I emphasized that I wanted *Mrs. Davies's* hotel; each time, he understood only that this was not the hotel I wanted. After finally finding Mrs. Davies's, we parted in mutual disgust, he demanding a tip and I giving advice about learning his way about town.

This relic of the Empire had been recommended as a climber's sort of place: cheap, run-down, not quite in the district, but possessing a tremendous charm and friendly personnel (most of whom had been there since the British left in 1947). By the next day, when the newly arrived expedition members were getting their first taste of the ovenlike air of Rawalpindi, I was feeling like an old-timer, only too glad to show them around the hotel and as proud as if I had built it. After breakfast, when it was already too hot to venture outdoors in direct sunlight, we spent our time alternately soaking in a cold bath and lying half naked under the ceiling fans, keeping simultaneously cool and free of mosquitoes.

Those ten days we spent in Pindi brought our foreignness home to us, as we struggled to cope with various bureaucracies and supply ourselves for the approach march. The search for plastic bags for wrapping our porters' loads gave us fits, and we ended by essentially making our own. A canvas wall tent was purchased in one shop, but we had to go to another to have wooden poles cut to length. Some of the packaged food we bought turned out to be five years old. Most of the grains were half gravel. But we muddled on, and each day a small expedition of two or three of us would go out in search of another item to cross off our list of essentials.

We were able to shop like this, one item at a time, because we were unable to leave Pindi: eddies had occurred in the torrent of paperwork that would allow us to proceed legally toward the summit of Masherbrum, and so, mired in phone calls, triplicate forms, and trips to the Ministry of Tourism, we waited.

The minister himself, Mr. Naseerullah Awan, had been described to us by his underlings as a "very big boss." He was, indeed, both portly and autocratic, and deference was the required style in his presence. He assured his American friends that the problems we had encountered in getting approval for Scott Hobson, our doctor, to accompany us, were being resolved by him with all due haste (here I noted the ancient, cobwebbed tomes in their wooden bins that constituted the filing system), but that we must understand the limits as well as the ex-

tent of his domain: there were other, bigger bosses before whom he must bow and scrape with our petition, so we should prepare ourselves for a possible stay of "no more than" two or three weeks in Rawalpindi, *insh'Allah.* If it is the will of Allah. We would have groaned had it not been indecorous; as it was, our frustration showed in a brief change of countenance.

Two days later, having demonstrated both his power and his mercy, Mr. Awan gave us final permission to get on with it, and our liaison officer arrived at last. He had been on secret maneuvers along the Afghani frontier, and his absence had been the second major tether on our departure. Our gear had already been shipped to Skardu by road (this very one down which we are bouncing home; I hadn't realized what an epic journey our equipment had made while we flew, so simply, so comfortably). Our last bureaucratic stumbling block was Pakistan International Airlines, our transport to Skardu. They, we were told, were booked solid for the next six weeks. Translation: you can go tomorrow if you keep bugging us.

JULY 1, 8:00 A.M. It's hard to remember, from the smoky confines of this van, how exciting that flight was. For all of us but Scott, it was our first view of the Himalaya. Trying to equate that one-hour flight with this two-day carnival ride is a real synapse-stretcher; yet we flew almost exactly along this route, minus the meanders. Nanga Parbat, invisible due to our location at the bottom of the Indus Gorge, served as a pylon to the plane: we banked around it at the level of its navel. Looking down, I would have been surprised to learn that those scrubby foothills enclosed a gorge more than 5,000 feet deep, and even more surprised to learn that a road—the fabled Karakoram Highway—managed to thread it for 500 miles.

Yesterday we passed several monuments commemorating those persons killed or injured during the construction of this marvel. Nor has the toll ended: merely keeping the road open through the constant assault of landslides and flash floods is an affair of bulldozers and dynamite. Army maintenance crews are stationed about every twenty miles to remove the debris.

This morning, after a brief hour's sleep, I awoke to the first sepulchral light of day and noticed the road was wet. We had driven through an early monsoon storm; only total exhaustion allowed me to sleep through its fury. Our driver, still speeding, is looking more at the Captain than at the road as he chatters on. Around one sharp curve, the brakes slam on. We stop. A pile of rocks occupies both lanes.

The sudden deceleration wakes everyone; I hear

Framed by ethereal clouds, the Trango Tower soars toward the heavens. ALLEN STECK.

Anne and Renny cursing. They are trying to catch a plane to the States tomorrow morning, to meet a deadline to start work. We have several hundred miles to go, and thirty miles per hour might be our average speed. There seems to be only one solution: we jump out of the van and start moving stones with shovels, hands, and ice axes. In forty-five minutes we have a narrow swath cleared on the outer edge of the road, close by the cliff overlooking the Indus. None of us dare get in the van while the driver roars through, tilting precariously on the uneven surface, almost flipping into the abyss. Then we pile back in, round the next curve, and stop in front of the next rockpile.

Did we really expect that a road that traverses the barren, steep sides of a mile-deep cleft for its entire length would have only one gully to disgorge earth and rocks onto its surface after a storm? From here we can see a dozen rockslides further down the road. Not wanting that much exercise, we decide to wait for the army crew to clear it. While we are waiting, my thoughts, perhaps triggered by the sight of the rockslides, turn to memories of the first days of the expedition.

Our approach march began in Skardu, after the flight through the Indus Gorge. I suppose we could

be considered far more fortunate than the Duke of Abruzzi, who, in 1909, traveled overland from Bombay to reach the Baltoro Glacier. Some romantics might denigrate our shortened approach, but I, at least, considered our own journey quite arduous and interesting enough.

The emerald oasis of Skardu has a spectacular setting: 10,000 feet of relief above a flood plain as gray and flat as the slate for a billiard table. Here the Shigar and Shyok rivers, braiding through a valley five miles wide, come together to form the Indus. The town sits behind a monadnock of rock that rises incongruously 500 feet in the middle of this plain.

The former jeep track through the business district has recently been paved; flanking it is a myriad of three-sided shops, like miniature garages, each of them selling the same few items. The few two-story buildings have balconies that threaten the street. No women are seen anywhere. Here, after the lassitude of tropical Rawalpindi, one starts to feel the mountains tugging at one's sleeve.

Word travels fast in Baltistan; on our second day there, we were swamped with people looking for work as porters. We told them all to be present at noon on Saturday, when we would hold court and formally hire perhaps forty of them.

Almost two hundred showed up for that session. Chas, as expedition leader; Scott, as examining doctor; and the Captain formed a tribunal outside our cell block of a hotel, on chairs borrowed from the restaurant. The police were there, with swagger sticks for beating the mob into orderly lines, and the local minister of tourism stood by to make sure that we were fair in our hiring practices. The Captain ran the show, and for the first time we began to think of him as a useful ally rather than a bureaucratic encumbrance.

Fascinated by the exotic appearance of the crowd, we watched the porters' frantic scramble to be noticed and selected. The job was obviously very desirable: we were paying five dollars a day, plus food—a royal wage indeed. Baltis who had worked with previous expeditions waved their conduct books, pointing to recommendations written by expedition leaders. The brown, lined faces of the porters strained with the desire to work; I was suddenly sorry we could not hire them all. As it was, many of these faces were to become good friends, wonderful people to work with.

When we were done, I avoided the gaze of the disappointed, ashamed that we had the cultural advantages to hire any of them at all. Some of the Baltis had walked a hundred miles to Skardu, looking for work. By the time the expedition season came into full swing, almost anyone who could stand would be hired, but for now we were one of the first employers, able to choose the best of the lot. The Captain gathered the elect around him and made a short speech in Balti about their duty to the expedition, the moral virtues of hard work, and so on. He then instructed them to meet us in Dasso early Monday morning, ready to go.

Dasso is a village at the end of a fifty-mile jeep road from Skardu. Since none of the porters owned a jeep, it was safe to assume they would be walking there, and so they did, in the day and a half available. Meanwhile, we finished purchasing supplies, packing our gear, and hiring vehicles. We left Skardu at dawn on Monday, feeling like Rommel's troops as we stood in the back of two overloaded Willys, heading up the Shigar Valley. Back then, at the beginning of our trip, the hardships of a five-hour beating over ruts and potholes with the wind blowing dust in our hair, eyes, and mouth seemed romantic. Verdant wheat fields lined with shade trees, waving villagers, and squealing children—all evoked our love. Everything was new and fascinating, and the fresh colors of the mountain spring enhanced the image of an Eden newly created.

Between the villages nothing grew; bare rock

and sand spoke of an extreme climate and of the people's dependence on irrigation. Along the way we passed a tractor, moving at a crawl, which was carrying most of our baggage. Ten miles short of Dasso, we came to a fresh ravine that split the road, leaving tire tracks dangling in midair. We braked just in time and slowly realized that today this was the end of the road.

JULY 1, 12:00 NOON. Roads in the Karakoram are fragile things. Rivers swell and wash them out; landslides take them away. Heavy rains cover them with mud and rocks. Maintenance is a constant battle against rapid geological change, and yet every year the roads push on deeper into the mountains, like the roots of a desert weed desperate for water. We were told that a road is planned beyond Dasso, up the Braldu Gorge to Askole. With luck it will be passable one month in twelve.

The army has arrived, and we are all out of the van, like kids at a construction site, watching the big machines at work. Traffic has piled up behind us. A carnival atmosphere prevails: radios blare as people stroll by in groups. Down the road we see a sudden burst of dust before we hear the explosion—a particularly large boulder has been blasted out of the way.

Anne and Renny are concerned about the delay, but not too much so. The work of clearing proceeds rapidly, and we seem to have plenty of time left to make their flight, though it means another sleepless night on the road.

Unfortunately, the road to Dasso was not a military priority, and so no one came to clear it for us. Instead, we sent one of the porters who had finagled a ride with us on to Dasso, at a run, to have the rest of our crew come back and meet us. We were now looking at an extra day's approach march, which had us worried, since both money and food for the approach were calculated carefully. I wondered at the intelligence of porters who would cross this break in the road and still expect us to drive to Dasso; I later discovered that this particular landslide had occurred only hours before.

One might expect a group of employees who had just walked fifty miles to be surly, if not downright hostile, when told they had walked ten miles too far. But less than four hours after our runner departed, a train of men started arriving; their good humor and effusive greetings removed all the gloom from this setback. We were old friends already, and I looked forward to starting in the morning with more than my usual enthusiasm for long walks through sand and rock.

That evening, camped by the silt-laden river and

cooking a dinner of mud and rice, we heard a rumbling, slithering sound and excited voices down the road. Running to look, we saw that a dry little gully had become a torrent of water, mud, and boulders knifing through the road. No storms had marred this torrid afternoon; only a collapsing snow-melt pond far above could have released so much water. I began to sense that the mountains here were younger and more violent than those in the sedate regions we came from.

In the algid light of dawn, shaded by a glaciated range of nameless mountains that would have had no equal at home, we gave each of our eager porters a fifty-five-pound load. With cracked leather thongs or old remnants of rope from other expeditions, they lashed their loads firmly and fashioned makeshift shoulder straps to carry them. We were finally under way.

The first few miles were just a track in the snow-colored sand, and, as the sun rose, its reflection began to scorch us. Renny, Scott, and I dropped farther and farther behind as we stopped frequently to rest in patches of shade; it seemed likely the temperature was already reaching a hundred. But our excitement kept us moving, with the feeling that we were walking away from everything that was known and comfortable, toward what was reputed

to be the most spectacular mountain range on earth, visible only to those who would spend a difficult week getting there.

The following days were a marvelous procession of novelty and awe-inspiring scenery. We passed into the Braldu Gorge and threaded its granitic narrows from village to primitive village, each one separated from the next by miles of naked, rocky gorge, each one utterly dependent on the irrigation ditches full of muddy water for its emerald existence. I had read a lot about expeditions into this area in an attempt to build up a thin shell of familiarity against the onslaught of new impressions I was expecting. But they had been wasted hours; I was overwhelmed.

It was not just the scenery that was unique. With our porters we formed a self-sufficient, mobile community, hardly smaller than the ones through which we passed. Hiking from six in the morning until noon, we avoided the worst heat of the day. The afternoons provided a time for relaxing under our tarp, reading, or joining the Baltis in their endless celebrating. We came to love the porters for their

This group of magnificent Karakoram peaks is dominated by Paiyu, at left, and Uli Biaho Tower, right.
ALLEN STECK.

penetrating happiness, so easily shared. At every opportunity they would gather in a large circle, and whoever felt moved would be up singing or dancing or acting out a tale, while the rest would sing along and clap in time. They seemed especially to love Ali's dirty jokes, Gulam Rasul's impersonations, and our own comic attempts to imitate the Balti style of dance. If there had been arguments or difficult stretches of trail earlier that day, they were now forgotten.

The villages through which we passed, terraced oases in the midst of some of the most barren mountains on the planet, took us out of the twentieth century entirely. I was reminded of Anasazi ruins I had found in the backcountry of Utah—one- or two-story houses with dirt floors and roofs of wooden beams. From these windowless dwellings, smoke seeped out through the roof. Dark, hollow eyes would stare at us from the shadows; the women would cover their faces, run, and hide. Their giggling children were bolder, approaching us tentatively in the safety of little groups. I was surprised at the lack of evidence of earlier expeditions; for these people, we were still an utterly foreign sight.

And the mountains themselves, as we went on, enclosed us. Each day the trail would wind and climb around spurs that ended in cliffs above the river, so that although we followed a single valley one had the impression of having crossed innumerable watersheds. As we approached Askole, the last and highest village—seemingly the last habitation on earth—our sense of distance from the phantasm "civilization" approached infinity. When we thought about home, which was rarely, it was something of a joke, for the direction it lay in was down, through 8,000 miles of rock.

But Askole was only a halfway point for us; beyond it, in the ever harsher climate that effectively prevented agriculture and habitation, stretched valleys that contained the longest glaciers outside the polar latitudes, hidden somewhere behind the twists and turns of the Braldu Gorge. Our goal was still thirty miles distant.

In the first few miles of our fifth day of walking, just after Askole, the gorge widened, and along its bottom the river meandered through a flat gravel bed. We were approaching the toe of the Baltoro Glacier, the lower end of a vast conveyor belt that crushed mountains at one end and deposited them as sifted heaps of stones fifty miles distant. We had a foretaste of the tedium to come as we crossed the snout of the Biafo Glacier, an equally large system flowing down a broad valley from the north. One hardly would have guessed it to be composed of ice; instead, we crossed a mile of loose rock formed like the peaks of a meringue, with sand, pebbles, and blocks of all sizes shifting underfoot. On the far side

we descended a steep hill of scree and rested in a level, pleasant grove of scrubby trees watered by the network of streams flowing out from beneath the bulk of the glacier looming above us. Other than scattered thorn bushes, this was the only vegetation we had seen since Askole, and it was starkly beautiful against this mountainous desert.

That night we camped on a sandy bench just above the river, and the wind blew gustily, filling clothes, packs, and the dinner pot with grit. With binoculars we watched a herd of markhor on the bluffs across the river, realizing that if these wild goats were not a new, miniature subspecies, our sense of scale was all wrong. Looking down the valley, I found I could not conceptualize at once all of the distance we had come—from Askole, from Dasso, from Skardu, from Pindi. I felt lost in this immensity, and when the stars came out in the silence that strangely included the river's roar, they seemed new, brighter.

Drawn by the increasing isolation, I struck out ahead in the morning, wanting a chance to absorb this great loneliness. Soon after leaving the porters behind (they had a habit of stopping frequently between breathless spurts, when they practically ran up the trail), I was puzzled to see a set of footprints going in our direction. Only one other expedition had preceded us this year, and all their porters had already come out; the prints could be from a mail runner, but he would be equipped with good footwear. A small stretch of mud revealed the prints in more detail: they were bear, not Balti.

Tremendously excited, I became obsessed with catching a glimpse of this rare creature in such a wild setting. The tracks looked fresh, they were going in my direction, and they followed the trail much of the time, since it was the least arduous route in this rugged country. I walked faster, but the bear seemed to know where we were going, and to be going there first. The country was so open that I had good hopes of seeing the animal in the distance; perhaps it was preceding me on the trail by only a quarter of a mile. So I walked faster yet, not even stopping to rest.

Topping an alluvial rise, I was instantly distracted from the elusive bear. Ahead, many miles distant, the space between the mountains was filled with frozen waves of glacier rubble—not calm, orderly swells, but a choppy, wind-racked sea that washed on either side against the granitic prows of suddenly familiar mountains. The triangular facets of the Lobsang Towers, the romanesque Trango Group, and, unrecognized until now, the more gothic Paiju formed a crenelated skyline. In the extreme distance the pyramidal tip of K2 showed for a moment before clouds enveloped it.

I savored for a while the achievement of one of

my goals: just to see, like the promised land, those fabulous mountains spread out before me. Only now could I allow myself to start thinking about climbing one of those peaks.

Our goal, Masherbrum, was still concealed in a bay around a distant corner. We would not see it until we were literally within avalanche range of its flanks, several days hence. Meanwhile, the exhilaration of the day led me to loosen my imaginative restraints; already, without having seen Masherbrum, I was nearing its summit, kicking steps very slowly in an icy wind on the west ridge. The dream that had been suppressed while we dealt with all the preliminary aspects of the expedition returned. Excitedly, I noted that it had a salience more of precognition than of wishful thinking; we were assured of success, *insh' Allah.*

JULY 2, 3:00 A.M. We all are in various stages of wakefulness and beginning to get the motorist's equivalent of bedsores. Anne and Renny have been fantasizing about the satisfaction of getting out of this van and onto the airplane; Eric is hatching a plan to join them. Chas, as leader, must be debriefed by Mr. Awan; Rick and I, in less of a hurry to leave the country than the others, elect to keep him com-

Baltis in the remote mountain villages of the high Karakoram greet expeditions with wary curiosity.
ERIC REYNOLDS.

pany. Scott has already flown to Rawalpindi, and we guess he must be home by now. All of us are cursing the luck that kept the planes from flying this past week; not only is it more expensive to go by road, it obviously takes far longer.

But a part of me has enjoyed this leg of the trip immensely (stop hogging the pipe, Renny). The thrill of traveling overland through this spectacular country, witnessing the subtly changing vegetation, architecture, clothing, diet, and physiognomies as we descend, is well worth the hassles. For me that comes as a confession, for I was not fond of the idea when it was first proposed in Skardu. But we have been fortunate: the weather has been cloudy and cool, and our vehicle has been more reliable than the road.

As these reflections are running through my mind, the driver pulls to the side of the road. We seem to be out of the mountains entirely now, on a moonlit agricultural plain. The Captain speaks to the driver in Urdu, then asks me to loan him my headlamp. We have a flat tire. The driver tells us it is three more hours to Rawalpindi; the plane leaves in six hours.

Holy shit! Rick and I had both looked up when we heard the familiar booming crack. The sickle-shaped ice cliff under which our route had to traverse had calved, at only eight in the morning, and with us still 200 feet below the bergschrund in which we had hoped to find protection. For a precious few seconds I stood and watched as the ice turned into a cloud that seemed to be growing out of all proportion; it did not seem to be channeled to the left, as we thought a potential avalanche would be. With a strange lack of fear I turned and ran. Out of the corner of my eye I watched the cloud accelerate to unbelievable speed. I never thought I could move so fast with a full pack at 18,000 feet!

I saw the avalanche envelop Rick just before it overcame me, and at that moment I gave up running and plunged my ice axe into the slope. Below was a crevasse into which I expected to be swept, if huge blocks of ice didn't eradicate me first. The cloud arrived with a fury of darkness, wind, and driven snow; I closed my eyes as my goggles and ears filled with powder. I could feel the rushing snow pressing against me, but as yet it was not forceful. Cringing, I awaited the arrival of more massive debris, certain it was coming as the darkness deepened. The only thought in my mind was to survive and then get the hell off Masherbrum. No more than a very long minute had gone by when I began to detect more light through the whipping snow. Soon I was overjoyed to see that the worst had passed. As the powder cleared, I could see Rick; he was also all right.

Anne, Chas, and Renny had just left the cache 500 feet below and were carrying loads up to join us when they saw the ice cliff collapse; they were able to run back to safety. Now all five of us ran out into the debris, each group convinced the other had been caught. I nearly fell in a crevasse while bounding down the slope. Our reunion at the cache was a joyous one.

The subtle convexities of our route and the 4:00 A.M. start had not provided the safety margin we thought they would. For thirty seconds a debate raged about whether or not to give up the route. Part of my mind was opposed to going down, but this part abstained from the voting. The others felt the same, apparently, and soon we filled our packs to the brim with the most important items from the cache and started down.

Gasherbrum IV, the striking 7,980-meter peak at the head of the Baltoro Glacier. ERIC REYNOLDS.

We had known the route would be perilous —the north side of Masherbrum is not approached lightly. But the photos we had seen had not shown quite so many ice cliffs, and we had needed firsthand convincing of the route's danger. With that assurance under our belts, we conceded gladly.

But one day's relief is the next day's disappointment, and from our camp on the Mundu Glacier we looked back at the peak in a different light, certain now that we would not be climbing it. We cheered on those avalanches that approached our route; extra vindication is always welcome. And we decided, then, as a salve for our discouragement, to go ahead with a plan we had tucked away for just such an occasion: if we could not climb Masherbrum, we would circumvent it. Masherbrum La, a pass just east of the peak, would bring us, with a few days' travel, to the village of Hushe, from which we could return to Skardu without retracing a step of our approach march.

JULY 2, 6:00 A.M. A hot, sticky dawn is growing across the sky. We are close now to Rawalpindi, and the bodies sprawled on the seats of the van are beginning to stir. I have managed an hour of semistupor, but the discomfort of being imprisoned too long in a bent position has prevented real sleep. It is much warmer down here on the subtropical plains.

We pull into a hut that serves as a gas station. Its owner sleeps outside on his string bed, coverless; the air itself provides a thick enough blanket. When we are not moving with the windows open, I feel like I'm in a greenhouse, and the damp air smells much the same.

Our driver wakes the owner; I see him shake his head. No gas here. We drive around, stopping five or six more times, but fail to find gas. The driver informs us that we do not have enough to get to Rawalpindi, twenty miles away. Disgusted, Anne surmises that we might have had enough if he hadn't driven in circles looking for more. We have spent half an hour in the search. It occurs to me that we are acting out one of Zeno's paradoxes: the closer we get to Rawalpindi, the less progress we make. I have to think of our adventures on the Baltoro for consolation.

Our "official" base camp, abode of the Captain and the faithful Mustaq, his cook, had been at Urdukas, a traditional camping place along the Baltoro route. Though the terrain was steep (flat spots being almost nonexistent in this country), the campsite sported the only grass and flowers for miles. It was to this charming spot that we returned after our failure on Masherbrum. Our real base camp had been five miles from Urdukas—two miles up the Baltoro and then three miles up the Mundu Glacier.

That five-mile section formed the most tedious hike any of us had ever known.

In the end each of us made at least three round trips, carrying heavy packs, over that awful terrain. Slipping, stumbling, moving in virtual circles around rubble-filled mounds of ice that for some nefarious reason thrust higher here than anywhere else on the glacier, we exercised our abusive vocabularies as much as our already weary bodies. We detected signs of our porters' trail in every slight leveling of the gravel, though knowing that no superficial track would survive each day's melting and shifting of the ice; these illusory trails led us a different way each time. Once, after a snow squall set in, we found ourselves plodding aimlessly down the glacier. Then it cleared slightly, and we realized that we had nearly passed Urdukas. Finally, though, having brought the last load down from our advanced base camp, we could prepare for the journey over Masherbrum La.

We decided to send most of our gear and all our remaining porters back down the Braldu Gorge, accompanied by the Captain, Mustaq, and Scott. The rest of us would retrace, one final time, the hated terrain back toward Masherbrum. If our pass should prove uncrossable due to bad weather or glacial evolution (its few previous crossings, involving rappels, had been made years earlier), we still might have to endure the never-ending sand and pebbles of the Braldu.

Our consolation prize may have been a gamble, but the attractions were great: we would see new country, arrive at a jeep road in five days instead of eight, and complete a wild and lengthy circuit of the peak that had sent us scurrying. We closed our eyes to the first well-known miles . . . or tried to.

"Every step I take on this glacier pisses me off." As my own faltering steps propelled me yet again onto my back, turtlelike, I was prodded into grudging laughter by Renny's well-timed comment. Gasherbrum IV, having flown out of my vision, returned to its proper place as I struggled onto my feet. I chided myself for silently agreeing with Renny; there was, after all, a certain fatuousness in the presumption behind the complaint. Who were we to curse the Baltoro for its untidy surface? The Karakoram's reputation as one of the more inaccessible mountain regions of the world had been one of our primary reasons for coming here. Firsthand, now, I was finding that inaccessibility to be more tedious than romantic.

We were unable, that afternoon, to cover the five miles we had hoped to. We searched for a campsite in the moat between the glacier and the cliffs, finally finding a patch of snow into which we were able to carve level platforms for our tents. Cooking on a large, flat rock as the sun went down, we watched the panorama from Paiju to Concordia go through its evening metamorphoses. Soon the primitive light of the stars was all that remained to delineate the looming silhouettes surrounding us.

No air traffic traversed these politically sensitive skies; the silence of the night was complete when we, like the nomadic mammals we were, ceased our bustling for the day and huddled on our rock in awe. The occasional report of tumbling boulders only enlarged that quietude.

In the morning we struggled onward to the mouth of the Yermanendu Glacier, flowing down from Masherbrum La, itself out of sight around a corner. Masherbrum, from this distance, seemed larger than it ever had from the foreshortened perspective of base camp. We searched the area for a campsite, still thinking we might take the opportunity to visit Concordia, twelve glacier miles away. If we had been forced to camp on the rubble, we might have, but instead we found what was probably the only level, grassy plot anywhere above Urdukas—a tiny vale squeezed between the lateral moraine and the vertical granite. It looked so restful, so inviting—we had been carrying loads across highways of rubble for a week—that we decided to remain there, lying in the sun, reading, and eating. Only Eric retained the strength and determination to spend these two "rest" days in a marathon effort to reach Concordia and return.

One afternoon we heard a tremendous splashing sound, like water buffalo at play, echoing off the overhanging cliff above. Investigating, we found, just fifty feet from our camp, a growing lake that, as it rose, was loosening boulders that slid into the water with a resounding crash. Its level was well above ours, and only the dike of the moraine kept us from being inundated in a most ridiculous fashion. We kept a nervous eye on the lake and were relieved when unknown factors halted its rise. By morning the constant splashing was replaced by an incessant noise like windows breaking as the draining lake left its lamina of ice behind.

One afternoon's rest had quite altered my feelings about walking. The next day I was determined to hike, without a pack, as a means of recreation while we awaited Eric's return. My goal was the spot, six miles distant, where Vittorio Sella had taken his famous photograph of the Mustagh Tower in 1909. I found the absence of sixty pounds from my back to be a wonderful restorative. After two miles the glacier became somewhat more level and

Rest stop en route to Masherbrum La; the Biarchedi Peaks rise in the background. RON MATOUS.

easier, leaving me free to enjoy my surroundings. Like an ant in an art gallery, I strolled, absurdly alone and unburdened, through the immensity of this canyon between some of the earth's highest peaks. I had no thoughts of the world I had left to get here; it seemed to have no relevance.

When, a few days later, we crested the 17,600-foot Masherbrum La and looked out at the corrugated jumble of ridges and gorges into which we would be descending, toward fruit trees, human habitation, and tropical desert heat, we were sorry to be leaving behind the desolation of the Baltoro. Its hardships had worked their magic on us, turning misery to fond memories. We didn't know if we would ever see it again.

More tribulations lay ahead, but first came the ecstasy of our descent, after a month's absence, into the world of trees and copious life. By most standards the Karakoram is a desert range, and its valleys are sparsely vegetated. But to us this new valley was an Eden whose lack of undergrowth made it only more gardenlike, its greens bright against the sun-scorched soil. Large, pink roses with yellow centers bloomed profusely, and we walked through their bowers like children in a park, sniffing. As we approached the village of Hushe, ripening terraces of wheat waved at us in greeting, and when we finally encountered a black-garbed man and his radiant little granddaughter, we knew we had left the inhospitable regions behind.

As we entered the district where many of our former employees lived, we met many of their parents, children, and families. The porters, for the most part, were now with other expeditions; we had even seen some of them coming up the Baltoro with another group. Mustaq, the cook, lived in Saling, twenty miles down from Hushe, and we had arranged to meet him and the Captain in a few days.

The villagers must have wondered about us, coming down from the mountains without porters, when they had not seen us go up. They marveled when we tried to explain that we had crossed from the Baltoro, whether at the feat itself or just at our clumsy sign language, I'm not sure. With pride they showed us their dark and soot-stained houses, all of them built by hand with a great deal of ingenuity. The villagers hospitably served us cup after cup of tea, and in due course most of us were sick again with the ubiquitous local forms of dysentery.

I let myself be guided around Hushe by a young boy, the son of the village headman and brother of one of our porters. He took me to the house of Gulam Rasul, one of our most enthusiastic singers and dancers, and introduced me to his father. Gulam Rasul's father had the same twinkle in his eye, the same button-nosed face as his son; the only difference was that his countenance was lined with the cumulative weight of decades of living in this valley. When the old man died, Gulam Rasul would inherit that wrinkled visage. It was a face that knew nothing of any other world; it was as unchanging as Masherbrum, standing at the head of the valley as a monument to immutability. I felt sorry, briefly, to be part of a society that knew nothing but change and was likely to bring its values here, infecting the villagers and beginning the transmutation of their ancient faces.

The father beamed when he heard his son had done a fine job; he grasped my arm and took me upstairs to show me Gulam Rasul's room. It was just that, a room, with not a single possession or stick of furniture in it; everything he owned was on his back. One picture graced the wall, a Polaroid of Gulam Rasul with another expedition. Neither the walls, nor the door, nor the windows were straight; I feared my weight might collapse the floor. It was like a house built by children, for children. The ceiling, incongruously, was made of embryonic Coca-Cola cans: flat sheets of tin, never cut or shaped, printed with the familiar trademark in repetitive rows. I wondered where he had found them: progress incarnate. The father smiled at me toothlessly.

I followed the boy to his own house. The first floor was given over to a few sheep, a small pig, and some chickens; the family lived above in rooms reached by a ladder. Only the boy's mother and grandmother were home. The old woman, blind, sat spinning wool on a small hand spindle, giving no sign that she knew I was there. The mother, crouching by a fire in the center of a dark, smoky room, offered tea and a bowl of ripe yogurt; I accepted the tea. The four of us sat quietly, unable to communicate. In one corner of the room were some shelves with two copper pots on them. In another was a pile of rags that may have been a bed. When I finished the tea, I arose, thanked the woman, and followed her son outdoors.

An exceedingly rough road led from Hushe almost to Saling. This track, only recently completed, already showed signs that it could not be adequately maintained. We had located only one jeep at Hushe, and its owner took advantage of the opportunity to charge us double the official rate, for which he consented to drive at double the maximum speed along that narrow, twisting, rutted road. For the six of us, standing in the back of the jeep ducking overhanging rocks and branches, it was an interminable twenty miles. We realized we had not left all the danger behind yet.

We were delighted to rejoin the Captain and Mustaq in Saling. Mustaq's hospitality was not diminished by the fact that we all were sick during our two days there. We did our best to eat whatever he gave us, as our illness was no fault of his. Sumptuous meals were served on his best china; Mustaq was a wealthy man by Balti standards. His father owned a jeep, horses, and many acres of land. Each of Mustaq's five brothers, as he came of age, would receive land on which to build a house. Mustaq offered land to any of us who would want to live there and build. It was, I realized, a serious offer.

Mustaq's house, the newest in the village, was not quite complete: window glass was hard to come by in Baltistan. Four large rooms, each with a woven carpet covering the floor, bordered a large garden. The kitchen had a fireplace and a Baltistan rarity, a chimney. On the floor of the dining room a plastic tablecloth was spread to protect the rug. A small bookcase held a copy of the Koran and one other book.

Mustaq would neither eat with us nor serve us. Custom dictated that he work in the kitchen while his cheerful brother brought dishes in and out. (Mustaq's wife was a wraith we never met.) Only when we were finished eating did our host join us for tea and conversation.

Scott, we heard, had already flown from Skardu and should be out of the country. The rest of us began to feel the drawing power of familiar things, though they still lay 8,000 miles beneath our feet. The Captain brought me three letters and teased me about the love they contained. Our time in Pakistan, I started to realize, was ending.

Unfortunately, the jeep ride from Saling to Skardu was about to begin. Sixty-five miles this time, and it would take five hours. Once again we would be compelled to stand in the back, choking on dust and being beaten against the metal railing by the violent bouncing. One of us at a time, besides the Captain and driver, could sit in the relative comfort of the cab. Mustaq came along, and he was even worse off, hanging from the rear, standing on the bumper. Eventually he acquiesced to our urgings and squeezed in with us.

That ride lacked the anticipatory excitement of our ride from Skardu to Dasso; we yearned for the torment to end. The stops for apricots or tea now were joyless. It was as if we had dreamed we were home already, the hardships over, and then awakened to find ourselves crammed in the back of that jeep, the temperature rising as we descended to the desert.

We arrived in Skardu on a blazing afternoon toward the end of June. We immediately checked into our old hotel, Stalag Shangri-La, and sought refuge from the sun in our bare little rooms. In these whitewashed concrete ovens the flies swarmed so thickly that one could not lie still. Skardu had lost its charm.

For two days we lay in Skardu with the heat and the flies, waiting for deliverance by airplane, but none came. We stormed the airline office across the street, to be told that "mechanical trouble" was keeping their only plane grounded. When would they fly? They did not know. The list of clamorous passengers grew longer and longer.

With July 2 approaching, Anne and Renny began to get nervous. We had heard of people waiting weeks for a flight out of Skardu. Yet after our most recent jeep experience, we could not bear to face a 500-mile drive as our only means of travel. Stalling, we hoped for a flight, but when, on June 30, Anne returned from a morning foray to the airfield to report that the day's flights had been canceled, we suddenly decided to hire a vehicle to take us to Rawalpindi. We all would go; the flies were driving us out. We had enough time, we reasoned, to get there the day before the July 2 flight; the rest of us, lacking reservations, would leave when we could.

So began this seemingly endless journey down the Karakoram Highway. Our hired van was loaded and so were we, passing the pipe in honor of our forthcoming misery, bouncing down the road past the deserted airfield at fifteen miles per hour.

JULY 2, 7:00 A.M. The sun is up now, palpable, and I am beginning to recognize streets and buildings. We are close to Mrs. Davies's, and the city is already humming. We did obtain a small amount of gas, finally, but time is running out for Anne and Renny: they are going directly to the police station to register for departure, then on to the airport. Eric will try to join them. I no longer have any desires but to sleep; Rick and I will stay with Chas for the debriefing at the Ministry of Tourism.

Finally, forty-one hours after leaving Skardu, we reach the hotel. We are shocked to find Scott in one of the back rooms, his corpselike and rawboned body lying under a single white sheet, eyes protuberant, red hair disheveled. He has been sick for a week and unable to leave the country because all flights are booked for the holy month of Ramadan. I remember a bumper sticker I had seen earlier: Pakistan—Love It or Leave It. Is neither going to be possible?

But several days later our luck changes and, with several hundred pounds of excess luggage, we catch a standby flight to London. Just before we board, a customs officer asks if we have any hashish; Chas confesses and pulls a fragment from his pocket. The officer laughs at its size and returns it to us with a smile: "Here, I think you will need this on the plane." You bet we will, buddy.

On and Around Denali

Above: Two climbers descend a spectacular section of Denali's west buttress. Olaf Sööt.

Facing page: Mist surrounds the northwest face of The Rooster Comb, a satellite peak of Denali. Lance Leslie.

Opening page: Moonrise over the Ruth Gorge, as seen from the flanks of Denali in late March. Galen Rowell.

Right: Climbers and cornice, French Ridge, Mount Huntington. Lance Leslie.

Denali at sunset, from Nugget Pond. GALEN ROWELL.

An icefall on the Muldrow Glacier. GALEN ROWELL.

Denali from the southwest. The West Buttress Route lies at the
left center; the Cassin Ridge, casting an enormous shadow onto
the south face, drops down and right from the summit.
Bradford Washburn/Boston Museum of Science.

Right: Twilight on the summit of Denali.
Alan Kearney.

Below: An Italian skier powers his way through
sastrugi (wind-sculpted snow) at 20,000 feet on
Denali's west buttress. Brian Okonek.

Mount Foraker looms in the background as a climber descends
from the top of Denali. JAMES BALOG.

David Grimes

The Mountain Beyond the Cabin

O N A SUMMER EVENING IN JUNE 1976, Dave Johnston was looking through the picture window of his wilderness log cabin, aiming his spotting scope across the sauna and the beaver ponds, the lush spruce and birch forests, past the Teton-like Tokosha Mountains, focusing on a point forty-two miles distant and nearly 20,000 feet above him. At the same moment that his CB radio crackled with the news, Dave thought he saw a speck fall from the summit of Mount McKinley and skim down the south face: an insignificant mote dropping down one of the greatest vertical escarpments on earth. An adventurer, Bob Burns, had just begun the first hang-glider descent from the mountain, and Dave was observing its shaky start—a wing tip had brushed the mountainside on takeoff and Burns dropped 600 feet like a card on edge before catching his airfoil, thus saving himself for the ethereal 13,000-foot glide to the glacier below. From afar Dave had witnessed history of a sort.

Though thrilled by the sight, Dave wondered what was happening to the mountain he knew so intimately. He had first climbed McKinley—or Denali, to use a native name—in 1963, when, with a little effort, one could learn the names of all those who had ever set foot upon the summit. Dave was again

on the mountain during the first winter ascent, in 1967. In a single decade he had watched the mountain evolve from a wilderness scarcely different from that experienced by the pioneers to one so accessible that a sixty-pound hang-glider could be launched from the summit. Denali had entered the late twenti-eth century.

My relationship with the modern mountain began at the Johnston cabin, and that view of Denali remains my favorite. One wants nothing more than to sit in Dave's rocking chair when the evening sunlight strikes the Alaska Range and oblique golden rays reveal the smaller mountain worlds nestled below the great ridges and flanks of Denali: Foraker and Hunter, giants in their own right; the chipped white blade of Silverthorne; the immense granitic fang called Moose's Tooth; the soaring walls of the Ruth Gorge; and the wild, corniced ridges of Hunt-ington. Still, Denali dwarfs them all.

At 20,320 feet, Denali is the highest mountain in North America; it rises 17,000 feet above its base, and by that measurement it is one of the earth's highest peaks. It is also the coldest of the planet's major mountains, and it has winds that can literally pick up climbers and throw them to the end of their ropes. Yet this hostile polar environment is now often crowded with mountaineers. The attraction of the tallest peak on the continent, the accessibility afforded by ski-equipped planes, and the unfortunate myth that an easy route leads to the summit combine to lure a remarkable assortment of oddballs to the mountain. One Denali guide thinks the peak provides the "greatest social climbing experience on earth."

For years I avoided the mountain and its crowds, preferring instead to know Denali only as a pristine mythical presence sometimes visible on the northern horizon. Then, in the late 1970s, I spent an autumn and winter in the Johnstons' cabin, in the kingdom beneath the southern shadow of the mountain, and Denali became a familiar friend, often visible beyond the orange juice on the breakfast table. In the daytime I skied through the forests—with rambunctious dogs at my heels—to haul water and cut firewood; in the evening I threw birch logs into the stove and leaned back to watch the pale green curtains of the aurora illuminate the mountain. What did I really know of Denali? Nothing. It was time to visit it firsthand.

Midday heat and the occasional cracking thunder of avalanches. In the long lulls of silence we hear the hiss of cascading meltwater on rock faces miles away. The world smells of ice and zinc oxide.

From below come singing voices and a blast from a cowhorn. Jon Robbins, Roger Robinson, and Lance and Lori Leslie climb into view, each carrying sixty pounds and hauling sixty more on their red sleds. "The north country," Lori laughs, "where men are men and so are the women."

The Kahiltna Glacier landing strip lies two days' travel behind us. We are heading north toward Denali's most popular route, the west buttress, a climb pioneered by Bradford Washburn and others in 1951. The main fork of the Kahiltna Glacier sweeps upward past hanging glaciers and icefalls and vast fields of white. The route ahead vanishes in drifting mists, and I wonder what lies beyond. Occasionally we pass people coming down. Some are quiet and some are cheerful. Some are haggard, as if returning from a great quest or battle. The world above begins to take shape in their reports and rumors. Avalanche over the route at 12,000 feet; two frostbite cases at 14; thirty-five below at 17, 120 degrees colder than on our glacier. We continue trudging upward, like jolly minstrels marching to extinction.

As I plod along toward Kahiltna Pass, I witness an apparition. A tiny jeweled bird approaches me, surreally hopping down the rope like a mechanical toy. It is a yellow-rumped warbler, seemingly unafraid, but more likely disoriented and weak. Gently

Looking south from the summit of Denali; Mount Hunter, the third-highest summit of the Alaska Range, is visible at the left center. OLAF SÖÖT.

I pick it up and marvel at its exquisite beauty. It is the first of five small passerine species we will see in two days: rusty blackbird, white-crowned sparrow, junco, tree sparrow, and warbler. Migrating through the mountains or else following insects on thermals rising from the lowlands, they have landed on the glacier, and many will be unable to escape. Their presence is startling in this landscape of ice, and, despite our desire, we can do nothing for them. Tomorrow, or the next day, they will freeze.

The ravens are different creatures altogether, strong and clever and of good cheer while raiding food caches up and down the mountain. "Goraks," we call them, using the Sherpa name, and they wheel over the ridgetops executing back flips and barrel rolls, addressing us with a hollow sound like rocks falling into the bottom of a well. Alaskan natives believe that these birds are magical.

Popcorn is pinging in the pan; frosty tent walls sparkle and fade in the candlelight. The six-day trek to this huge basin at 14,300 feet has been surprisingly easy—no terror at all. We have slipped smoothly into the rhythm of life on a big snow mountain. Most of us here at 14 are acclimating to the altitude and have little to do but assemble for yarn spinning, philosophizing, and popcorn. The village of clustered tents contains Brits, Scots, Kiwis, Texans, Japanese, Germans, French, Swiss, Americans, and Alaskans. Tonight, this small company of vagabonds gathered inside the Morning Glory—the "cultural affairs" tent—seemingly represents all available earthly knowledge: history, culture, and lore of the species—all stored in a few minds. It is a gathering of riches. The astrophysicist and the fundamentalist describe their worlds of science and salvation; the banjo player fresh from the Cassin Ridge recalls bits of Catholic doctrine suggesting the salvation of scientists. And so our time passes smoothly between the heavens and the earth.

Outside, in the spring air, a fattening moon and the luminous face of the mountain gaze down onto our glowing camp. The village guitar rings through the tent walls, and a Frenchman just arrived at 14 strides by. His voice is richly accented. "A guitar? A guitar! I play the viola!" He slaps his head. "I did not bring it!"

On the other side of the mountain a solitary man endures the same night with growing despair. He is more than alone: he exists, barely, on the skin of the glacier, but his thoughts are locked beneath him in claustrophobic walls of blue ice. Seven days have passed since Jim Wickwire and Chris Kerrebrock fell with their sled into the same crevasse. Kerrebrock, conscious and apparently uninjured, was wedged upside-down so tightly that Wickwire, with a dislocated shoulder, could not release him. After many hours of painful struggle to free Kerrebrock that first day, Wickwire began to realize the unthinkable: he would be forced to leave his partner to die in the crevasse. The two men talked. Kerrebrock calmly made a verbal will and left messages for his girlfriend and parents. He made his partner promise to wait for rescue on the spot, afraid that if Wickwire tried to cross the heavily crevassed glacier alone, he too might perish. When there was no more to say, they said good-bye. Sometime during the night Kerrebrock died of exposure.

The days that followed were a torment. Wickwire's line-of-sight radio was ineffectual on the north side of the mountain. There was no food—it also was buried in the crevasse. Hopes of rescue diminished with each new sunrise. Wickwire at last decided he must move or die.

Two weeks after the accident, Doug Geeting, the pilot who had originally flown the two men to the mountain, heard a faint voice and clicking on his radio. Geeting was involved with a separate errand, yet overflew Peter's Glacier on intuition. "If that's Jim and Chris," he radioed, "click three more times; your signal's very weak." Geeting searched the glacier, spotted Wickwire, then brought the plane down and taxied a treacherous mile along the glacier. Wickwire, near to abandoning hope, lay on his back, exhausted; he had eaten almost nothing for two weeks. Trying to escape from the glacier, he had managed to solo only a few miles over its undulating surface, in constant fear of the immense blue chasms yawning somewhere beneath him. When Geeting reached him, Wickwire's first words were Kerrebrock's last.

Low-angle sunlight illuminates the tent at 14, cheery pastels of light and shade. Outside, snowflakes stream through the yellow light like moths on the wing. After carrying a load to 16, I'm weary, yet I feel pleasure in being here in this wild place where I must consciously, every day, reaffirm my will to live.

As I slip off my wind parka, my thoughts turn to a discussion I had earlier in the day: what is the proper name of this mountain? McKinley, after all, never saw Denali. But when prospector William Dickey named the mountain in 1896 after his favorite presidential candidate, Senator William McKinley, the name stuck. The Tanana Indians north of the mountain knew the peak as Denali, the Great One. The natives never saw Mr. McKinley, who hailed from Ohio and wasn't much interested in mountains. (Denali's 17,400-foot neighbor, Mount Foraker, was named after yet another Ohio politician.) In 1981 the National Park Service changed the age-old name, Mount McKinley National Park, to

Denali National Park and Preserve. This, we all agreed, was an enlightened gesture that recognized the value of original native names. One of these days, I predict, the U.S. Board on Geographic Names will restore the name Denali to the mountain itself. The politicians of Ohio might not approve, but then, like President McKinley, most of them have never seen Denali either.

I am grinning as I unclip from the fixed lines and step onto the spine of the evening world—what Lance refers to as the Land above the Clouds. Up ahead Roger moves with the same leisurely pace of one of his after-supper strolls into the Fairview Inn in Talkeetna. A beer would taste awfully good, indeed, but I'm not sure I'd have the breath for it. Our substitute stroll leads up through the spring evening toward an airy campsite on the ridge at 16,400 feet. The ridge plummets steeply on either side; we are perched above vast corridors of twilight.

Looming out of the deepening shadows in the south are the other two giants, Foraker and Hunter, their summit ridges sharply etched between blue shadows and light. Their snowslopes radiate quiet color into the dusk. To the northwest, we can see all the way into summer: 14,000 feet down the mountainside, the green floor of the Interior is potholed with shining lakes. In the west, undercast beneath us, a blanket of blue clouds stretches to the horizon and the sea beyond. I clap my hands in the thin air, greeting the great bowl of the evening sky.

I also notice that we are standing in a field of turds. And, near where the ridge drops off, empty fuel cans and an abandoned food cache have been scattered by the ravens and the wind. The contrast between the magnificent distant view and the sordid near view makes me wonder: what would the Sourdoughs think of such a view? In 1910 several hardy gold miners ceased their prospecting long enough to make a matter-of-fact first ascent of Denali's 19,470-foot north peak. In so doing, these men performed what Terris Moore, in his 1967 book *Mt. McKinley: The Pioneer Climbs*, called "the greatest *tour de force* in the annals of mountaineering on this continent—the amazing feat of climbing from 11,000 feet to the top and back in one day." The men—nicknamed the Sourdoughs—transported a fourteen-foot spruce flagpole with them on their jaunt; the two who achieved the summit planted it on top in order to verify their climb to the townspeople of Fairbanks. The pole was not visible from that distance, however, and the Sourdoughs' story was doubted for this and other reasons. Three years passed before the Stuck-Karstens party, scaling the higher and still-virgin south peak, spotted the flagpole atop the north peak.

On our spring evening three generations later,

lightweight stoves deliver their blue flames and familiar purr, encouraging us to relax and even enjoy our sluggish efforts at this altitude. The evening remains ethereal. It occurs to me that the mountain might look better if modern Denali climbers left behind spruce flagpoles instead of pudding cans.

Denali's popular routes have suffered environmental degradation in the last decade or two. Recent efforts to clean up the mountain have met with considerable success, though the latrines, litter, and abandoned food caches sometimes seen along the twelve-mile-long West Buttress Route are hard to believe. Even the difficult routes show obvious signs of past climbers: the Japanese Couloir, on the Cassin Ridge, appears to be strewn with colored spaghetti, so much rope has been fixed and abandoned.

The mental and physical strain of high-altitude mountaineering has often persuaded climbers to jettison their excess baggage. On Denali that didn't used to matter much. The park had fewer than twenty climbers a year during the 1950s and only twice that number during the 1960s. But during the single week of the American Bicentennial, about eighty mountaineers were positioned to reach the highest point in North America. Storms trapped most of those climbers on July 4, but two days later, when the weather cleared, a waiting line formed for the summit.

Seven hundred climbers a year now visit Denali, mostly during the late spring and early summer. This is not an excessive number when one considers the 200,000 souls who attempt Fujiyama each year, but it's enough to change profoundly the character of a wilderness mountain such as Denali. On a nice summer's day, when skiers carve telemark garlands at 15,000 feet and a hot-air balloon drifts serenely past the summit, the Sourdoughs wouldn't recognize the place.

"How can you get closer to a mountain than by living inside it?" Lance is whimsically philosophizing as he leans back and stretches in the relative comfort of our igloo at 17,200 feet. Our relationship with this frozen mountain is certainly a close one: we drink from it, we sculpt and build with it, we live inside it in our snowcaves and igloos. Though we have temporarily insulated ourselves from one aspect of the mountain's reality—the elements outside—burrowing into the giant's skin seems a satisfying way to survive. Our enclosed hemisphere of warm air is awash with exotic colors from half a dozen sleeping bags, red rubber balls, and paperback novels. In one corner Lori Leslie is working her hair into a braid long enough to rappel with. Jon and Roger are hidden behind the steam of dinner: shrimp and crab, rice, a stick of butter, and the last of the brandy.

Tranquil blue light filters through the snow-block walls, and on this unusually pleasant evening it's hard to believe I'm on the same mountain that Bradford Washburn warns has "a climate around its summit which may well present the most severe year-round average of any spot on earth.... I know of no spot where wind and temperature can be more powerfully combined than on McKinley's upper ridges—and I am referring to the summer months. The [upper reaches] of this peak in the great winter storms ... must be fiendish."

At our igloo's elevation, summer temperatures often fall below minus thirty; six feet of snow has fallen *in one day,* only to be removed the following day by savage winds. Stormy weather has persisted for two weeks at a time. In winter the summit has been reached only three times, in 1967, in 1982, and in 1983. The thermometer registered minus fifty-eight on the evening of March 1, 1967, when Dave Johnston, Art Davidson, and the late Ray Genet stood on top after a month of climbing. The night was calm, and on the descent the weary climbers chose to bivouac at Denali Pass, at 18,200 feet, rather than return to their camp at 17,000. Their bivouac turned into a six-day polar hell, with incredibly violent winds and temperatures of minus fifty and sixty degrees. The trio somehow clung to the mountain, living inside a tiny snow cave and surviving through courage, luck, and moments of individual heroism. They learned more about the wind speeds later from pilot Don Sheldon, something of a legend even then. He had flown near the pass, looking for them in the storm. Art Davidson, in his book *Minus 148°,* described Sheldon's reaction to the storm: "Yea, I was huckledebuck'n on up there to take a look at ma boys, when I look out the window .... Whoa ... I seen this ridge just standin' still. I look down at my speedometer and it says 140 mph. Yowza, I had to fly 140 mph just to keep even with that ol' wind."

Accessibility is what currently enables folks with money to fly to the North Pole for the purpose of sipping champagne. In a like manner folks can be found guzzling beer while sitting in lawn chairs alongside the Kahiltna Glacier landing strip. The pilots come and go: Kitty Banner, Doug Geeting, Lowell Thomas, Jr., Cliff "Hanger" Hudson. Green leaves and ice cream and the Fairview Inn are what the planes offer if one is headed out; if one is leaving Talkeetna with a month's climbing supplies, the plane allows an instantaneous entry into an icy universe.

Denali must now be the most accessible of the earth's major mountains. In the early 1900s just getting to the foot of the mountain—or to any of the vanishing blank spaces on the world map—was a major exercise in wilderness survival. If the Sour-doughs' problem was to get in and out of the wilderness, our modern challenge is to find it. And in order to rediscover even a semblance of wilderness, climbers must be responsible for their actions.

So far as I know, the first expedition to be totally responsible for their garbage arrived on Denali in April 1971. Seven climbers, led by Gary Grimm, then director of the University of Oregon Outdoor Program, set out to climb the mountain with what was a novel mountaineering idea: they would carry out all their litter and leave nothing behind on the mountain. This was not at all in keeping with the venerable expedition practice of discarding items once they no longer proved necessary to the primary object of reaching the top.

When that first expedition proved successful, Grimm and others created the Denali Arctic Environmental Project, which organized a number of Denali clean-up climbs in the mid-1970s. The DAEP's work rippled outward: in 1975 the cosmopolitan garbage dumps at the Everest base camp were receiving clean-up attention. Closer to home, the National Park Service responded with environ-

Frances Randall, manager of the Kahiltna Glacier base camp and member of the Alaska State Symphony, plays her violin in an unusual setting. GALEN ROWELL.

mental regulations for Denali guides. Additionally, Park Service mountaineering pamphlets were translated into several languages in order to pass on an environmental ethic to foreign climbers. Army helicopters assisted with clean-ups, and ranger patrols aided in educational work. The DAEP's initial efforts clearly demonstrated that expeditions could live on a severe mountain for extended periods while maintaining sound environmental practices.

If litter is ceasing to be a problem on Denali, the same cannot be said about human waste. The heavily used campsite at 17,200 feet on the west buttress is periodically scoured by incredible winds that remove snow and expose frozen human waste scattered like fossils. Down at the Kahiltna landing strip a communal seat has been suspended on a platform over a deep snow trench. Its construction has eased the problem of contaminated drinking water at base camp; human waste once randomly deposited is thus replaced by huge, frozen balls that move down the advancing glacier, spaced like tree rings, a year apart.

A current technique for disposal high on the mountain is to put human waste into a garbage bag and drop it into a deep crevasse. Edward LaChapelle, avalanche expert and student of glaciers, wrote me concerning such disposal: "Future scientists no doubt will rejoice at recovering well-preserved climbers' shit so they can analyze it to determine the 20th-century diet of this peculiar human subspecies." LaChapelle's words are not entirely tongue-in-cheek: junk *does* acquire value when it becomes sufficiently ancient. Imagine the excitement of recovering the Sourdoughs' flagpole!

Sometimes I wonder if the mundane sanitation problems of a remote mountain really matter at all. I once told a friend about how the strain of climbing at altitude turns some people into slobs. My friend replied, "People are slobs when they're born. You know, genetics." He raised his arms. "All those years living in trees. We didn't worry about garbage; we just threw the stuff over our shoulders. The only problem today is that we can't tell the difference between our banana peels and our plutonium. And that," he added, "may not matter up in the mountains, but it sure does down in civilization."

Stragglers from the summit return throughout the quiet evening. Meanwhile, two of 17 Camp's reprobates are preparing for an unusual night ascent: Jon, our expedition ornithologist, and Peter, a lanky guide from New Zealand who has somehow convinced his present clients he has been on Denali before. To ensure warm feet, Jon borrows my military VB boots, promising he will return alive with them in the morning. Two merry souls set off into the twilight.

Later, those of us remaining in the igloo listen to the faint sounds of wind and imagine the bitter cold outside. The nylon parka pressed over the entrance is covered with frost, tiny stars that sparkle with each breath of air. Thinking of Jon and Peter, we read aloud a passage from *The Narrow Road to the Deep North,* by the seventeenth-century Japanese monk, Basho: "I myself have been tempted for a long time by the cloud-moving wind—filled with a strong desire to wander.... I walked through mists and clouds, breathing the air at high altitudes and stepping on slippery ice and snow, till at last, through a gateway of clouds, as it seemed, to the very paths of the sun and moon, I reached the summit, completely out of breath and nearly frozen to death. Presently the sun went down and the moon rose glistening in the sky."

The moon rises, and Jon and Peter climb and climb. Across steep traverses, ridges, and slopes, past the gables and towers on the wild, broad roof of North America. Icicles grow from frosted beards; the two climbers' teeth suck in the pain and dull ecstasy of frigid air. Ice axes and crampons squeak and crunch. And always, in the back of their minds: will the mountain let us pass? But the night remains peaceful, and the cold air has great clarity. A nibble of chocolate, a handful of nuts, frozen orange juice slush. At 19,500 feet Jon drops a mitten. It drifts away in the mild breeze and he sprints after it, amazed he has the energy to run. He stoops to pick up his mitten and smacks into the wall of oxygen debt. His body is overwhelmed by violent, desperate breathing, but he stands his ground, heaving and panting until he recovers enough to delicately curse the mitten and follow Peter.

Rolling terrain leads to a long moonlit plateau and a steep rise. At 20,000 feet Peter stops and suddenly pulls down his pants, an unexpected and urgent movement. Frozen cobblestones roll down the slope and disappear. Within the subtle context of competition Jon sees his chance to gain a little ground on his companion. He passes Peter but then, thirty feet beyond, also suddenly halts. The competition ends with both their pants down.

These final difficulties behind them, they climb upward together. The moon sets, but at 4:00 A.M. and minus forty degrees, the dawn light breaks over them on the summit.

Sunrise on the rooftop. The wind is still. Jon holds a picture of a special friend up to the light. Peter fumbles with his camera and smiles through his icicles. Well, Yank, we're mates now.

In the morning I awaken to Jon's cheery face. "Hey, let's trade. Quick, crawl out of your bag and put on your boots so I can jump in while it's still warm." I cannot fight him; so I crawl out the door into morning. And so it is that soon I find myself

heading up alone into the cloud-moving wind wearing a pair of boots still warm from the summit.

The Okoneks have a family business in Talkeetna. Jim is a glacier pilot who flies climbers into the Alaska Range; Julie helps run the business in town. Brian, their son, is a veteran mountain guide, and Jamie, their daughter, is becoming an experienced pilot herself. Over the years Jim and Brian have been involved in many climbing rescues and have experienced rewarding moments in which a frail network of miracles has allowed humans to help their comrades. Unfortunately, some rescues have not been such uplifting experiences.

I was having dinner at the Okoneks' one evening in the summer of 1979 when Jim returned from a rescue mission on Mount Foraker. He was unusually drawn and quiet; later that evening he explained his mood: "It was the hardest rescue I think I've ever done." Since Jim had been flying helicopters for twenty-five years and was a superb mountain pilot, I listened carefully. Jim had located the five climbers on Foraker who had radioed for a rescue, but squirrelly winds and poor visibility made his landing

This aerial view of Denali shows the entire West Buttress Route, the chief focus of this article and the two that follow. The thin, wandering line visible on the lower mountain is a shallow trench made by the hundreds of climbers who attempt the popular route each year. Windy Corner, a well-known feature of the route, is located near the center, at the base of a prominent, left-diagonalling ridge. The route continues upward behind the ridge, then ascends a curving ridge to a relatively flat snow basin at 17,000 feet. Immediately above this is Denali Pass, the rounded saddle lying between the north summit, at the left, and the main peak. BRADFORD WASHBURN/BOSTON MUSEUM OF SCIENCE.

hair-raising—once he had been thrown into a wall of clouds on the far side of a ridge and had to dive blindly back out. When he finally was able to set the craft down, three climbers requested rescue and Jim asked no questions. The flight back was treacherous; sometimes the chopper lurched down the back sides of passes in stomach-floating dives to avoid clouds. The cruel black-and-white world soon receded; ahead lay green forests and silver rivers leading to Talkeetna. After landing in town the three climbers emerged without assistance, suffering from no apparent problems. Jim was amazed; he wasn't used to rescuing healthy climbers. Why had they called for rescue? The trio explained that their group had overextended itself to reach the summit and had run low on food and fuel. The three men had decided to radio for evacuation. Rather than descend their nontechnical route with patience and self-deprivation for a few days, they had risked another person's life. Jim wonders even today if the climbers have ever comprehended the magnitude of their irresponsible act.

The National Park Service performs numerous rescues each year on Denali; most of them, unlike Jim's "rescue," involve climbers genuinely in need. In some seasons one out of five Denali climbers falls victim to injuries and illness; one out of a hundred doesn't survive. To coordinate rescue operations, the Park Service employs one dedicated, full-time ranger, Bob Gerhard, and three seasonal rangers. Since the Park Service has only a minor budget for rescue operations, past rescues usually involved army helicopters funded out of the army's training budget. But in a surprise move in 1982, the army presented the park with a $67,000 bill for the use of its Chinook helicopters. Since most climbers can't afford the cost of a rescue, taxpayers must cover these expenses.

Gerhard has for many years concerned himself with the various aspects of rescuing mountaineers. In 1976 he visited Doug Scott in Anchorage, where the British climber was recovering from an exhausting climb he and Dougal Haston had made on the south face of Denali. Gerhard posed a question: "What do we do with all the inexperienced climbers who don't belong on the mountain? We believe in the freedom of the hills and don't want to tell them they can't climb. But then they get into trouble and need to be rescued. What do we do?"

"Don't rescue them," Scott replied.

"We can't do that."

"I know," said Scott, wistfully. "It's the Decline of Western Civilization."

It is well known that dozens of irresponsible climbers, incapable of self-rescue, set off each season for Denali. Some of these people, thinking to be responsible, may bravely tell the rangers in advance that they don't care to be rescued if illness or injury strikes. But the Park Service, of course, feels obliged to attempt to rescue anyone who is reported to be in trouble.

Scott's remark came in a watershed year for Denali rescues. Prior to 1976 there had been very few rescue missions, but that year thirty-three mountaineers were involved in accidents or evacuations from Denali and Foraker. In the following years such incidents became commonplace; Denali accidents filled sixteen pages in the American Alpine Club's

1983 publication *Accidents in North American Mountaineering*. It is obvious that because of the crowds on Denali and the illusion of a safety net, modern climbers have a nonchalant and disturbing attitude about climbing and rescue.

Wind had plagued the seventeen Germans all day, a constant adversary looking for signs of weakness. Now, through the night, it would slowly try to destroy them. It rolled down the hidden slopes above them in powerful gusts, driving spindrift through the white-out in the shape of great, whirling creatures. Seventeen bundles of warmth lay scattered over a wide area; a few were hidden behind rocks and snow hummocks, but the wind found them all. It pried open bivouac sacks, stripping away heat, numbing the bodies. Slowly it began to narrow the difference in temperature between the bodies and the mountain.

These impossible conditions were forcing the Germans to endure a night in the open at 17,300 feet. The group had spent the entire day struggling to reach the summit in deteriorating weather; in the evening, at 19,500 feet, they had finally acknowledged the seriousness of the weather and turned back, exhausted. The downward traverse below Denali Pass had been treacherous because of the incessant wind, the near-zero visibility, and the unconsolidated snow that lay over ice. One climber had fallen 1,300 feet and was lucky to be alive after fracturing three vertebrae. Others fell also but managed to self-arrest. The camp at 17 proved impossible to locate in the white-out. With cold fingers stuck in armpits the Germans lay down where they were, fully exposed to the night and suffering from the mind fog of altitude, fatigue, and fear.

At dawn the Germans struggled to their feet like tottering old men. Miraculously, they were still alive; the storm had prevented nighttime temperatures from falling well below zero for the first time in weeks. The clouds had lifted in the night, and the camp was visible a quarter-mile away. The wind, however, had increased to nearly a hundred miles an hour.

While other climbers lower on the mountain marveled at the beauty of the sunrise, the Germans stumbled into camp. Many of them, with desperate efforts, entered their tents and crawled into sleeping bags. Hypothermic, they were probably going to die unless someone came to their aid, quickly.

The camp at 17 was comprised of several small snow caves, ten tents, an igloo, and nearly thirty-five people, including Roger Robinson, leading his Park Service patrol, and Nick Parker, another Alaskan, guiding a group of ten. Roger helped the less exhausted Germans remove the center poles from their pyramid tents to prevent these shelters from totally failing. The wind instantly flattened the tents; the climbers underneath looked like corpses covered with shrouds. Nick tried to take down his most exposed dome tent, but the wind was so extreme that the poles could not be removed. Inside this tent, climbers huddled silently, as they would inside a balloon about to vaporize. A tiny tear appeared in the ceiling as the paralyzed climbers watched. Then they were sitting outside: the tent had disintegrated.

Nick looked at his last two domes, horribly stressed in the ferocious wind. Somehow he must get them down and get people into snow caves. A client moved forward, pulling up an ice axe to brace himself against the wind. This axe, however, had been the last major anchor for the tents, and Nick lunged instinctively as the tents took off, dragging him in their wake. Face down, he careened through the basin, heading for the drop-off. Near the brink, half airborne, he finally let go; the tents grew small and vanished to the north.

Roger and Nick quickly organized the survival efforts: the Germans must receive liquids and adequate shelter if they were to survive. Ten of the Germans were packed into an igloo built for four: it was paradise. Work began on a large snow cave, to be made by joining two small, adjacent caves. The enormous wind speed persisted, and after a while the climbers accepted it as an environmental constant, something like horizontal gravity. They could not easily exhale facing into the wind, nor inhale facing away; breathing, such as it was, worked best at ninety degrees. Climbers lumbered through the camp with deliberate, Frankenstein motions, moving gear and people, their breath frost turning to heavy rime on beards and eyebrows. Inside the caves one person shoveled snow at the head of the tunnel, while those too hypothermic and exhausted for vigorous work assisted from their slumped positions by paddling the snow down a foot-wide trough toward the exit. Others began melting snow for hot drinks. Free from the wind, people began to calm down.

Of the original ten tents at 17 Camp, nine had been destroyed or dismembered or had disappeared. All that Nick Parker had left of his three domes was in his pocket—a single grommet attached to a shred of fabric. The only surviving tent was a sturdy dome surrounded by four-foot-high walls of snow. Except for those inside it, everyone at 17 was living inside the mountain.

Roger woke in the night, drowsy and content. He looked in wonderment at the crescent of sleeping bags that disappeared up around the gentle curve of the cave: eighteen climbers were sleeping side by side. The raging wind outside was reduced to a whisper. Roger went back to sleep, dreaming spindrift dreams of ocean surf.

The incident involving the Germans was unusu-

ally dramatic, to be sure, but Denali is more famous for the less sensational problems it causes climbers. As a result, the mountain is an ideal site for the study of altitude- and cold-related medical problems. In the spring of 1982 the High Latitude Research Project of the University of Alaska-Anchorage set up a medical research camp in the basin at 14,300 feet on the West Buttress Route. As part of a multiyear study, researchers have collected data from hundreds of climbers and, additionally, aided climbers with serious medical problems.

Dr. Peter Hackett checked the barometer one morning at the research station and observed to Brian Okonek that they seemed to have climbed 800 feet in their sleep—overnight, the air pressure had dropped dramatically, a not unusual Denali occurrence. Hackett had used the same instrument for three months on Everest, but he had not observed such radical barometric fluctuations. In addition, the *average* barometric pressures in the Himalaya versus the ones in the Alaska Range were quite different. Allen Carpé, leader of several Alaskan scientific expeditions in the 1930s, wrote that "the atmospheric pressures on the [Alaskan] summits has corresponded to elevations about 10% greater than the actual." This apparent anomaly is the result of gravity and centrifugal force, which cause the shape of the earth's atmospheric envelope to flatten toward the poles and bulge out from the equator. The effect is further enhanced by temperature and season: the great heat of the tropics expands the column of air upward over the equatorial regions, whereas the cold of the Arctic contracts the air mass downward over the high latitudes, especially during polar winter nights. In essence, a climber ascends into thinner air more quickly at high latitudes than at low latitudes. Terris Moore feels that the combined effect

A hastily assembled group of mountaineers works to right a plane that had an unexpected—and fortunately minor— accident. BRIAN OKONEK.

of these phenomena is such that in midsummer the atmospheric pressure on Denali's summit corresponds to an elevation in the Himalaya some 1,500 feet higher. And, in the colder seasons, Denali's summit may be equivalent to a summer Himalayan elevation more than 3,000 feet higher!

Hackett and Okonek, living at the medical research camp, had ample time to acclimate to the altitude in 1982. Brian occasionally rambled up to the 17,000-foot camp just to visit folks for the evening; to those unacclimated climbers plodding along a ridge near the upper camp, it was more debilitating than even the cold and the wind to see a bright-eyed fellow literally running by, dispensing a cheery "Nice evening, isn't it?"

Peter and Brian had lived at 14,300 feet for nearly a month when they left camp one morning, bound for the summit via the upper West Rib Route. They reached the top of Denali eight hours later. The most impressive aspect of this climb was not their speed but that the two men felt uncommonly good the entire time, not at all as if their limits were being pushed. Unlike other climbers who stagger onto the summit burned out and without the reserves for a safe return, Peter and Brian were strong and confident on the descent. Such were the benefits of superb acclimation.

From 17 our group descends through morning clouds and wind to the camp at 14, where the sun is beginning to shine. We have entered a cushion of thick air, or so it seems, and Jon delights in his full lungs. In a frisky mood he composes an imaginary letter to his mother: "Hi, Mom. All my toes fell off last night, but the views up here are great. All the guys are jumping bottomless crevasses and showing off. I haven't been able to get up the nerve yet, and everyone's teasing me; so if I have to do it at two in the morning, I will. But don't worry. Bye now."

It's late afternoon; blue shows through the wet clouds, and we are bathed in a pale golden light. A fellow named Wolfgang has just descended alone to 14 suffering from that all-too-common Denali affliction, pulmonary edema. He has had this disease twice before, in the Andes and in the Himalaya, and by the time of this climb he felt he knew his safe rate of ascent. He says he did not anticipate problems so

"low" on the mountain. I do not tell him that a Japanese climber on the west buttress acquired pulmonary and cerebral edema at only 11,800 feet and died a bit lower during an evacuation attempt.

Wolfgang's condition is not critical, though occasionally he is doubled over by a fit of coughing. He waits patiently, chatting and wheezing, while we break camp; we will accompany him to a lower elevation, where he should recover quickly. We amble downward together through the peaceful evening sky, by now a luminous, mother-of-pearl blue and gray. Snow gives way in places to cloud-blue ice; the crystals underfoot reflect tiny flashes of light. Pleasant conversation ebbs and flows.

A large caravan on its way up is camped at 11,000 feet. We settle in for the night between the Fantasy Ridge guided expedition and four sixty-year-old gents who call themselves the DUMB (Denali Upper Mountain Bunch) Expedition. I ease into my sleeping bag next to Wolfgang. A gentle breeze puffs on the tent door. Memories drift in, and I can't quite place them—the night odors of the spring wind in my childhood? I smile to think that it's almost summer.

At midnight I awaken. Roger is widely considered a world-class snorer. He has been dormant for a week, but now, with his head only inches from Wolfgang's, he erupts, and incredible sounds bang into the walls, shaking the tent. In the brief silence between "storms," a tiny moan escapes from the stuporous Wolfgang, who seems to be having a nightmare. Roger snores, Wolfgang moans: if he can survive the night with Roger, surely he will survive the mountain and his pulmonary edema. I ponder his fate as I seek my own escape in sleep.

The air smells of moss and wet ferns. I rise and step out the door of the Johnstons' cabin. At 3:00 A.M. it is half light, and the world is calm, unhurried, turning in its imperceptible motion toward morning. A loon whistles from the nearby lake; a breath of wind stirs the wet birch leaves and sets them dripping. I gaze up at the canopy of leaves while my calf muscles stretch, supple after a month on Denali. The sky above is pale and clearing. Northward, the big mountain basks in the first light, the color of a good peach.

*A campsite on the Northeast Fork of the Kahiltna Glacier;
the southwest side of Denali rises in the background.*
OLAF SÖÖT.

Paul Willis

The Kahiltna Open

RAY GENET WAS A HYPERACTIVE Swiss climber who for many years guided people up Denali. Long ago, I read about him in a book; one glossy photo showed him chugging up a snowy ridge in thin air, ice axe in hand, a bound-for-destiny look all over his face. His destiny, at least on that trip, was to complete the first winter ascent of Denali, but he almost froze to death in the process.

He went on to help other folks bound for destiny. Genet himself put it more crudely: his profession, he said, was selling ego trips. Hundreds of men and women across the country can proudly claim to have conquered the highest peak in North America. Simply great for their résumés. And Ray helped. But high upon Everest destiny returned, and he froze to death at last.

At the time of this story, however, Genet was still selling ego trips. Which made me hope I had better reasons to climb Big Mac. But they eluded me like trout in a pool, none of which I could quite catch.

In the meantime I had to settle for being bound for destiny. I'd heard that the culmination of every North American climber's ambition was to stand atop The Great One. My own seeds of ambition secretly grew in a crumbling quarry north of my high school, a half-hour bicycle ride on any warm summer evening. The quarry walls were forty feet high, quaintly embroidered with blackberry vines and poison-oak creepers. Garter snakes roamed the quarry floor. We hid behind an alder when the owners drove by in a gravel-spitting pickup. With the coast clear we rappelled the cliff in great leaps, again and again. Clearly, the finer part of climbing lay in rappelling. Just as clearly, this quarry was but a few logical steps, leaps, and bounds from Denali, the natural apogee of my desires.

And so one day I found myself encamped on the Kahiltna Glacier, an eager member of a fledgling expedition.

The Kahiltna Open

I had rolled up a hundred peanut-butter balls for our trip. They were about the size of golf balls, and, when frozen, they even felt like golf balls, which gave us the sportsman's incentive.

After dinner one evening, as the sun was poised for its deep-freeze dive behind Mount Foraker, we dug a cup-size hole in the ice and marked it with a bamboo wand. Then we assembled a wonderful assortment of clubs: snow shovels served as drivers, snowshoes as irons, and ice axes as putters. One sled, pulled by an able caddy, held the clubs in readiness.

It seemed like an easy course, although a bad hook could send the ball into a nearby crevasse.

Eager to try my skill, I stepped up to the tee. "I recommend this Sherpa Lightfoot, Sahib," said my caddy. "Sir Edmund Hillary once scored a hole in one on the eighteenth using this model." That's good enough for me, I thought, taking the club from my barefoot assistant. I lined up on the ball and shifted my weight as my college instructor had taught me. "Everyone should learn to play golf," he'd informed me. "You never know when you'll be asked to play a few rounds with the boss."

I pulled back and swung hard. The ball soared sharply right in a high arc, catching the last rays of the Arctic sun—a flaming comet bound for destiny. At last it plummeted to the glacier, bounced once, and rolled neatly into the crevasse.

"See," I told my caddy. "I was aiming for that, you know."

"Sahib knows best," he replied.

An Igloo

Igloos come in handy. One day we encountered a three-day blizzard (although, of course, we didn't know it was a three-day blizzard until it stopped) and pitched our tents in the middle of the vast Kahiltna. Tents are easier to set up than igloos —that's why we set up our tents. Wind blew; snow fell. We cut out salt-lick-size blocks of snow and stacked them wall-high to the windward. This would keep snow from drifting over the tents in the night.

That evening the wind and snow blew dirty gray, with grim, knuckle-down energy. We sat in our tents burping half-cooked Japanese noodles. All at once the tent walls caved in upon us, and through the little ripstop nylon squares we felt salt-lick-size blocks. And we said, "Hello, wall." We said this because one of us had worked at a ski factory with a fellow who faced the wall every day and said, "Hello wall; hello, hello wall" in a quite friendly manner. So actually we were quoting.

The wall had broken two poles. We splinted them with bamboo and, rather than rebuild the wall, decided to get up every two hours and dig out the tents. So, every two hours, someone braved the storm and shoveled off the drifted snow. The tent walls crack-snapped fiercely, like American flags on March afternoons—but louder, much louder. Sometime after midnight everyone fell asleep. How could we have fallen asleep?

I woke up before dawn in a bear hug. If I moved, the tent poles would snap. My tentmate was under

A threesome approaches Windy Corner, at 14,000 feet.
OLAF SÖÖT.

the same pressure. We called to the next tent and heard someone throw up. Expeditions, I thought. What are expeditions for? A shovel squeaked to the rescue, bravely digging a hole through one tent wall. Before the snow was cleared away, another pole crumpled.

I began to think of sitting on the sunny south steps of the student union, a chocolate-mint cone in hand, bare feet baking into the warm concrete, ivy-covered dolomite walls rising above green lawns, Frisbees wafting about, professors nodding hello. But it was not time to think; it was time to build an igloo.

We took most of the day to cut rotten blocks from the storm-softened snow and form them into an in-leaning spiral. No air remained in the air; it was all displaced by flying snow. "When our eyes we'd close, our lashes froze / Till sometimes we couldn't see." We stumbled from quarry to igloo, snow blocks crumbling in our hands, fingers numb, feet frozen. Our mason stood within the spiral; we'd hand him our blocks and he'd pack them into place. His skill would be tested when the walls began arching toward each other; that is, when walls became ceiling. He would have to guide them delicately to the final capstone before they collapsed. A partially built igloo wouldn't count.

The walls closed inward, yearning to meet. Completion looked imminent, yet impossible. By abrogation of the laws of gravity we reached the point where only a head-size hole remained. The wind tore at the hole wildly, tearing away chunks and slivers of snow. We passed the final block through the ground entrance and watched as two mittens popped it out the top, righted it, then settled it down slowly, slowly, like a trap door softly closing.

It stayed.

We crawled quickly through the entrance, fat little snowmen all, to congratulate our mason. Heavenly silence filled our crystal palace. The storm had lost its voice. We warmed our hearth with a flaming stove, brewed the good broth, and blessed the hollow ringing in our ears.

Kahiltna Katie

While we wandered up the Kahiltna Glacier, a Japanese expedition was attempting Mount Foraker. This we knew because we heard them on our radio. The word *follicle* always came up in their conversations. This identified their peak, of course, although the metaphor was inappropriate.

Hearing our counterparts through the static bolstered our belief in Kahiltna Katie. At times we knew we heard her sweet, stilted voice come faintly over the air: "Mountaineer boy, hey there, moun-

taineer boy. Come bottom of crevasse, have rice soup! Make you safe, make you happy, mountaineer boy." We took pride in steeling ourselves against her beckoning. Yet her invitation came again and again, warming our radio. It was that last "mountaineer boy" that always got to us.

One night, tossing and turning in the igloo, I almost met Kahiltna Katie in my dreams. A great crevasse opened beneath my sleeping bag, and in I swirled like a feather, coming softly to rest in a dazzling cavern far below. On the snowy floor beside me, a beautiful Asian girl dressed in white sealskin knelt beside a purring stove. The pot smelled rich and steamy.

"You must be Kahiltna Katie," I said, pinching myself.

"Solly," replied the girl. "Katie retire last week. Now live in mobile home in Palm Springs."

"I'm very sorry to hear that," I said.

She looked at me with a Mona Lisa smile and pressed my hand affectionately. "But Katie ask me to give golf ball back," she whispered.

In my palm was a well-fondled ball of peanut butter, half thawed. "Thank you," I breathed. "Thank you so much."

"Make you happy, mountaineer boy," she said.

Mountain Medicine

The blizzard I mentioned earlier was in its prime when visitors arrived. Two men, ice-beaked and ice-bearded, snowshoed into camp and asked to borrow our radio. A diabetic in their party, they said, had let his insulin freeze. We gave them the radio, and they walked back into the blizzard toward Kahiltna Pass, from where they hoped to transmit a message.

Three days later, on a shining morning, we came upon a dome-shaped tent, blue and green. No one was in sight; so we rang the doorbell. No one answered. Slowly, we zipped open the door. No one home.

Sleeping bags lay crumpled on the floor, looking as if people had just crawled out of them. Scattered about were ice axes, mittens, stray socks, pots, candy bars, and syringes. Syringes lay strewn in every corner. Realizing that the tent was abandoned—and the diabetic and his party now evacuated—we moved inside and helped ourselves to lunch. The tent walls reeked of private terror. Here the angel of death had hovered and seemed to hover still.

But we soon got used to the hastily abandoned tent. Someone found a dandy pair of overmitts and decided to borrow them. Someone else discovered a fine pair of goggles. And some knee socks, too. And more candy bars couldn't hurt. We plundered and then left, zipping the door shut once more.

Shining morning had become gray noon, and we plodded away with bleak, disjointed steps, syringes strewn in the corners of our minds.

Garden Stakes

As the expedition proceeded, I studiously plunged green bamboo garden stakes into the snow every 150 feet to mark our path. During blizzards, we could barely see from one to the next. A grand procession of garden stakes would follow us to the top. Along the sown furrows of steps, crampon-punched seed holes would soon sprout. If we didn't return quickly, the way might become wildly overgrown.

Each wand, as they were called, was decorously capped with a little orange flag. I had tied these flags on, one at a time, in the basement at home. My high-school girlfriend had come to help, and asked about the girls at college. "How are the girls at college?" she asked. I quickly attached one flag to three wands stuck together. Which was crazy—I had nothing to hide. From the summit, perhaps, I would see all the girls from college lined up behind me, carrying little orange flags.

Shining Medusas

Wonderful it is to stride downhill with an empty pack at day's end. Hips and shoulders float in stray bubbles, feet ripple downslope, and the mind does country dances. The eyes drink in, not columns of kicked steps, but wide-flung world views, complete philosophic systems in terrestrial flavors. Sun glows upon cream-cracked domes, sprouting like crystal gopher mounds, far and near. At the brink of kind winter, soft in gold haze, glinting rivulets descend canyons of brown and braid into shining medusas upon a dark plain. And the dark plain stretches outward, outward, but never to a horizon. Across the plain one can see all the way around the world, to Denali.

Dr. Livingstone, I Presume

One morning, high on the mountain, I heard British voices outside the tent and feet squeaking on the snow. Fast in the grip of altitude stupor, I took a while to decide if it was worth getting up to meet

Convocation at 17,200 feet; these mountaineers are enjoying the social scene as well as the visual one.
ROGER ROBINSON.

the newcomers. When I did crawl out, I saw two figures crouching over a stove. Their bright blue jumpsuits were tucked into sleek orange overboots. Their calves looked enormous.

"Good morning," said I, tentatively.

"Good morning," returned the shorter man. I thought his long, scraggly hair was silver at first, but then I saw it was brown, flecked with ice.

"Want some tea?" he offered.

"No, thanks," I said, and cringed, recalling the time I'd eaten Sunday dinner at a British professor's house and refused the same offer four times. The professor had finally risen from his chair and thundered, "Will you get civilized and drink some tea with us?" But this fellow with the icy hair evidently wasn't civilized; he just liked tea. He didn't care if I did or not.

"Where are you from?" I asked.

"He's from Edinburgh; I'm from Nottingham."

"Nottingham," I repeated. "As in 'the Sheriff of'?" I received a glacial stare; a change in subject seemed in order. "And your names?"

"Haston and Scott." He pronounced them crisply, precisely, like they were the title of a business establishment. I realized I had heard these names before, but I couldn't place them. He didn't ask my name.

"And what do you do for a living?"

"Climb," Scott said. "We're professionals, you know. We just did the south face—six bivouacs, with a variation of our own." He added this last detail with emphasis. They both looked exasperated.

"Amazing," I said. "You must be tired."

Scott seemed bemused and sipped his tea in silence for a while. He nodded toward the summit and murmured, "It's Mordor up there." Then, in a scrappy voice, he said, "First brew we've had in a long while. We've run out of fuel messing around with this bloody stove. Just a bag of prunes left. The altitude's got us ringy-dingy. We're just pretty bloody fucked up, mate."

"Me too," I nodded. We seemed to have something in common.

Mr. Haston had nothing to say. He put in a distant, clean-shaven nod now and then, as befits a strong, silent type. On his head sat a gray balaclava, floppy and unfolded—his wild hair emerged through the hole on top.

Upon finishing his tea, Scott fumbled with his Whillans harness, dropping it three times as he reached between his legs for the elusive crotch strap. Then the two Brits staggered unroped toward the west buttress, Haston in the lead. One of his feet was markedly pigeon-toed.

West from the summit of Denali. OLAF SÖÖT.

It's Lonely at the Top

The day came to climb to the summit. But I didn't get there. Like a penultimate stanza, I stopped 800 feet below the metal pole marking the highest cornice. I had so wanted to touch that metal and yell, "Free!" But I was dizzy, walking in circles, falling down—and the pole was out of reach. Behind me the wands stuck out of the wind-packed snow at crazy angles; I'd put them in crooked. Tears seeped out and froze, and I turned back.

Earlier, I had considered stopping twenty feet below the summit, for a hair-shirt effect. But I'd reconsidered—self-imposed false summits only nourish false humility. Now, humility faded. I was a vaguely disappointed lotus-eater stumbling down the mountainside. I was a Second Street wino in Corvallis, Oregon, peeing in my pants. I was a small boy walking through a Cascade clearcut at dusk.

And the clearcut became suddenly dark. We weren't down yet; so my companion dug a snow trench for us to sleep in while I rendezvoused with oblivion. In the morning, as I gripped an ice-filled water bottle, my frozen fingertips felt like mushy Popsicles.

"We've got to get down," said my companion that morning. "Yes, we've got to get down," I agreed placidly as I tottered after him.

Below Denali Pass the terrain steepened. I possessed a residual fear of falling downslope into a crevasse, but this did not stop me from trying. My knees crumpled, and I sailed blissfully downhill on my back. After several moments of yielding to destiny, my arms recalled the use of the ice axe. Languidly, beautifully, I turned over, brought the pick to bear upon the speeding ice, and halted serenely, taut at the end of the rope. And so we arrived, eventually, at our two yellow tents.

The next day I descended further. In the late-afternoon sunshine, time stood still inside my head. I shuffled down a narrow ridge on a forgotten mountain and came upon a ghost town of two igloos. Who's there? Staring black doorways, whitewashed sepulchers. I sat down on the snow; glistening plastic baggies blew round and round, and the wind puffed decadently. The sun pierced my eyes, and the baggies swirled round my head.

Panel of Experts

Others were frostbitten, and worse than I. We radioed for a helicopter and sat back to wait in our igloo at 14,000 feet. We were twelve strong, including our guests Doug Scott and Dougal Haston, who had helped us down the upper slopes. Two pillars supported a sagging roof of hard-snow masonry: the igloo resembled an ancient crypt. We sat on benches cut around the sides. Soup steamed in a bottomless caldron, and we poured it down the throats of our badly frozen comrades. We were worn, wondering, through. Yet expectancy lay in the air, though a worn sort of expectancy. We all sat, hunched over in archetypal waiting positions, listening for the beat of a rotor, the whistle of a locomotive, the clatter of hooves, the pattering of feet. Four of us were departing on an important journey; the others had gathered to see us off.

The two professionals crouched next to the entrance, smoking cigarettes, their gaze not quite reaching the floor. Out of nowhere, someone asked a question: "How does being married and going on expeditions work out for you?" Scott gave a funny start, then answered promptly. "Works out just fine," he said. "My missus does her thing; I do mine—we give each other that freedom. We each have our own interests and don't begrudge the other's. It's no problem at all." Even by the end of his reply, he still sounded amazed at the question.

Suddenly, Haston crawled out the entrance to take a leak. Smoke and steam hung quietly in the igloo; yet the air still held an Arctic pungence, almost too sharp to breathe. "Now, Dougal," said Doug in a more thoughtful tone, "that's another story." He shook his head sadly and mumbled something I didn't catch. No one said anything for a while.

When Dougal entered, we were talking about climbing literature. "Don't you think *Annapurna South Face* was poorly written?" I blurted. "Seems like Bonington just cranked it out to meet the expedition debts." Haston startled us by opening his mouth. "A straightforward account of the expedition," he said firmly, looking at me as if my fly were open. Then I remembered—Dougal was a hero of those pages. Too late now. "Chris wrote the book after the expedition was paid off," snapped Doug. I hoped someone would change the subject.

At last someone did, after a silence of perhaps one or two years in duration. "What do you read on expeditions?" came the question. Scott allowed that he had paged through all of Hesse on his visits to Everest. "I took a class on Hesse," said the questioner. "I received an A+ in the course." Doug grunted politely. The person went on to show his understanding of Hermann Hesse, Lit. 462, Section 1, until Scott stepped out to relieve himself.

Later, after we had become accustomed to pestering the immortals, someone popped the big one: "Why do you think you climb?" A pause ensued. Everyone looked at Doug. Doug, in turn, looked reflectively at the green twisties on the floor before replying. "Mostly," he said, "because I'm grumpy when I'm not climbing." Well put, I thought.

"And," he added, "my wife can't stand me when I'm grumpy." It all made sense: I saw how neatly climbing and marriage fit together.

Deus Ex Machina

One early morning the helicopter came to snatch us up. It circled half a dozen times as we stood outside the igloo in the aching cold. When the machine finally touched the glacier, we were instantly caught in a breath-plucking blast, a hurricane of snow needles. We groped for the chopper like blind men, one by one, forging slow-motion steps against the screaming, lacerating cold. It was far worse than any blizzard we had met with. Suddenly I reached the eye of the storm, clambered in, and kicked out a bucket of Kentucky Fried Chicken for those who remained.

As the helicopter rose, the snowscape enlarged: the igloo receded into the massive mountain. I sat on the floor of the helicopter and sank into numbness, thinking that I would remember sitting on the floor of this helicopter and sinking into numbness. I watched the Alaska Range pass by; I didn't even point a finger.

We landed. The door by my head was ripped open and a face appeared. It was Ray Genet. His forehead was wrinkled in consternation, and he stared at me for a long time without saying a thing. He seemed to want to know where I was bound.

The Perfect Bulrush

Two years after our visit to Denali, I went to a slide show given by Doug Scott in the Los Angeles area. The crowd in front of me popped up and down like grasshoppers, trying to see over the people in front of them popping up and down like grasshoppers. Under someone's hind wing I saw a piece of the southwest face of Everest. Scott was explaining his drive to climb in terms of an episode from *Through the Looking-Glass:* Alice floats through the bulrushes, looking always for a more perfect bulrush to pluck up. He talked about high-altitude euphoria and always wanting another—and better—taste of it. The audience quieted; no one popped up for a few seconds.

Scott switched continents, and a picture of a large igloo appeared on the screen. A bundle of green wands with orange flags leaned against the entrance. Scott began talking about the frostbitten climbers he'd helped down Denali. "Plucky lads, but over their heads," he commented. "They said it was Divine Providence that we happened along. I say they were just bloody lucky." And the grasshoppers roared, as if he had spoken the punch line to a cosmic joke.

Eric Sanford

Roughing It on Denali

BIG MAC IS THE AFFECTIONATE NAME given to 200 trillion tons of rock sandwiched between 100 trillion tons of ice and covered with half a trillion tons of garbage. Some have called it Mount McKinley; the natives named it Danolly, the Smelly One. I called it crazy while wondering what the hell I was doing in the village of Talkeetna, waiting with three friends for the flight to the base of the great white mountain. I knew I would be in for some strange experiences; McKinley is not only noted for its weather but for its oddball human element.

The undeniable fact that Denali—to use the more proper native name—is the highest peak in North America, as well as the continued misconception that a "tourist" route leads to the summit, lures an endless horde of naive mountaineers to Talkeetna each spring and summer. A more comical mishmash of misfits could be found only in Chamonix, Kathmandu, or JFK International. Misfits are basically harmless at those places, but at Denali a forty-minute flight deposits unprepared and bewildered climbers smack in the middle of 10,000 square miles of rock and ice; the shock when arriving is substantial. (At

least in the Himalaya one must spend a few weeks walking to get to the mountains—there's no other way.) Technically, Denali offers a choice: the purists and the foolish walk, but the lazy ones, say ninety-nine percent of the total, choose to fly.

April 16 brought good fortune. After only one day of waiting in Talkeetna, Cliff Hudson, fresh from a nonstop, thirty-eight-hour poker game, shoved the four of us and our gear into his two-seater plane. My headrest was a can of "Chateau de Chevron."

The bobbing and weaving airplane made a final dive and slammed down onto the glacier. I plopped out of the plane like the cork from a bottle of champagne and rolled off into the snow, stiff and green. Cliff lit a cigarette, gazed wistfully into the sky, and wondered if he could get in at least ten more trips before dark.

Suddenly the horizon was alive with commotion and color. Running and stumbling toward us, screaming insanely and waving their arms wildly, were ten Japanese. We stood staring in amazement; it was a sight reminiscent of northern Iwo Jima. As they got closer, I tried to decipher their spirited yelling: it sounded like "sticket" or "cricket" or, perhaps, "picket." Picket? Aha, that was it. Picket! But what did it mean? Were they all on strike? Were they building a fence? Was it the name of some Cau-

The eastern escarpment of Mount Foraker dwarfs a plane approaching the Kahiltna landing strip. OLAF SÖÖT.

43

casian general who had offended their ancestors? I got ready to dive back into the plane.

Our visitors were climbing all over themselves, each trying to be the first to grab our attention. A leader emerged and, in his fastest and most polite Japanese, recited the history of the world, or something similar. When I appeared puzzled, he started all over. One word kept popping up in his story: picket. And the crazy fellow kept pointing up at the Cassin Ridge.

Finally it dawned on me what was going on. Pickets! The guy wanted our pickets. When I pointed questioningly toward our pile of gear, the entire group began jumping up and down, jabbering all the while. Planning their trip in Japan, they had misinterpreted the Park Service equipment list and brought two dozen tomato stakes instead of climbing pickets. Finding them somewhat unsuitable for ice belays on the Cassin Ridge, the Japanese were willing to barter anything in their possession. I declined their offers until I was hoarse. I didn't plan to create an international incident, but what the hell were we supposed to use if we gave them our pickets—tomato stakes?

Hudson, standing by his plane and ready to leap in if a rumble developed, had a don't-you-little-devils-even-consider-it look on his face as he watched one of the Japanese troops fondling a wing strut. The leader launched into another tirade that I was sure was his technical explanation about how easily the plane could fly minus those cumbersome struts. Wouldn't Hudson enjoy seeing his struts put to the honorable cause of helping conquer the mountain?

Finally we escaped. Hudson escaped. The contingent from the Land of the Rising Sun retired to their huge, camouflaged World War II tent to plan their next move.

The next day began late. Actually, the day began on time, but we were a bit slow realizing it. The temperature at eight o'clock hovered at thirty below; since it was early spring, the sun didn't hit our edge of the glacier until midmorning. We spent the late-morning hours warming up and organizing our loads; we knew we should take advantage of the clear weather to move some gear up toward the mountain.

It was easy traveling along the glacier, and we sang and laughed and snapped pictures. The singing and laughing ceased, however, as the route began attacking the mountain in earnest. Above the first

Canine climbers take it easy after making the first dog-team ascent of Denali. GALEN ROWELL.

rise—the first of several thousand to come—was a rather strange sight: either the Park Service had set up a raven feeding station or else someone's food cache was being vigorously and thoroughly trashed by the huge scavengers. Half a dozen immense birds, obviously well fed, were screeching and fighting over every scrap of food. What had once been the supplies for ten climbers was now a chaotic mess strewn over several acres. I made a mental note to bury our supplies ten feet deep, not wishing to face the embarrassment of later having to explain that our failure was due to ravens.

As we wearily approached base camp late in the day, I looked up and spied a large, self-suspension dome tent slithering merrily down the glacier toward us; a moderate breeze and slight incline made its journey easy. Then, stumbling over the horizon, came a wild-eyed, half-naked man, one hand holding up his knickers to his knees and the other gesturing wildly for the tent to stop. As he frantically yelled at us, his trousers dropped to his ankles and he crashed onto the snow.

We quickly surrounded the mischievous dwelling and towed it back to its owner. It seemed he had stepped out for a quick trip to the latrine, and the tent, held down solely by the weight of his sleeping bag, had decided to go for a stroll. You can't really blame the tent; lying in the same place all day long can get pretty boring. Later, I heard the man mumbling something in Russian about "capitalist pig air currents."

Early the following morning, as we grimly ate our breakfast of sweet, sticky gruel, the crisp morning air was shattered by an explosion. I quickly analyzed the possibilities: the Japanese had decided to take our pickets by force; the mountain was actually a dormant volcano and had picked this day to erupt; or perhaps a monstrous crevasse, filled to the brim with garbage, was experiencing heartburn. But I hadn't considered reality.

We watched in awe as two Polish climbers flew out of their tent just moments before it burst into flames and was vaporized. Smoldering in the charred remains was a large, double-burner propane stove that looked like it had been pilfered from a Winnebago. The five-gallon propane canister fell to earth a few minutes later, having completed a speedy orbit of the moon.

The crafty Japanese, never ones to miss a trick, immediately converged on the hapless Poles and began chattering, "Pickets?" Pickets?" Within minutes the dejected Poles had lost most of their climbing gear.

That day, while trudging up the glacier over endless and deceitful hillocks of snow, I was reminded of factory work. If trudging were a job, you couldn't pay me enough to do it. Clever me, I do it for free.

As we approached Camp 2, I noticed that we had some new arrivals: a young couple who must have been on their first outing, since their clothing and equipment appeared brand-new. Any conscientious climber will let some favored piece of ancient equipment slip into his wardrobe to demonstrate he's been around forever.

I slumped down on the snow and said hello to the young folks. Noticing that the woman's face was beet red, I offered her some sunscreen. "No, thanks, we've got plenty," she replied, pointing to a large bottle of Johnson's Baby Oil. We talked some more and I discovered that the couple had been traveling along the glacier for eight days from base camp, having gotten slightly off course: their first two camps were actually located *below* base camp. I figured it would take them eight months to climb the mountain at that rate. I didn't mention it, just wished them luck.

The sun was appearing about five minutes earlier each day, much to my pleasure. One morning, as we luxuriated in the warmth, two skiers appeared on the horizon. We watched enviously as they carved smooth, graceful turns down the fresh powder covering the glacier. As they got closer, it seemed that only one was making smooth, graceful turns; the other was apparently practicing survival skiing.

They soon reached our camp, and the wobbly skier collapsed in the snow. The other delivered a more formal greeting: "Hello. Nice day, isn't it?"

"Yes, it certainly is," I replied. "Say, is your friend there okay?"

"Well, actually we had a bit of a problem up above, and he seems to have a slight cut on his face. We don't really have much of a first-aid kit. Do you think you could look at him?"

We gathered around the moaning man and rolled him over. A little problem? His face was split open from eye to chin, and his swollen tongue stuck out where he had once had some front teeth. We spent an hour stitching him up. Since he was close to going into shock from the loss of blood, we lashed him to one of our sleds and headed down toward base camp to arrange to have him flown out.

His companion mentioned something about trying to ski up the mountain in a day and his buddy falling at Windy Corner and grabbing a fixed rope that turned out not be be fixed and tumbling a thousand feet down the glacier tethered to a pair of windmilling skis and stopping five feet above a huge crevasse by digging his elbows into the ice. Skiing around Windy Corner? For an encore maybe he'll try riding a bike down Hoover Dam!

Soon we arrived back at base camp, which by

For some climbers, at least, a portable stereo enhances the base-camp experience. ALAN KEARNEY.

that time resembled Grand Central Station. Twenty new arrivals from a Seattle-based climbing school had just been dropped off, presumably by a 747. As we approached, they all stopped whatever they were doing and stared at us with a hey-what-are-you-guys-doing-here? expression on their pasty white faces.

After the novelty of our arrival wore off, they went back to the matter at hand—issuing ice axes and crampons to everyone. Most of them stared at this gear as if they had never seen it before. One lad insisted his pack was already too heavy and that a friend had told him he didn't really need those spikes anyway. Still another chap emerged from an army-surplus pup tent wearing full camouflage fatigues, an olive-drab helmet complete with netting, and a belt canteen. I hoped I would get to see him drink out of a metal canteen at twenty below. The Park Service questionnaire had asked, "Do you have your own equipment?" He had undoubtedly answered, "Affirmative, sir."

As we sat and waited for the rescue plane to arrive and take the skier away, a plump, assertive woman approached me, apparently assuming I had something to do with the Seattle expedition. "Say," she said angrily, "what's this about sharing a tent with someone else? I didn't pay $1,900 to share this stupid little tent. There's hardly enough room in there for me! What do you mean by supplying only ten tents? I told you people I wanted a private tent, and I mean to have one. I don't care if you have to go out and buy one! You hear me?"

I assured her I totally agreed and that I would rectify the problem right away. She stomped off across the glacier.

Nearby, four climbers were clumsily setting up their tent while roped together. Obviously, they had heeded the advice in *Freedom of the Hills:* one *never* walks on a glacier unroped. Like the action in a three-ring circus, so much was going on that I found it impossible to absorb it all.

As we continued to wait for the plane, our casualty kept staring into a mirror, tilting his head this way and that, and asking if we thought he'd still be good-looking. And did we think he'd have much of a scar? And did we know the name of a good plastic surgeon in Anchorage?

The plane landed in the fading daylight, and we loaded the poor wretch into it and headed back to Camp 2, arriving at midnight. An entertaining day.

Another morning, another tedious haul. As we flopped down after the exhausting carry, we realized we were not alone: a hundred yards away, a large party was putting the finishing touches on a gigantic igloo that must have taken a full week to build. We set up our modest camp and went to visit.

Their igloo resembled the Astrodome. I poked my head inside and saw room for twenty climbers, though only two were dozing at the moment. "Howdy," I greeted the occupants. "Did the game get rained out or am I here on the wrong afternoon?"

One of the men propped himself up on an elbow, squinted in my direction, grunted, pulled his sleep-

---

An injured climber is readied for evacuation from Denali Pass, at 18,200 feet. In a few hours the victim will be in a warm city hospital. GALEN ROWELL.

ing-bag hood over his head, and flopped back down. Perhaps he didn't speak English.

Outside, another member of the party appeared, and we all sat down and had a cup of tea. "Say," I began. "Those fellows in the igloo seem rather beat."

"Ya, they're not going any further. I told them for six months to get into shape, but no way. All they wanted to do was eat and drink and play cards and watch the 49ers. To hell with them. They can sit here and freeze for all I care. I hope they end up in a crevasse. The rest of us are going to the top!"

As we sipped tea in the soft evening light, another climber appeared on the glacier above us and began threading his way down through a maze of crevasses. For several minutes I watched him weave in and out of the creaking mass of ice.

"By the way," I asked my host, "is that fellow with your party?"

"Ya, that's George. He just went up to have a look around."

"Alone?" I queried.

"No one else wanted to go."

"Isn't that a bit dangerous?" I continued.

Taking advantage of a perfect Denali day, numerous mountaineers, having left their camp in the 17,000-foot basin, begin their pilgrimage toward the summit.
BRIAN OKONEK.

"Dangerous? Why?"

"Well, what if he should fall into a crevasse?"

"Oh, that's no problem. He's wearing his beeper."

"His beeper?"

"Ya, you know, one of these." He reached into his pocket and pulled out a Skadie Avalanche Traceiver. "Haven't you ever used one of these before?"

"Well, yes, I've used it before, but not in crevasses."

With a bored look he continued to explain. "It's simple. If anyone falls into a crevasse, we know just where to look for him. See, you simply turn this dial and put this earplug in and listen for the beeps from his unit. They'll lead you right to the crevasse. Using the Skadie means you don't need ropes anymore."

"Oh. Now I understand. . . . Yes. . . . A good idea. . . . I wonder why no one else thought of that before?" I turned my attention back to the wandering climber, thinking that at least he wouldn't be dead *and* missing in some bottomless crevasse; his friends would know exactly where the body was. I also wondered if they had access to a 100-mile extension cord—the battery life of a Skadie is only five days.

We bade the group good night, not wishing to wait around for the inevitable rescue.

At Camp 3 we decided to make only one carry per camp until we were in place for a summit bid. The thought of trudging up and down Big Mac simply to shuttle our food a little farther up was not at all appealing. I was beginning to feel—and probably smell—like a burro.

We packed huge loads and began to trudge up the 3,000-foot wall to Camp 4. Since we didn't have our Skadie beepers, we opted for a more conventional style of climbing: we used ropes.

At 13,000 feet we reached a long, icy traverse above a steep drop. A series of reddish brown blotches just beneath the ice fell into the abyss. I immediately flashed on the climber with the broken face and shuddered as I peered downward.

Farther along, I came upon the fixed rope that the "beeper bunch" had installed earlier and told us about. I gave it a tug; it seemed solid, but force of habit made me ask for a belay anyway. I clipped into the fixed rope, which was secured at the near end by a shiny new ice screw, and gingerly started across. As I reached the opposite end, my heart missed a beat: the rope wasn't attached to anything. It had simply been stuffed into a hole, where it had frozen into place. Fixed? Those idiots had "fixed" only one end of the rope! It reminded me of the last time I had my car "fixed." I gave the rope a sharp tug, and it popped out of the hole and dangled uselessly in space.

We had been on the mountain more than a week, and it was time for a rest day. I slept until the first rays of the sun hit the frozen tent, then turned over and slept another hour until the tent was a dripping mess. Finally, I oozed out of my bag and stepped outside into the brilliant sunlight. Clad only in my red long-johns and huge, white bunny boots, I decided to wander around. Climbing to the top of a nearby rise, I was surprised to see other signs of life: garbage lay strewn around a crudely built igloo.

Feeling sociable, I strolled over to greet the occupants. As I reached the entrance, a scruffy head appeared, followed closely by a raggedly clothed body. He spoke first. "Like, hey, man, how's it goin'?"

"Er, fine," I responded. "How about you?"

"Hey, man, it's a real bummer, you know? You got a cigarette?"

"Ah, no. I don't. Sorry."

"Hey, man, that's okay. Like, I've been trying to get off this hill for like two weeks, you know what I mean?"

"Er, no, not really. . . . What happened?"

"Well, like, I had to kill all my dogs, you know, man, and. . . ."

"Dogs?"

"Yeah, man, my sled dogs." He motioned over to the far side of his igloo.

I glanced down and swallowed hard. Scattered about the igloo were pieces of dog. Bones and tails and feet and eyes and ears were frozen in the snow like the fossilized remains of a slaughterhouse. My gaze continued to the top of the igloo. There, impaled like a pagan war token, was a dog's head. My jaw dropped a foot.

Dog Head Bob, as we later named him, caught me staring. "That's Charlie, man. He's the best dog I ever had, so, like, I gave him the best place, you know?"

Nauseated, I shook my head in agreement. "How come you killed your dogs?"

"Well, man, I ran out of food, you know, and then I got my feet froze and the sled's stuck up on the hill, you know, and my old lady can't get it down and. . . ."

I turned toward the steep slope rising behind us and could barely make out a solitary figure struggling with something next to a mammoth crevasse. I turned back to Bob, took a step back, and tried to comprehend the situation.

"Yeah, that's my old lady up there. She's still trying to get that old sled down so we can get outa here."

I found myself staring at his feet. His huge boots looked like someone had taken a shotgun to them.

"Yeah, man, I borrowed these boots from this guy, you know, and he said not to worry about the holes and stuff. But I guess they musta leaked or something because I froze my feet."

He pulled one of his feet from the worthless boots, and, indeed, it was swollen and discolored. "Man, like I can't even fit any socks on, you know?"

We conversed for a few more minutes and he told me how he had heard about this guy who wanted to drive his dog team up Denali, but that he, Bob, a trueblood Alaskan, had decided to ace this other guy out, but he had run out of food halfway up on account of his dogs, who weren't exactly keen for this trip, and so here he was with no more dogs to eat, and did we have any extra food he could have?

I told him we were fresh out of dog meat but that perhaps the expedition right behind us might have some.

I returned to camp and related my amazing tale. Everyone thought I had finally gone off the deep end this time; but one by one they ventured out to talk to Dog Head Bob, and each returned shaking his head in awe. We spent the rest of the day drying out our gear and trying not to think of sled dogs.

Both the sun and Dog Head Bob were still asleep the next morning as we pushed on up the icy slopes. Several million miso-secs later (on a long climb, each day is divided into many millions of "misery-seconds" instead of hours; each miso-sec is slightly longer than the preceding one), we crested a ridge at 16,000 feet and slumped into the snow for a rest. Above us, a weary-looking threesome were making their way down a steep, wind-sculpted ridge. Their progress resembled a slapstick version

Detail of the middle portion of the West Buttress Route, showing the infamous Windy Corner (at the base of the sharp ridge at left center) and the extensive basin at 14,000 feet. BRADFORD WASHBURN / BOSTON MUSEUM OF SCIENCE.

of tug of war: the leader would stumble forward, pulling the rope taut and yanking the following two climbers off their feet. The last man would retaliate with a violent yank. The poor fellow in the middle was being cut in two by the oscillating antics.

Assuming they were returning from the summit, I inquired about the conditions. It seemed that they hadn't made it past their camp at 17,000 feet: their summit food had been packed next to the white gas, and the escaping fumes had permeated all the food, resulting in a pile of inflammable mush, some rather strained relationships, and a terminated expedition. I urged them to raid our small supply of emergency food at 14,000 feet and give it another try, but the

thought of retracing their steps up Big Mac didn't appeal to them. We said good-bye and watched as they started down, tugging and swearing with each step.

We continued to inch our way up the mountain: one step, one breath, one step, one breath. Rest five minutes, gather some energy, then one step, one breath. At 17,000 feet we came upon an abandoned snow cave piled high with candy wrappers, torn plastic water bottles, and pieces of frozen Ensolite. It wasn't an appealing place, but we were glad to set up camp out of the frigid wind. The wind howled all night, and no matter how often we plugged the cave's tiny chinks, spindrift spread over everything.

The summit day at last. At six o'clock, as we left our cave, the thermometer registered a toasty minus twenty, and the winds were of the gale-force variety. The snow swirling around my feet made the ground itself appear to be moving—a boiling caldron. Time became meaningless, movement imperceptible. Each step forward was an instinctive movement as my toes felt for the incline ahead.

At some point my ankles didn't flex quite as much; the angle had eased. The top? I eagerly peeled back my furry hood and looked upward for the first time in hours. A few yards away was a pile of junk: the summit!

Clouds and snow swirled around us. Razor-sharp crystals attacked every spot of unprotected skin, but I couldn't complain: this was the experience I had come for. The sweat and toil and uselessness of struggling to the top of this inelegant mound was the ultimate act of nonproductivity, and I had loved every minute of it.

The view? Well, I'm sure it would have been quite magnificent if there had been one, but, alas, the mist was thickening by the moment; the only view I had was of my own feet as they turned and pointed downhill.

It was time to undo it all and head back down the mountain. Down past the cluttered snow cave and the wind-scoured ridge. Down past the gaping crevasse with the woman tugging at an ice-encrusted sled. Down past the dog-head igloo and the unfixed rope. Down past the climbers who would not move. Down past the beepers and the creepers, the eager and the tired, the friendly and the fierce. Down past a dozen expeditions, large and small, fast and slow. Down past rotting supplies and quarreling ravens. Down past tugging guides and submissive clients with sunburned eyes and ears. Down, down, down. . . .

David Gancher

ILLUSTRATIONS BY DEBRA SMITH

The Ascent of Typewriter Face

MIST SWIRLED AROUND THE towering column that climbers call Coffee Cup as the party of fingers began the arduous ascent from the lap's floor. The first reach gained us the overhang; then we followed the cracks of a desk drawer, then a technical reach to a brass pull outcropping onto an unbroken blank wall of flawless mahogany. Though the total height was something less than a foot, the fingers still had to surmount an altitude equivalent to more than four times their own elevation. Too low for a helicopter rescue. Just as dawn broke over the Selectric Range, our party of eight fingers and two native thumbs finally gazed up at the column-figured complex formation of Typewriter Face: the final frontier.

How many other fingers, hands, had climbed this same formation? Thousands perhaps. Perhaps many thousands. But still it remained virgin territory. Though the routes were known and touch-typing was an increasingly respected technique of finger-mountaineering, the variations on the same theme—fingers versus language—were endless. Royal "Typewriter" Ribbons put it best: "Give a million monkeys a million pitons," he theorized, "and some day one will write an article for *Ascent.*" And design a backpack for REI, I bitterly added as my thumb stumbled across the space bar for the thirteenth time in as many sentences.

The weather was calm, luminous yet ominous as the index took the lead for the first ten-pitch, forcing its way up the crack between the *n* and *h*—a route pioneered years before by Remington, Underwood, Olivetti, giants of a bygone era. Finger-mountaineering had been different then, was the thought that suddenly invaded my mind, like ants, or maybe wind. It was cruder, more mechanical. Carriages had to be thrown by hand; ribbons were made of unwieldy cloth. Often a single paragraph could take a full week.

We were luckier, smarter, richer, and better-fed. But still a deadly acid torpor, unseasonable and unwelcome, rapidly spread across the keyboard. We had reason to fear. We had our fear to reason with. We had corrasable bond, pitons—and Ezerase if all else failed. We hung our hammocks then from the forks of the *y* as the sky lowered, and nounless adjectives—flabby, pointless—poured down on us.

I was cold, very cold. Until that moment, I had thought that *cold* (adj.) was a synonym for *frigid* or *chilly*. (The noun was a different story; perhaps I will tell it one day.) I knew nothing. I had not experienced real cold, the cold that lives in the mountains and only comes down to pick up its mail. The real

cold that pours up your sleeves, the cold that won't go away. My fingers were growing numb. The question was, Would hypothermia win? And if it did, could I spell it? Would the fingers fall from the keyboard with tiny, wordless screams? Would my final paragraph end in a jumble of meaningless, descendingly lower-case consonants?

I suddenly wondered what I was doing here. Why was I not at home, warm, snug, whittling pitons before a warmly flickering television? What were the deeper typos that drew me back, time and time again? I wondered if I couldn't write only about solo climbs and hole up in Chowchilla with a typewriter, a moll, a sun lamp, a tub of ice, and a full case of mumps instead of trying to type on a freezing mountain ledge in the middle of the alphabet. Sleep was slow to rappel from the summits into the chimneys of my mind.

The next morning, things looked better. I was in Miami. But no—that was a rogue phantasm, a brain-edema illusion. I cleared my head. I cleared my throat. A sudden break in the clouds revealed, far above, our goal: the paper—pristine, unblemished, untouched, and other adjectives too tedious to recount. It seemed balanced in the glacial grips of a dread, granitic roller. Exactly a century before, at 8:27 A.M., John Muir had described this unusual formation: "Though the hands of angels running through the hair of the infinite," he posited, "might pause while all nature in conclave solemn the spirit of the mountains themselves in glee ecstatic proclaimed," he proclaimed, "still would I climb. And climb I still," he still continued.

As the sun rose on the eastern horizon over the distant peak that climbers call Beige Telephone, our spirits quickened. Unseen, on the horizon, a helicopter restlessly prowled like a phantom dragonfly. Its flat, tropical flap came to us like rumors of war across a documentary, Baltic skyline.

We were in trouble, and we knew it. Our ropes were unshown. Our period was faint. Our ribbon was running out, our tabs were cramped, our slots unfilled, our stamina severely taxed by Proposition 13, our credulity taxed by the state. Our advances had retreated, our royalties were overthrown. Our enthusiasm waned as our ears waxed. The ice was as rotten as Canadian wine.

Now, as the fluffy adjectives and blunt metaphors gave way to the stinging sleet of adverbs, we began to wonder. Would the final, the ultimate attempt on Typewriter Face remain frustrated by the rain of apathy, the rein of inhibition, the reign of tears? Or would the sky finally clear, the platen rolling, phrases falling from the frigid digits of creativity, the glacial wall of editorial license scoured clean by freshets of springlike verbiage amid the granitic pronouns?

Friends had warned me about this climb. "Your fingers will never make it clean," they said. "Don't do it. You'll never get past the rapid backspace, and even if you do, the mountain gods all speak Bulgarian." Again, Royal "Typewriter" Ribbons put it best: "The Selectric Range has seen them all, and still it remains unqueried." Nonetheless, we persevered.

Six drafts it took, and one finger had to descend—it had an early train to catch. Many an adverb met early excision, and the bindings on our semicolons broke repeatedly and had to be mended by makeshift conjunctions. Too bad. But finally, one last stormy paragraph in the middle of the Fallible Galleys, we stood—humble, yet arrogant; wordless, yet prolix—on the very summit. We had withstood all the challenges, the heavy weather that the Selectric Range throws at every finger-mountaineer—Index, Mar Rel, Tab Clr and Set, Back Space, and Shift—yet here we were.

God, it was good to be alive.

*The existence of some terribly yawning abyss in the mountains
. . . was frequently described to us by crafty or superstitious
Indians. Hence the greater our surprise upon first beholding a fit
abode for angels of light.*

—Lafayette Bunnell, member of the Mariposa Battalion,
on discovering Yosemite Valley in 1851

Jeff Long

Angels of Light

Chapter One

ICE—A GIGANTIC, PRIMEVAL SHEET OF IT —peeled loose from the summit rim and fluttered by like a torn wing, sucking at the night air. It glinted once in the cold moonlight as it sank away, then exploded with a roar against a girdle of rock 3,000 feet lower and scourged the spidery forest with shrapnel.

"Jesus," breathed John Dog, a brief anthem of relief. His fingers were numb and he was tiny, a slight creature willing itself up the hard space and color that formed the vertical walls of El Capitan. "Veins like rope," he silently chanted as if to pull the rim lower. "Like rope, my veins." It was Christmas Eve, and all he was wishing was for an end to this killing beauty, for respite from this night upon this drifting continent.

Frost poured from his mouth. He was tired to the bone. Even his mane of black hair weighed heavy. But the summit was no more than a couple dozen yards now. And he had veins like rope. A chronic voyeur of his own possibilities, he told himself that again. Then, for the fifth time in an hour, El Cap's icy rim creaked like cast iron bending and sent a huge sheet knifing overhead, and he flinched.

Two ropes were knotted at his waist. One bellied out into open space, arcing down and then back into the wall where the far end was tied to his partner, Tinkerbell. The second rope fed through a series of rusting pitons and nuts fixed into the wall. It was this second rope that was supposed to catch John Dog if he fell.

Three thousand feet above the dark soil of California, he pinched a slight granite flake and shifted his weight from the toe of one foot to the other. It was a wintry motion, slow and brittle. The moon, carved white, hung beside John Dog's poised feet, searing the vertical rock and starving his shadow. Fifty feet more, he coaxed himself. Fifty feet into midnight and he'd be up, just ahead of the approaching storm. Then he would haul their gear up one line while Tinkerbell ascended the other. Fifty feet to reentry, to the horizontal globe where trees grew upright and gravity was not a mortal consideration. It had been an endless five days of climbing. The days had been short, the nights arctic. Now the distant storm was boiling to a soft crescendo. A tidal wave of clouds engulfed half the sky, bending to flood the moon, his only source of light. The sense of urgency was not unfamiliar.

He'd been here before, muscling against the elements, hugging close to walls while exhaustion or fear or storms or the mountain itself conspired to dislodge him. He had always survived, sometimes just barely, but never stupidly. "Skin like a condom, veins like rope. . . ." He caught the echoes more fully now. That's what a sports magazine had once written about him, drafting a portrait of a witless barbarian. He should have known better than to talk to that journalist. "The grandson of a Chiricahua Apache shaman, half Apache and magician himself, he can stick a finger or toe to almost any surface—granite, brick, or the sandstone of his native desert spires—and it will stick like a spot weld. One of the nation's premier rockclimbers, a natural-born mountaineer. . . ." A grim, cold *cuate,* shivered John Dog. Beat, frozen, and fifty feet short. But no barbarian.

He eased upward, locking his taped knuckles inside a deep fissure. The way it felt, the movement it invited, the very smell . . . all were echoes of a thousand similar cracks. There were other echoes, too, other dimensions as he pulled higher and edged the inner toe of each worn rubber sole against new crystals. Not all were as immediate as the bite of stone against his fist or the urgency rearing high in that cloudbank. Some of the resonance was so old and persistent that it was next to silence. There was, for instance, no ignoring the Chiricahua advice that no one is your friend, not even your brother or father or mother; only your legs are your friends, only your brain, your eyesight, your hair, and your hands. My son, echoed the void gaping under each toe, you must do something with those things.

He fell.

It was that sudden.

As if skinning off a glove, John Dog felt his hand slide from the crack. His toes lost their granite purchase. He gave a reflexive slap to the rock, and then he was off, flying toward the ground, far, far below. The wall overhung, and so he drifted, mute and free, full of fear. The air was clear, a buoyant, sucking emptiness. I'm falling, he registered. It was a soft moment, which allowed him thoughts.

This shoulder, he predicted without question, this hip. They'll hit first. Christ. You've done it this time. He glimpsed the cadaverous moon tilting sideways, then rapidly upside-down. He heard a thin, metallic pop followed by a second one. Oh, Christ. He gritted his teeth, his dread deepening. There go the pins. One by one the ancient pitons that he'd clipped into as he climbed by them failed. Pop, pop. The sound of crystal exploding. Or breakfast cereal. Pop. His protection jerked out of the rock like joints from sockets. He had nothing else to do as he unzipped; so he counted the pops.

He passed Tinkerbell. He saw the moonlit boy as an instant of mercy. Spare me, thought John Dog. Catch me, Tink. Please. But not a sound passed his lips. He felt the rope tighten at his waist and counted two more pops. With each pop the rope relaxed

again. Gone, he thought without astonishment. I'm gone away.

But suddenly, with a long, dreamlike bounce, he stopped. The rope stretched elastically, snatching him away from the abyss, and then he was slammed pell-mell into the wall, his shoulder and hip striking first. His lungs emptied with a frosty *whoof.*

Tink had caught his fall.

He felt pain, but it was a distant, unflowered sensation. John Dog didn't care. As if in supplication, he reached both hands above his head and grasped the rope, gasping. He touched his forehead to the rough perlon line. *"Padre nuestro,"* he started the prayer, then gave in to his adrenalin and simply sat there. Still clutching the rope, he dangled above the inky forest floor. He raised his head, listening for the stars to twinkle audibly like a chandelier just barely disturbed. But all he heard was the abrupt, mossy burp of a faraway frog. In a slow, noiseless spin, the world began to accumulate around him again. The same moon was gleaming across the same cold acres of vertical granite, illuminating John Dog's long, black hair, washing the whiskers on his face quicksilver. It was like him to watch himself dangling there, tied to a puppet string far too close to God.

At an even six feet he was barrel-chested with aboriginal legs that were longer than Apache but slightly bandy all the same. He didn't have to wonder what his mother had looked like; one glance down his hybrid body and he could catalog her features. Besides those long legs, she'd carried narrow feet and small hands that looked almost delicate on him. He was self-conscious about those hands. They seemed so inadequate for all the gripping and grabbing and pliers-tight pinching that climbing demanded.

Certainly his hands seemed less than true to the desert savagery that was the other half of his heritage and had stalked and worried his younger self like a scorpion. The Indian in him was prominent: straight hair, black eyes, and huge, Mongolian cheekbones. What he most often recognized in the mirror, though, was neither the Anglo nor the Indian. What he saw was the impact of one culture upon the other, something quieter than intercourse, the mark of history all over his face. And it never failed to shame him: smallpox scars. The pockmarks ruined his wide, angular cheeks. He saw himself as a bad invention, the product of too fierce a seed or a not quite certain ovary. The pitting scars were proof that his mother had vanished into mystery, marooning him and his brother with a dusky, nomadic man who knew roughnecking and bars and a thousand stories of his father's fathers and who could track bobcat from horseback and cut water from cactus and coax crude oil from the barren earth, a man who'd struggled like a hero to be both father and mother to two dusky sons but never quite got it down. His pa had forgotten to get John Dog immunized, and by the time he'd remembered, the disease had finished with his younger son. John Dog didn't blame his father.

He'd even quit blaming himself for the ugly scars. He could look in the mirror now and touch the pockmarks and accept that he was marred, but that it wasn't his fault. With a sort of reverse vanity that had infuriated his Jesuit high-school teachers, he carried humility with him everywhere. He was reticent in crowds, shy around strangers, and coeds had never quit teasing that he must be retarded or mute. The pockmarks gave him a vigilance. When he looked at people, his dark eyes always saw them looking first, studying his face, his skin, his fallibility. Lately, he could say it wasn't his fault: maybe they weren't looking critically, just out of interest. But that still didn't take the sting out. Too many years had gone into feeling marked. Maybe, he sometimes smiled in the mirror, maybe he carried *penitente* blood in him along with the Chiricahua and Anglo and just enjoyed torturing himself. Sort of like climbing with knees he could scarcely bend some mornings and hands plagued by arthritis and wrists with tendinitis. Or hoping for Harvard when Berkeley had proved too much after three short semesters.

The moon floated perilously close to the billowing cloudbank, and frost drifted from his nostrils.

"John?" Tinkerbell's voice floated down and clutched him in midsentiment. John Dog looked up toward the paltry cobweb of nylon straps and ropes that anchored both their lives to El Cap, but didn't answer.

"Hey, John," Tinkerbell repeated blindly, more urgently.

"You okay?" John Dog called up, stealing the initiative. His voice quavered a little, which annoyed him. He scolded himself with a hiss.

"Fine," Tinkerbell called down. "You?"

"Crazy, man. Crazy." But John Dog was not amused. It was cold, he was exhausted, and the summit was much more than fifty feet away now. He'd have to climb the pitch all over again. Glittering overhead, liquid in the moonlight, hung the icy summit. The holy fucking grail. He sighed. Now it would take three hours to get to the top, maybe four or five. They'd be lucky to get off by dawn, and luckier still to beat the storm. John Dog moved his limbs one by one, checking his shoulder and hip for damage. Bruised, he knew. He studied his taped hands as if they were traitors, his body a Judas.

Ten months into his twenty-eighth year, he was hanging on the very brink of adulthood. It was high time to quit climbing but difficult to let go. More

than the lifestyle of a rock jock tiptoed in the balance; it was also a heritage, a full-blown past rooted in centuries of simple lust for the mountains. On both sides of his family, Anglo and 'skin, ancestors had loved and coveted their abrupt landscapes. More than anything else, the defiance of gravity guided his thoughts about heritage and gave him license to think of himself as a mountain man. The thought of leaving these walls and mountains caused him pain—pain, he sometimes rhapsodized, like the fur-trapper Hugh Glass must have felt, grizzly-scarred and lame, bidding adios to his people at the 1824 rendezvous in Jackson Hole. Like Maurice Herzog, the great French alpinist, must have felt as he watched the doctor snip off frostbitten joints in the jungles below Annapurna. Echoes. The thought of turning his back on the mountains and never returning was as terrible to him as it was romanticized. That was all part of it, though. The overblown melancholy. The power and glory.

"Be up in a minute," he called. He wanted to rest and digest the adrenalin, draw in the moment. Once this climb was over, he'd forget these thoughts about mortality or, better yet, would fish the thick spiral notebook out of his backpack down in Camp 4 and jot down his confessions under Mosquito Wall, the name of this route, just the way he had under Muir Wall, North America Wall, Bonatti Pillar, Super-couloir, Walker Spur, Ama Dablam, and all the other major routes he'd done. "Fingerpaintings" he'd called the journal, the stuff of his never-ending childhood. His eyes followed a lone set of headlights creeping along the valley floor. An orange satellite floated up beside Sagittarius, then sank into storm clouds.

And then, for just two or three moments, between wisps of sharp breeze, John Dog heard something new and separate. A faint, irrelevant buzz, like the drone of a gnat. Then it was gone, next to imaginary. It was an airplane, off course and sliding to its doom, but John Dog didn't bother wondering about the source of the sound. He didn't care. He sniffed the air and wondered how Tink could have put up with the stink for so many days. He grinned a small one at that, then grabbed the rope. Up, he commanded. Up so you can go down. Up. Down. The no-exit, alpine-circle game. Sisyphus never had it so good. He pulled hard.

Chapter Two

ON THE NIGHT BEFORE CHRISTMAS the Sierra Nevada set in motion columnar inversions over lakes that served as constant temperature sources. Through such whirlpools of air, an aging Lockheed Lodestar, off course, tried to thread the mountain range. Near the crest a fierce and sudden battle of physics ensued, during which the aircraft sacrificed its right wing in order to maintain a temporary equilibrium of its whole.

Seconds later the greater part of the plane came to rest at the bottom of Ophidian Lake, an oval tarn coiled just below treeline. As if closing one contented eye, the lake slowly froze over in the following weeks, covering the dead machine with a thick sheath of ice, snow, and pine needles. It would have been a perfectly kept winter secret except for one thing: seven telltale feet of the tail section jutted above the lake's surface.

On February 28, more than two months after the crash, a party of snowshoers discovered an airplane wing with the obituary N8106R emblazoned on its metal skin. On their way back out of the forests high above Yosemite Valley, the snowshoers forgot exactly where they'd found the wing, but that was all right. For the time being, the call letters were quite sufficient.

The Federal Aviation Administration was first. Contacted by the snowshoers, they pieced together a background report on the plane. It was a Lockheed Lodestar with a 5,000-pound load capacity, registered to a fictitious person in Albuquerque and purchased in Bartlesville, Oklahoma. Beyond that there seemed to be little information: no flight plan had been filed. The news of an unknown plane crash puzzled the FAA only mildly. The rationale behind a flight over the Sierra in a snowstorm at night was odd, but not so odd that the plane's purpose was totally mystifying. Smugglers rarely file flight plans.

The FAA contacted Customs. The presumption that drugs were involved was automatic; therefore Customs contacted the Drug Enforcement Agency. What exactly was being smuggled, how much, and where it was at present remained unanswered questions, but three federal agencies were now involved. That, the respective authorities felt, was a good start.

Had the crash occurred in warmer weather and closer to the highway, representatives of the three agencies no doubt would have examined the site themselves. But given the fifteen-foot backcountry snows, it was deemed wise to contact the National Park Service. The Park Service jumped to life and on March 10 dispatched ten rangers from its winter staff to pinpoint the wreckage. The rangers were rebuffed once, then twice, by blizzards. Finally, on March 27, a young ranger by the name of Elizabeth Jenks unlocked the mystery of N8106R.

A bright, large-boned girl from a southeastern Oregon cattle ranch, and a graduate of the University of Washington's forestry program, Jenks was the sole woman in the company of nine men, some taciturn about their doubts and two or three openly delighted to have her along. Sex discrimination was a brand-new term in the Park Service in 1973, a buzzword associated with hairy armpits, equal opportunity, and forests of clenched female fists. She had been hired to satisfy a trend; that's how most of the men lived with it. For them, her rationale was simple: she was on a husband hunt. Besides doing a good job and keeping it, however, what Jenks wanted most this first year was to make it through without having to grow testicles. She was a methodical skier, nicely attuned to her own pace, and as a result was the first to close in on the lake.

No one knew exactly where they might find the downed plane, or if they ever would. After fourteen miles and seven hours of travel, the general feeling was that if they hadn't yet skied ten feet above the buried wreakage, then soon they would, and would never know it. They had found the wing, of course, but the plane could be anywhere. Another commonly held opinion was that an airplane filled with dope would not be going anywhere until spring thaw, at which time two hippies on a leash could locate it with minimal effort. The party stopped for the night, made camp, and resumed the hunt the next morning, cold and grouchy about the task at hand. Nevertheless, they continued to search all day, devoting themselves to cursory probing into likely looking humps of snow and occasional glances into the surrounding forest for signs of sudden trauma: broken treetops, torn metal, dead bodies.

By six o'clock most of the rangers were neatly burrowed in snow caves, snug and drowsy. But before she surrendered the search—and, even more importantly, missed the subtle red alpenglow that had blossomed without warning—Jenks skied toward the crest of a nearby ridge. The ridge was bare, its vegetation long ago slaughtered by the wind. At the north end of the ridge a gentle decline swept out through a miniature forest of stunted pines and introduced Ophidian Lake. Perhaps a hundred feet from the drift-covered beach, she saw the upright tail section of an airplane. It jutted like an unflagging erection, the sole clue that something larger and more stimulating lay locked beneath the ice.

The day had been long and aggravating, and Jenks's glide was a trifle more aggressive than it should have been. Her speed picked up on the crusted snow. She tried unsuccessfully to telemark, but the powder was too deep. A suitcase-size mound loomed in her immediate path, threatening to snap her wooden ski tips. With a last-minute twist she managed to ram the object broadside instead of tips first and ignobly toppled over.

Jenks's first reaction was to look toward the ridge to make sure none of the men had witnessed her graceless halt. "Hell," she sniffed in irritation. Her second reaction was to brush the telltale snow off her clothing and check her skis and poles for fractures. Her pride and equipment accounted for, Jenks stabbed at the offending lump with one pole. To her surprise, the tip penetrated what she'd thought was a rock. Curious, she brushed a little snow off the lump, then more.

The lump was burlap, and under that, showing through a gash in the corner, was yellow plastic. She dusted more snow off, enough to uncover black lettering stenciled on the burlap.

On the first line was the word *Especial.*

The line beneath consisted of three red X's.

And beneath that was an ostentatious, hand-size outline of a marijuana leaf, its five toothy fingers splayed like a partial sunburst. Jenks exhumed the bundle and stepped back, amazed. It was a cubic foot of grass. On the butt end were painted the numerals 23. Twenty-three pounds, she wondered, or the twenty-third bale? Or, more likely, twenty-three kilos. Fifty pounds of pot? She lifted her wide, gray eyes from the bale. Only then did she notice that on every side, upslope and all the way down to the lake, she was surrounded by lumps of snow, all of them just like this one.

Chapter Three

THEY WERE EXPATRIATE RABBLE with their hair in leonine disarray and their clothing either unwashed or so old and patchy that washing was a questionable expense. A dozen or so of them lorded it over two tables shoved together in the middle of the Four Seasons restaurant in Yosemite Lodge. Some wore tennis shoes with the soles taped to the toes; others sat bundled in lifeless parkas devoid of down feathers and repaired with crude X's of white adhesive tape. Legwear ranged from ankle-length knickers to navy-surplus wool pants and blue jeans; on their heads were caps, wool balaclavas, and one or two bandanas wrapped pirate-style. What little money they had came from misused student loans, odd jobs in the park, and the dumpsters, which yielded aluminum cans worth a nickel each at the local grocery. "They were typical mountaineers," John Dog had blithely resurrected from a century-old paragraph. "Outcasts from society, discontented with the world, comforting themselves in the solitude of nature by the occasional bearfight."

They were too loud that night, radiating the sort of vulgarity beatniks and hobos used to, their behavior so outrageous it set the jaws of the family men, mothers, and honeymooning couples straining to enjoy a civilized meal. Known to the park rangers as C4B's, or Camp 4 Bums, they weren't a gang, and many weren't even friends. If anything, the label designated a lifestyle, a willingness to live in a tent or cave year-round, to subsist in order to climb. They put ordinary hippies to shame with their hardcore devotion to the rock, with their biceps, poverty, and voyageur ways. As tedious as they too often proved, they were, in effect, John Dog's extended family. He sat among them, his eyes on the notebook in his lap.

Like clockwork, whenever the weather turned nasty, a glut of C4B's could be expected to show up at the Four Seasons, in the adjacent bar, or in the lounge next door. To the few tourists who actually analyzed the source of their indigestion, the climbers' nonchalance was galling. They were so ruthlessly, generally nonchalant, it seemed; nonchalant about their golliwog appearance, their forest odor, their machismo, their awkward, narcissistic shuffling about. They seemed indifferent to everything but their vertical outland, that frontier hugging Yosemite like Cossack steppes. They were horsemen down from the walls, Natty Bumpos slung with perlon rope and sporting a disdain for Winnebagos. About that they were proud.

At the head of the two tables sat Matthew Kresinski, self-delegated liaison between the C4B banquet and Connie, a gland-rich waitress who had worked in the Valley for years. Kresinski had arms the size of calf flanks and a nose as straight as an English war helmet, with a temper to match. Just now he was happy, temper smooth as bourbon. Each time a tray arrived heavy with beer and California wine, Kresinski praised the service and doled out a tip with ribald abandon. By evening's end they'd be lucky to have money for half the bill, not that they were extravagant with their choices. The only menu item cheaper than a cheeseburger was a burger without cheese, and that was precisely what most had ordered. "And lots of ketchup," trailed a shout. "And hot water." The hot water was for the ketchup, which was for the few with no money at all. Tomato soup with free table crackers.

With each visit Connie found the climbers looser and louder. The talk was incessantly climbing talk. Kresinski she knew, and Broomis, and a few others. She'd met John Dog, with his mustang looks and white T-shirts, always brooding or buried in serious-sounding discourses. And who didn't know Arthur, the squat, hairless Austrian infamous for his drinking binges? Tinkerbell was her favorite, though, what little she knew about him. He was everybody's favorite, the wild child of any gathering because of his naiveté and gullibility. Thin, with wide shoulders, black home-barbered hair, and acid-green eyes, he stuttered every time she tried to talk with him. Word was that Tinkerbell had the hottest streak going in the Valley, at least this past climbing season. Word also had it he was a virgin.

At the moment, Tink was seated in the middle of the proceedings, subject of the evening's roast, in agony while Eddy Delwood wove an exaggerated tale about him. It was a story about the day's big climb.

"So the gumby's up there fifteen minutes now,"

boomed Delwood with his foreign New Jersey accent. "He's not movin', just standin' there like so. Like this." He spread his arms high and wide, his fingers just so. "I'm standin' on this little ledge right underneath, get it, scared to death. Hey, like he's sixty feet out on a piece of 5.11 lichen and a foxhead, okay? I could just see him take a dive right on me, right?"

Across the table Tinkerbell held his saliva, afraid to swallow, far too aware he was blushing under his windburn. Nothing would grant him the dignity he yearned for, not this night, with these people, anyway. They wanted their little babe-in-the-woods Tink, their hayseed spectacle. He wanted out, but the rush of eyes held him tight and his corduroy pants felt stapled to the chair.

"So he's up there fifteen minutes, I don't know, maybe half an hour, not a muscle movin', on the crux, man, like he's stuck or dead. I'm prayin', don't you fall, you mother. Then I see somethin' that really put God in me." Delwood tapped at the flaccid veins on his forearm. "Tink's veins were turnin' green! Green, man. The strain. We're goners; I knew it then. I got all shaky like a big titty." Like an ass, Tink silently appended. "I was so scared I couldn't even yell at him. Fuckin' Tink." Delwood toasted Tinkerbell across the table with his glass of flat, warm beer. He'd been talking a long time.

Never, thought Tink. I'll never climb with you again. He searched for poison, but all that would come was "jerk." He didn't say it aloud.

With a tattered sleeve, Delwood swiped his mouth dry and launched on. "But real, real slow, Tink crawls his fingers up to this little dime hold. And zoom. It's done. Flashed it like lightning then. As for me, man, I was so drained from my nerves and all. . . ."

But nobody was listening anymore. Delwood was not popular. Indisputably the worst climber in Camp 4—some insisted in all America—Delwood was blessed with the largest, newest, and finest collection of gear, bar none. He never lacked for partners, but he rarely returned from a climb with all his gear; as long as he tolerated the petty thefts, he was tolerated. The thought had never occurred to Tink that Delwood was easy pickings. Just a jerk.

"Hot tamale, Tink," Kresinski pricked from the head of the table. "A first ascent. A brand-new line."

Tinkerbell shifted his gaze and nodded his head, glancing across at John Dog, who was absorbed in his notebook. I got to start writing poetry or something, he thought. Nobody bothers John. He watched the pen poise before descending to scratch out a word, add a passage.

Without glancing up from the page, John Dog picked a french fry from his plate and thoughtfully chewed at it, his eyes dodging through a fascinating footnote he'd unearthed concerning the original natives of Yosemite. For whatever reason, they had split the Valley into two territories, with the river as a border. North of the river, the tribe's totem was the grizzly; to the south the coyote.

"What you calling it?" demanded Katie, a petite Hawaiian girl with scars lacing every knuckle.

Leave me be, thought Tink, but "Naw" was all he could manage. His blush was engaging. Dumb, he cursed himself.

"Wait a minute," said Kresinski. "This climb doesn't start off the Dihedral Bench, does it?"

"Yeah," said Tink.

"And it's got a crystal near the middle that cuts your fingers?"

"Yeah," said Tink, looking at his lacerated index finger.

"And it curves left?"

Tink nodded.

"But I free climbed that three years ago," Kresinski said as he stared at the boy. It was suddenly a matter of possession.

The torpedo hit hard; everyone could see Tink's heart sinking. "You did?" he whispered.

"You bet," Kresinski pressed, his eyes glittering in the raccoon mask created by his ubiquitous sunglasses. He was daring to be challenged.

Dropping his head, Tink relinquished the route. If Kresinski said he'd climbed it first, he had.

"Tink?" Kresinski winked. "April fool!"

Not everyone laughed at the prank.

"Cool out, sport. Have a beer," Kresinski ordered. But Tinkerbell was only drinking water, and Kresinski knew it. No beer, no wine, no booze or pot, not even milk or soft drinks. He was, for one thing, trying to drive his weight down to 140 in order to accomplish a severe route that he wanted to call, for no reason but the color and slickness of the rock, Black Soap. He was also teetotaling on principle, having cultivated an overblown fear about the damage alcohol visits on brain cells, liver, and muscle tissue. For a young man who carried his toothbrush in his shirt pocket, this was a perfectly reasonable concern.

"Water's fine," he mumbled. Shamming indignation, Kresinski sprayed a mouthful of beer across the table. John Dog looked up, finally annoyed by Kresinski's buffoonery.

"I . . . I gotta go," Tinkerbell suddenly managed. He stood up, muttering to pave his exit. He left as unobtrusively as possible, a breadball striking his head just before he reached the door. No one expected Tink back; no one remarked on his departure.

"Hey, Cochise," Kresinski tossed downtable to John Dog. With Tink gone, he needed a fresh target. If not a mountain or rock, then one of the herd.

Kresinski had well-honed instincts, and he recognized John Dog as a subtle breach in his monarchy. Kresinski never quit sniping, probing, testing for the jugular. "We need four bucks."

John Dog glanced up again and sighed. The man was drunk or getting there, and that only made him more eager for return fire. John Dog didn't bother to flash his wild mestizo, switchblade eyes. It wasn't worth backing the King down every time, not even for the practice.

"I already kicked in," he said and returned to his notes. Coyote or grizzly bear—he burrowed into the dichotomy but for the life of him couldn't decide if there was more brain or brute in himself. He plucked another fry from his plate.

"Come on, dude," Kresinski brayed. Others were looking now. There was an uneasy titillation; no one was quite sure if there was humor here or not. The Apache versus the King: august figures. "All for one, right? We're group."

Qué jodón, thought John Dog. A nuisance. He stared across at the man. Menopause, he diagnosed, and almost said it aloud. We're getting old, he thought, but Matt's getting old and mean. Bad enough the barbarian had been out of the country climbing when that sports journalist came looking for a barbarian, bad enough that Kresinski had lost his partner that same trip. Now menopause was on him. That was no excuse for the malice, though. He reached in his parka pocket and threw some coins toward Kresinski's plate. "There's a nickel," he pointed out helpfully, as much for the congregation as for Kresinski. "And there's a dime."

It took an instant too long for Kresinski to make the connection, and it stole his thunder. "Hey, I get it," he snorted. All the same he flushed, and his scalp-hunter eyes bleached bluer. A black hole gaped in the bonhomie; everyone felt it and was confused. This was group. The King was king, fools were fools; that was part of it. For a bad moment they saw how trite the construct was and how obedient they were to it. Then Cortland "Bullseye" Broomis started up, relieving the tension.

"Me," posed Bullseye, so named for the pattern he'd painted on the crown of his ice-climbing helmet. Attention was flung toward his bankable good will. "I'm the guy. Stud, if you will. While you geeks were fighting over your Silver Surfer comic books last November, I was doing my duty. I'm the one who voted for Dick Nixon." More righteous lampoon from trusty old Mr. SDS, self-proclaimed mastermind of the Chicago riots. "Why Dick? That's my very point," he netted them, leading them into safer currents. Like a Baptist preacher, he evoked the so-called "pucker factor," that degree to which one's anus squeezes shut on thin rock moves, and speciously demonstrated how the pucker factor

had everything to do with his voting for Nixon as a means of voting against him, an act of absurdity in the face of absurdity. Jokes rained down; the bedlam resumed. John Dog returned, or tried to, to his fries and 3,000-year-old Ahwahnachee Indians.

Kresinski. A gadfly. The man shoved and bullied and baited, but in all the years they'd known one another, working the same walls, inhabiting the same campground, and sharing communal feasts like this one, he'd never shoved John Dog too far. For whatever reason—the color of his skin, the mystery of his temper, or both—John Dog knew the King was afraid of him. Maybe not afraid, he amended, but cautious, and therefore harmless. Over others, though, Kresinski had a disturbing power. For most of them, big walls and multicolored granite were the only things worth climbing on twice, and Yosemite was sort of a world capital. Kresinski confirmed that with his unfailing returns from far-flung mountains in places most people encounter only via *National Geographic*. Other locals, quite notably John Dog, had climbed throughout the planet's cordilleras, but none returned so loudly or brazenly as Kresinski, nor did anyone else have his heavy-metal gift for wrapping a mountain or wall or even a forty-foot crack in such hairy-assed terms. They liked that about Kresinski because he was diplomatically generous in making them feel bold, separate, and superior too. They were mainly white, middle-class boys on the lam from white, middle-class duties: school, marriage, the draft, or jobs. But with Kresinski they could perceive themselves as more rarefied beings: electric drifters cruising the high, bare angles, navigating the brute, psychedelic canyons.

More beer was ordered. With great reverence Bullseye proposed a toast. "Fucking Nam," he recited. "The war is over." He seemed mournful, not happy, and no one else cared.

A half-hour passed before an empty chair next to Kresinski was pulled out and occupied by a tall, deeply tanned woman with gray eyes and thick, golden hair. She was dirty and reeked of wood smoke, damp wool, and sweat. It was Liz Jenks, who had just returned, bone weary, from her five-day trip to Ophidian Lake. Kresinski leaned over and kissed her. He whispered in her ear and she laughed. "You're all tool, Matthew," she chided him and kissed him back.

"Matt," Liz crooned in her Lauren Bacall basso. "I'm beat." That was code for sex, sleep, and affection, in whatever repeating order. They'd been lovers for two months now, stealthy and private. She seemed not to fathom that theirs was the most famous of all the local romances, the lady ranger and the King of Camp 4. Nor did she know that Kresinski himself had made it famous. Leaks, he called his little tales to the lads. Deep background. They all knew the Amazon gave great head.

"A little longer," Kresinski coaxed.

"Then get me drunk," she said, resigning herself to the boisterous clamor. "I want to make you a rich man." It was her roundabout way of expressing discontent with his stubborn impoverishment. The impoverishment she could live with, but not all this passion spent—wasted—on such a useless, dead-end sport. Grow up, she was begging.

Before the hour was out she was very drunk and very certain that she was talking to her lover alone. But every ear was cocked as she detailed her trip to Ophidian Lake and described the bales of marijuana. A conspiratorial sobriety had descended at the two tables, a dead silence that was pleasant relief for the nearby tourists.

Tinkerbell stumbled through the darkness across the road to Camp 4, skirted a Standard gas station closed for the night, and passed a bulletin board bursting with scribbled messages: "Joe meet Henry in Site 14 until 3/8/73"; "For sale 1 pr. unused EBs size 43. $20. #6"; "Wanted, climbing partner. I lead 5.8. Jocelyn. #12." He crunched down the ice-spackled path past the log-cabin bathrooms and at a stump stepped off the path to his tent. The stars barked down, cold and glittery. Struggling to get his pants unbuttoned, Tinkerbell winced, remembering he'd torn off a fingernail during the climb that afternoon, and that in turn reminded him of Delwood and of Kresinski's April-fool joke. Absent-mindedly, he pulled the toothbrush from his shirt pocket for a dry brush. After a minute or so he spat, crawled into his tent, and zipped the sleeping bag snug around his shoulders. His eyes sealed shut with immediate sleep.

Hands woke him. He gave a soft yelp.

More nightmares? he wondered. Night was when he digested the risks and falls, excreting them as terrible dreams. It was very dark, he saw, which meant it was not yet midnight. After that the moon would candle the world. "What?" he grumbled, exorcising sleep, not even sure if he was talking with anyone.

"Tink," and he was shaken again. "It's me. Hey. Wake up, amigo." It was John Dog; he recognized the patois.

"What?"

"Come on. There's stuff in Ophidian Lake. You want some or not?"

"Tonight?" He was floating.

"You want some, Tink?" John Dog was a dark shape huddled in the door of his tent. A second, burly shape shifted behind John Dog. Tinkerbell caught a gleam of dull light off a bald head and guessed it was the Austrian, Arthur. Something was up. Ophidian Lake. That was eight miles in on the Illilouette Trail, guarded by ten feet of snow up in the backcountry.

"Naw," said Tinkerbell. "I'm training."

"Look," John Dog persisted, "the lake's full of pot. A plane crashed up there. A Customs helicopter came and scooped up everything that was lying around. But the lake's frozen over and there's pot in there. Liz Jenks said so. The feds aren't even going in there until spring thaw. There's no one there."

"Naw, I don't really have the time."

"Tink, here's your grubstake for that trip to Makalu." There was silence. John Dog knew he'd touched a nerve.

"Naw," the boy finally muttered.

John Dog accepted the statement. Training was training. And for the others, sleep was sleep. Except for Arthur, no one else was going up either. John Dog smoked little weed himself, and he doubted there was any money in the enterprise; but there was an element of adventure, a way to count coup on the long-knives. Besides, he'd never been to Ophidian Lake. It would be a nice distraction while spring shifted into gear.

"Adios, Tink."

Tinkerbell heard John Dog zip the tent shut, listened to the receding crunch of boots in snow, and floated off toward warm, liquid sleep.

Sleep—lots of it—was part of Tinkerbell's training. He was called Tinkerbell in honor of his boldness, but Clint Stanley was the boy's real name. A year and a half earlier he'd flashed Tinkerbell, the first known unroped solo of a 5.11 climb in history. He wore the title reluctantly. Barely nineteen years old, Tinkerbell was wiser than in those early days. If he had to do it all over again, he wouldn't dare repeat the solitary bravado of Tinkerbell. Not and tell others about it. But the reputation was there, and despite all his attempts to keep his climbing in a guarded perspective, Tinkerbell felt obliged to attempt nearly impossible routes in nearly impossible ways. He'd barely finished the tenth grade before rockclimbing had swallowed his life. Having thrown himself into climbing with blind abandon, he was at first well served. Purpose, recognition, a place in the world. Lately, though, only three years from his first roped scramble, Tinkerbell had grown disenchanted.

It was common wisdom that Tinkerbell would be dead before he reached his next birthday. He'd heard the rumor. As it was, fewer and fewer people would do a serious route with him anymore. John Dog was an exception, a powerful exception. He was a friend. Though Tink was the darling of Camp 4, he had no other friends, really. He was a jinx; that's how people treated him.

"Not enough protection, brothers. Shit, when

he goes, he'll take the rope, his partner, the anchor, and probably half the fucking rock with him. Not me. No thanks. . . ." So Tink often climbed alone these days, more often than he wanted to, which only added to his notoriety. He'd become, literally, the source of a superstition. His acts were charmed, but no one, including himself, believed in infinite luck. Someday his gifts would fail.

Death or serious injury he could handle, but not the loneliness and exaggerations. I'm quittin', he'd sworn. Soon. According to his elaborately planned training schedule, if he continued working on his ice climbing in the winter, could manage five consecutive five-minute miles in his running, and did 400 pullups every day for the next year, he'd be ready for Makalu, his 8,000-meter peak in the Himalaya, by the next spring. Then I'm done, he promised himself, a nightly prayer. He slept.

Chapter Four

JOHN DOG AND ARTHUR SKIED FOUR HOURS, then crawled under a rock shelf before dawn, husbanding their invisibility. Neither of them was certain about the gauntlet they might or might not be passing through; there could conceivably be any number of federal agents lurking in unlikely places, ready to stop just such a piracy. For all they knew, they could be skiing into a complicated trap designed to snare the Mafia or a gang of drug runners. They weren't too concerned, though; the whole enterprise involved risks, not the least of which was that, because neither of them had ever been up there, they might miss Ophidian Lake altogether.

Just before sunset, John Dog wiggled out of his sleeping bag and silently waxed both pairs of skis with a hard green klister for the April night's snow. Arthur continued to snore under the rock shelf until John Dog poked him and handed in a lukewarm mug of chocolate. Soon the two were stealthily sliding along what they guessed to be the Illilouette Trail. Alpenglow tinged the caps of the surrounding domes, then melted into blackness. With headlamps on, they continued to gain altitude. Just after midnight the moon rose, and they packed their lamps away. At two o'clock, alive with the cold, altitude, and exertion, John Dog topped a ridge and realized they'd found Ophidian Lake. The snow ringing the frozen lake was mutilated by footprints and ski tracks. Gliding still closer, he saw torn metal glinting like tinsel in the tops of several pines. He slowed to a halt, pausing for Arthur to catch up. The Austrian's smooth skull glistened in the moonlight. They agreed to split up at the first hint of a threat and meet each other back at Camp 4. They ghosted forward, quietly slipping through the trees, until they could determine once and for all whether there were any guards hidden or sleeping around the lake.

"What do you think?" John Dog asked.

Arthur stabbed at the snow with his poles, raised his eyebrows, and cleared his throat. "It doesn't seem possible," he said.

John Dog grinned. "Let's do it, then."

With a deep thrust of his poles he tucked low and hissed down the gradual hill, his black backpack fluttering in the draft. It was, he pictured, a melodramatic entrance—Errol Flynn looping out of the mainsail. With unnecessary speed, he crisscrossed the marks of a helicopter's skids and didn't stop until he was a good twenty yards out onto the ice. There was no challenge. Liz's incredible Arabian tale was so far on the money. Arthur quickly joined the Apache on the flat, soundless lake.

Having reached the lake, they felt the impetus momentarily disappear; just getting to the site had been the reward. No landmarks indicated the plane's underwater location. They roamed separately across the wind-packed snow that covered the lake's ice, searching for some sign, then met and roamed some more. On a beach stampeded by bootprints, the two men doffed their packs and fished out headlamps for the second time that night. "We make it quick," said Arthur, sliding away on his skis. Their headlamps bobbing in distinct cones across the lake, they separated once more, and immediately both of them spotted the truncated remains of the airplane's tail section. It was sticking through the ice like a black and silver leg bone. John Dog could only surmise that the authorities had cut the very top off in order to look down inside the submerged plane. Approaching the tail, they flashed their lamp beams in, and John Dog recoiled from the black water that stank of oil and stood like clotted blood inside the plane. Dead men: not even the Jesuits had erased the old Apache bugaboo. He forced himself to look again.

"Petrol," Arthur defined. "Now. Where to look?" He shone his lamp across the rippled snow dunes. Here was the lake. Here was the airplane. Where was the Mother Lode? "It's not up there, sure," the Austrian said as his light swept through the trees. "The Amazon was right. They taked it all in a helicopter. There's only one place, huh? Inside the plane or in the water. Under the ice. Maybe if we dig a hole we can see something in the morning?"

"Sounds good."

"Okay," Arthur spat, and shuffled off to the beach to collect their ice axes.

It took them all of one minute to regret not having brought heavier tools. Nevertheless, the two men kept at it, cutting into the lake's coarse, obstinate surface, stabbing and prying away splinters and chunks. At four o'clock the Big Dipper was just beginning to flatten out on the horizon, and John

Dog's axe penetrated the bottom of the roughly circular hole. Water immediately filled their handiwork, seeping up through the puncture. From then on each axe stroke splashed water up and out. At last, arbitrarily, the hole was big enough.

They held one lamp close to the water and saw nothing but a single brilliant eye beaming back at them. Arthur sat back on his heels and began to roll off his cagoule, sweater, and shirt. "There is nothing for it except...." He flopped out onto his bare stomach and sank his arm into the hole. John Dog clenched his jaw. He knew his fear was irrational. But committing your arm to a black lake afloat with bodies and in the dark night?

"Ah," grunted Arthur. "I am feeling something. It is against the ice.... It feels like ... crucifix!" He whipped up and backward from the hole. "My Christ," he hissed. "It move in my hand!"

John Dog stared at the shivering Austrian in horror. Snow clung to his chest hair and blubber. "What?" he rasped.

The Austrian closed his eyes, gritted his teeth, and dropped back onto his stomach. "Ave Maria," he intoned and pushed his arm back under the ice, groping deep underneath to pull in whatever he'd felt. "Now I got it again," he panted. With evident strain he began muscling it closer, visibly repelled by the possibility of dragging a corpse into view. "Okay," he said, shaking the water from his arm. "There it is." He knelt to the side while John Dog played his headlamp down the ragged hole. It wasn't a dead man. John Dog bent lower and touched the rugged brown surface. Whatever it was bobbed up and down, nudging at the hole's bottom. It was burlap. He stared up at Arthur.

"You know what this is, don't you?"

Arthur had an open knife in his hand. "Maybe," he answered. With a quick jab he pushed the blade hilt deep into the burlap and sawed a ragged incision. Below subcutaneous yellow plastic was a dark reddish vegetation. John Dog dipped his fingers into the cold, wet mass and withdrew a dripping handful of marijuana. The rich smell of resinated leaves broke across the ice.

"My ... my ... " Arthur uttered.

John Dog picked at the saturated leaves in his hands. There were hard, red buds and thick juice. He was awed by the voluptuousness of the weed; he could smell and taste the deep crimson color just by looking at it. "What have we found?" he whispered rhetorically. He knew how to clean a lid and roll a crooked joint, but this was magnificently larger. Arthur, too, was ignorant. It was marijuana, but they couldn't begin to fathom what value it might have.

A single, stately cloud lofted across the sky and blotted out the moon. Arthur furtively slumped to

the ice; John Dog snapped out his light. Suddenly they remembered where they were again and what risks accompanied that sweet, pungent odor. John Dog pawed at his sleeve and exposed his watch.

"It's nearly five o'clock," he said. Arthur was shivering wildly now and pulling his clothes on as fast as he could. "Should we dig it out now? Or haul ass out of here?"

"I think," boomed Arthur, "both."

By five-thirty they had dragged a monstrous bale from the icy water. It must have weighed a hundred pounds, saturated as it was. With mounting paranoia now that darkness was nearly gone, John Dog and Arthur dragged the bulky monster across the crusted ice, up the snowy beach, and into the trees. The feds would be coming soon—they had to—otherwise this treasure would surely evaporate into pure fantasy. They towed their catch deeper into the trees, then darted back onto the ice to retrieve their skis and ice axes. Impulsively, Arthur dropped to his belly and thrust his arm into the water again. "Yes," he grinned, and moments later they'd fished a second bale from the hole. Cradling the dripping behemoth in his arms, John Dog staggered toward the trees. Arthur followed with the last of their gear. Minutes later the snow turned a bright flamingo pink with the sunrise, but already the lake had returned to its innocence.

Chapter Five

THE VALLEY'S BARE FURNITURE, its conifers and massive, upright facets, and the waterfalls that had paused blue in midflight for the winter, stood quiet. John Dog was drunk; he could see himself drunk as he angled toward Camp 4, his long strides tormented here by a waver, caught there with a stumble. Several times he stopped to scout the woods behind. No hostile rangers lurking back there. The early light was a cold aquamarine that flooded the forest. The air was still. Too still, he slyly registered. He staggered on a little further. Mysteriously, the parking lot stood empty except for Arthur's ancient Buick. He passed the well-beaten pathway. The tents were there, but in subtle, unnerving disarray. The spines of some tents had relaxed and bowed; tent walls were limp, and some had collapsed altogether.

"What the devil ... " John Dog muttered. He and Arthur had stashed two full packloads of pot in a secret cave the Austrian had discovered some years earlier. Drunk with the knowledge that their haul must be worth thousands of dollars, they had proceeded to get drunk in fact. Now John Dog had come to announce a fabulous treasure to his sainted lost tribe, to elevate them and bring their souls back from the pit, as it was written in Job, to enlighten them with the light of the living. If only Father Michael could see him now. Jesuits, he coughed. Them and their twenty-five-cent Thomist propaganda —the Good, the True, and the Beautiful. No wonder he'd ended up here in the Valley. Drunk and very wealthy. But in his absence the camp had turned into a ghost town, eerily depopulated. "Hey!" he yelled. Empty, he softly concluded. He veered toward Tinkerbell's site, unzipped the boy's tent door, and peered in. The sleeping bag was gone. So. The evacuation hadn't been totally, relentlessly sudden; they'd had time to gather their essentials. Not overly concerned, and with all the caprice of a bird dog, he cast about, spot-checking other friends' tents. There were no sleeping bags or ropes anywhere, no valuables: Tavini's guitar was missing; Bill Fuller's typewriter was gone. There was no climbing hardware anywhere. Just tents. Very strange. Confoundingly strange.

"Wait a minute," he accused the silence, without a clue in mind. Out of nowhere he heard a sudden, fast, whistling noise. The next instant something struck him on the thigh, and he dropped to the ground, pole-axed, clutching his leg. A bullet? But why? It hurt.

"Get out!" he heard a reedy voice through his pain. "The area's restricted." He saw a stone the size of a golf ball by his foot. Someone had thrown a rock.

John Dog tried to locate the voice, but, before he could, a second rock kicked up pine needles by his head. "Run, go on. Get." Through his liquored fog, John Dog was certain he recognized that voice. "It's me," he called out. His quadriceps throbbed.

"It's me," taunted the voice. This time John Dog caught the accent: a pronounced British Columbia bray, thin and aggressive.

"Biscuits?" he called back. There was silence.

"Yeah," the voice finally answered. "What?"

A thin boy wearing a cast on his right leg levered himself to standing position on top of the huge practice boulder in midcamp. "Christ, Biscuits," John Dog complained, dusting himself off.

"Jesus. I didn't recognize you, John," Biscuits shouted down. "Sorry. Come up, then, but quiet like."

Despite his Bordeaux spin and bruised thigh, John Dog managed the gymnastic moves up and onto the top. Biscuits had already eased himself back and was tenderly laying out his casted leg when John Dog pulled over the edge. He was amazed to find that Biscuits, incapacitated with a broken leg—the wages of a popped bolt protecting a wet crack—had not only pitched a tent on top of the boulder; he'd also stocked an arsenal of throwing rocks and gathered together all the valuables missing from the tents: the guitar, the typewriter, several

cameras, a telescope belonging to some amateur astronomer, an assortment of cooking utensils, an immense mound of ropes, and the sum total of Camp 4's climbing gear. In all, there were several tons of equipment, valuables, and throwing rocks neatly stockpiled on top of the thirty-foot-high rock.

"What's all this?" John Dog summoned up.

Biscuits lay on his side on top of three foam pads. "Kresinski's plan, a cardboard camp to throw off the enemy. All fluff, no stuff." He was jovial. "You want a beer?" He pointed to three cases of beer. "I'm sentinel," Biscuits explained. "I been pelting bears and raccoons for two days and nights now. Yesterday, three turkeys from L.A. tried to lift one of the tents. I put them to flight."

"Where'd everybody go?" John Dog found himself copying Biscuits's low profile and muted voice.

"You didn't pass 'em? They all gone up to your lake. Some gone off two days ago, some yesterday, and some this mornin'. No one's back but you." He paused. "Not yet, but they will. How'd you not see them?"

"We came down the back trail." John Dog was puzzled. "But why now? How'd they know to go?"

"Same way you knew. They just all got bold and went. The weather's okay; so even the pansies gone up. All of 'em off to be millionaires like you and Arthur."

"No one stayed to climb?"

"Even Tink gone off. This mornin', last to leave. He's up there with the rest. They went in small groups. Axes, crowbars, and picks. They mean to empty your lake, if there's anything left. What you haul down?"

"It's there." John Dog tried not to smile. "A few pounds." Biscuits understood by "a few pounds" that John Dog and Arthur had probably brought down a good seventy pounds each. Understatement was a universal pastime among climbers.

"But the feds . . ." John Dog remembered.

"A risk, same as you took." Biscuits lifted his cast and set it on another of the half-dozen pads scattered about. "You want protection?"

"Protection?" John Dog still couldn't believe that the entire camp had taken off to the high country.

"You can leave your particulars with me. I'll baby-sit till you come home. Going rate's one ounce of stuff, man."

"No. I'm not going back up there. I got what I need. The feds have to know by now."

"Come now," Biscuits reasoned. "All Camp 4's up there. They can't bust you all."

Perhaps it was his exhaustion or the hangover or just the overload of good luck, but by the time John Dog arrived back at Ophidian Lake, he was filled with premonitions. In the full noon glare it didn't look like the same lake from which he and Arthur had thieved two mere bales. More than fifty people were laboring at the ice with the meticulous frenzy of a cargo cult. Some were pushing and pulling bales; others were probing and digging in the ice or drying marijuana on pieces of aircraft metal pulled from trees. An audience of scavengers, all strangers to John Dog, were standing well away from the slush that now covered the ice, waiting, it turned out, for a bale to surface and then converging for a free grab of pot. John Dog started to count the number of holes that had been gouged in the ice but lost track. As he stood there, two people stumbled and almost fell into holes that were hidden in the thick, creamy slush. One bellicose longhair was toting a Remington deer rifle as he strutted about, a one-man anti-fed army.

"*Carpe diem,*" Arthur breathed over his shoulder.

"What?"

Arthur motioned with his hand. "They have seize the day."

"In broad daylight they seize the day," John Dog groused. So obvious.

No sooner had John Dog reprimanded himself to mellow out than a sudden hum clamped hard on his privates, and he nearly dove for cover. Helicopters! But it was only a chain saw, which died, then kicked to life with another jerk of the starter cord. Christ, he thought, and scanned the horizon in all directions. At any moment a whole fleet of helicopters could come stabbing in from below the ridge. With luck a few people might manage to escape, but the patriarchs in uniform would be armed and ready for a massive bust. Biscuits was wrong. If they wanted to, the feds could arrest everyone. Down on the lake, Kresinski lifted the chain saw with one hand and inserted its spinning blade into the ice. An abrupt roostertail of clear water shot out the rear guard. The blade was withdrawn, then pressed down through another patch of ice. This time the roostertail showered a riot of dark red buds and chopped foliage. A bale. Five people converged on the site and began chopping furiously at the lake's surface.

"It's not good," John Dog complained to Arthur. He bent and scooped up a handful of heavy snow, compressed it, and took a bite from the clean, white edge. Too many, too audacious.

"Maybe, maybe not." The squat, bald Austrian grunted and started down toward the lake, leaving behind the smell of Wild Turkey. Let it be, thought John Dog. He followed Arthur down.

A caravan of burdened climbers skied by, preceded by a "clean" pointman, whistle in hand. Bent beneath huge, dripping packs were Tavini, Bullseye Broomis, and Bill Fuller. All were wearing dazed Mona Lisa smiles, their faces haggard but luminous. Bullseye greeted John Dog with a clenched fist, shook his hand, and trudged on.

On the lake John Dog was greeted by more Camp 4 neighbors. Carl was hanging his long neck over an opened hole in the ice. "Come see the glory train," he invited. John Dog stepped across the slush and peered down through Carl's window in the lake. The plane was clearly visible, only thirty feet down in the hard, sapphire water. It was tilted slightly off the vertical, its nose embedded in lake mud. Both wings were missing. One was in the trees down the trail. The other must have sunk into the rich silt at the bottom. The plane was pretty much as he'd imagined, except for its colors, a patriotic red, white, and blue striping the body from end to end. With a plane painted like Old Glory and every bale marked with a marijuana-leaf silhouette and weight number, the smugglers had not lacked style.

"Word is, there're fifty pounds of snort down in the cockpit," Carl confided. "We've got a guy from Santa Barbara bringing in his scuba gear tonight."

John Dog moved on, scornful of the rumor but unable to shake his premonitions. The center was bound not to hold. For an hour or so he went from group to group, now and then helping wrestle a bale from the reluctant water, and everywhere chewing over the rumors: cocaine in the cockpit, a bust in two days, a green light that had shone through the ice last night. Finally, John Dog admitted that he wasn't going to haul any more pot down from the lake. He had what he needed already.

He spied Arthur, with his thick legs spread wide over a hole in the ice, in the throes of manhandling a dripping burlap bale. His face was grim, not joyous, not young, as he grappled with the bale. John Dog didn't bother to interrupt. He didn't need to say good-bye. He'd see Arthur and everyone else in a day or two, back in Camp 4. With his pack as empty as it had been on the trip in, he turned from the scene and skied over and down the ridge.

Once, in the Andes, he'd come across a twisting vein of gold high on a mountain and then, just to see how it felt, had walked away and never mentioned the fortune to anyone. He felt that way now, like he was turning his back on Shangri-la. There was pain and contempt in the feeling, but also a relieved sense that if he was being honest he wasn't a complete idiot.

The world of fairy tales was very real for John Dog. Reality should always be something you can turn your back on, he believed. He'd climbed on Everest and wandered through sandy, crumbling castles in the deserts of Afghanistan; he'd seen the inside of jails in Kathmandu and risked his neck on peaks so beautiful they turned camera film blank;

and he'd outlived viruses and parasites American doctors had never heard of. He'd even traveled to Timbuktu. In short, he'd been to Shangri-la, seen its kings illiterate and guardians barefoot with polished bayonets on their polished, loaded rifles, smelled its diarrhea in the gutters, argued with its greed, and kept his mouth shut before the religions that insisted this life was not the only life. In Shangri-la, he'd learned, ideas were like the grit you picked from your rice. That was the paradise of Lowell Thomas and of *Lost Horizons*—bald, raw, unadorned. At its most dramatic, you took a bullet for thinking new thoughts; at its most tragic, little boys and girls starved to death far short of their first intelligent moment. If that was paradise, John Dog had decided, he wanted out. It was going to be tough as hell to leave. But by shunning gold veins and false lusters, he liked to believe some better frontier was just a valley away.

Tinkerbell was in the forest below.

John Dog had forgotten all about him. Then, barely a quarter of a mile from the lake, he heard someone yelling. Not calling for help or attention, just yelling. Circling a fat lump of rock and a crumpled window frame from the plane, he found Tink standing in a dark clearing, rooted to the spot and hollering in solitary bewilderment. In his hands, John Dog saw, he held a blue-and-yellow parka, its design more fashionable than functional.

"Tink?" he called, a little frightened by the boy's lonely howling. Tinkerbell's eyes were big. He was clutching the jacket fiercely.

"John?" He was staring straight at John Dog, bewitched.

"What you got there, Tink?" A gentle voice.

"Oh, man, John, look." Tinkerbell extended the jacket, the fingers of one hand stretching the pocket open. "It's my Makalu trip, just like you said." He dropped down to his heels and plucked a thick stack of money from the pocket. John Dog squatted in front of the boy. The bills were all hundred-dollar notes. He was astounded, even after his own score and the hundreds of thousands of dollars surfacing just over the hill. "Where'd you find this?" he asked.

"In that tree," Tinkerbell pointed. "I was just walking around and it was up there. Boy, oh boy."

The two hunkered down with the parka between them. Tinkerbell pushed his hand into the other pockets. From the breast pocket he extracted a large wallet made of Mexican cowhide, then a small red address book.

"Look," he whispered. A Washington driver's license showed a thick face with a sloping bandido mustache. It was, they both realized, the dead pilot or copilot, one of the men lying at the bottom of the lake; it had to be. The jacket had survived how many

destructions—and now Tinkerbell was plucking its secrets. There were other legal papers in the wallet—credit cards and licenses—so much paper and ink to identify the body and face now deceased. Then the two climbers turned to the address book, filled, naturally enough, with names, addresses, and phone numbers. The entries stretched from *A* to *Z*, common and ordinary, but in the Addenda section at the end of the small book, they came across a brief list of colors annotated with phone numbers lacking area codes: Red-547-3407, Blue-843-3094, and so forth.

"Mafia," Tinkerbell murmured knowingly. They turned to the very last page. There, neatly printed in pencil, was the legend "Laughing Christ: 250 M16, 350 M14, 145 Uzi. 1,000 ammo each." Guns. It held images of an alien, killing world.

"Burn it," snapped John Dog. "You don't want it. The stuff in the wallet, too." He took a plastic lighter from the top flap of his pack and handed it to Tink. "It's trouble." Overkill, he thought. It wasn't that significant. Just paper. But he was filled with foreboding and wanted to wash his hands of the lake. Something was going on here, temptations, illusions. He could feel it.

"Yeah." Tinkerbell set fire to the exposed pages and held the book by a corner until its pages were incinerated. "We never saw it, right?" He fired the papers in the wallet, then shoved the cowhide wallet and credit cards deep behind some loose tree bark. The money he tucked inside his backpack.

No more than five minutes had passed since the two had met in the grove. They put on their skis and moved out, down, and back toward the Valley. As they started off, the great mystery of it all weighed heavy on Tinkerbell. There were no words for the depth of it. Finally he had to speak, borrowing from the most recent mystery. "John," he asked solemnly, "what's a Laughing Christ?"

Chapter Six

NEVER AGAIN WOULD THERE BE A PARTY like this one, John Dog registered in the full-blown din. It was a rendezvous in the bygone fur-trapping tradition: no Hawkens rifles, no knives or pelts, but everything else. The frivolity and drunken recklessness was true to the spirit of that earlier forest bacchanalia. It was spring in Camp 4. There was a full moon, and the bonfire was rimmed with kegs of beer. When Grace Slick wasn't warbling full decibel about the white rabbit in wonderland, Gloria was being spelled syllable by pornographic syllable. Every handshake measured your grip. Around midnight the real huns had begun fire jumping, first in their thongs or blown-out Adidas, then barefoot through the flames. Somebody had fallen in and been rolled out, smoking, and was feeling no pain, nor would until morning. Air moves could be seen everywhere, with hands locking onto imaginary holds and toes twisting into invisible cracks. Vicarious flight. John Dog wove through the crowd, stoned, buffeted by the language, noise, elbows, excitement.

"Yeah, man, forty feet out on 5.10. No pro. I mean, like, runnin' on empty."

John Dog staggered. The voices were faceless. He moved on.

"Like glass. Friction city. Then you mantle off a bashie. Cool."

"No way!" thundered another voice. "Not to trash the event, man, but he clipped and grabbed. Grabbed, that's what I heard."

"Who?"

"Where?"

"5.12?"

It was a broth of climbing and dreams, talk of Uli Biaho in Pakistan and Mount Logan's Hummingbird Ridge, talk of tumbling over the roof on Psycho, talk of Kresinski's latest or Tink's newest, and talk of tomorrow's climbs. The scene had the feel of immortality and would continue until the drugs or liquor put the revelers out or the sun came up, and then they would be spiders on the walls again.

What made this party different and more reckless than any other, past or future, was the sense of stupendous unreality. One week earlier they'd been paupers; tonight they were, for their own intents and purposes, millionaires. Evidence of the new wealth flowered everywhere. New ropes and shiny equipment were shown off. Pristine tents, their bright colors not yet bleached by the sun, stood erect among the trees. Climbers were brandishing freshly purchased round-trip tickets to the Andes, Alps, New Zealand, or the Himalaya. The bulk of the so-called Lodestar Lightning, nicknamed for the ill-fated plane that had borne it to them, had already been turned in San Francisco or Los Angeles; what pot remained was either stashed for a rainy day or was being smoked in copious, pungent clouds around the fire. The night emphatically belonged to these Lake millionaires, these reefer bandidos. And there was one final proof of their success: federal agents had come.

There were an even four, two from the FBI and two from the Treasury Department. They had, apparently, agreed beforehand that disguises would only make them more conspicuous among people who carried crack scars on their hands and knew one another by sight or reputation. And so, opting for a modicum of dignity, the agents had come dressed as if for a chilly barbeque, the most liberal in pressed Levi's and a raincoat from L.L. Bean. One wore a wool scarf around his neck. Singly and in pairs, they mingled among the crowd, seeming for the most part like pleasant, bemused family men, aware of but not too discomfited by their incongruity in this lawless group. Throughout the evening they had been in attendance, chatting, even joking, but to a man declining repeated offers of beer and liquor and heroically ignoring the cigar-size reefers passing back and forth.

The agents were not the only characters strange to Camp 4. There were other new faces, most of them catalogued by John Dog as Hungry, Curious, or Awed. The climbers had scored coup, stolen a ton of pot from under the nostrils of the FBI, DEA, Park Service, and who knew what other bureaus, and they'd done it in a style Geronimo couldn't have bettered. Inevitably, the noisy celebration had drawn groupies, tourists, and dopers too late for the Gold Rush, and for this one night they weren't unwelcome. The xenophobia normally reserved for outsiders had been relaxed for this occasion; having an audience confirmed the tribe's cunning. A general good will prevailed, even after Kresinski and Broomis hemmed an FBI man against a ponderosa to loudly slur the director of his agency. "We take care of our own, by God," Kresinski boasted, flames mottling his face. "So forget your concentration camps."

"But don't forget Chicago," Bullseye threw in with corrupted passion. "And don't forget Madison, bub. Or Huey Newton. Or John Sinclair. Or Angela, or. . . ."

The agent remained unflustered throughout the harrangue, a smiling patrician among crude outlanders who knew no better. Soon enough the two climbers realized this ox wasn't going to be gored, and so disengaged to find the three ladies Kresinski had imported from a Carson City cathouse. Renting them had been as much for the shock value as anything else, and while the not-quite-lovely trio knew that everyone knew who and what they were, they pretended otherwise and had spent the evening so far flirting audaciously, being courted, and enjoying the vestal role of girlfriends at a sock hop. Kresinski had added to his legend and knew it; no one would ever forget the bearer of these dubious gifts—three hookers who would not hook, at least not this early in the evening. And come the next party, he would be telling in unsparing detail how he'd enjoyed each in ones, twos, and threes.

Just short of a dented aluminum keg muddy with dirt and foam, a pair of iron hands reached out from the shadows and intercepted John Dog. He jerked back, but the hands held him tight. It was Arthur, on his last sodden legs. "All the mountains," the bald man breathed in despair, leaning close and gripping harder. "They all been climbed."

John Dog understood what the Austrian really

meant, that there was no longer any proportion worthy of this fire-lit machismo. But he disagreed. Now that all the highest mountains had been tramped on, now that the age of colonizing and brute domination had come to a close, the age of aesthetics could begin. Elegance could take over. Elegance, not sheer muscle; that would be the new ethic. Out of that would spring a million new mountains on routes and lines never before conceived, mountains that Arthur could never climb because he was too old and drunk and had just plain missed out.

"It's okay," he told the Austrian. But there was no possible way to explain to him how it was okay. It just was. Part of his certainty that the spirit was alive and well came from his Indian ghosts. "A species of pauper," a general had once promised to make of the American savage, and so the great warriors who weren't killed had finished out their days growing watermelon like plantation niggers. And the enslavement had never stopped. John Dog's father had been an oil-rig slave, and his brother had been a big, strapping buck of a Marine Corps slave. Injuns, John Dog thought with drunken precision. They'd been made into that species of pauper, and not all the reservation oil and minerals and ski resorts could revive the demonic soul that glittered in the eyes in century-old photos of Cochise and Naiche. The closest thing to that hungry, egotistical, earth-loving demon that John Dog had managed to find was right here, frolicking all around him in Camp 4. He pulled Arthur's grip off his shoulders.

The fire was high and white, littered with broken glass, and surrounded by dancing forms. A group had joined arms and begun stomping in a tight circle, crooning a Bing Crosby song as if their salvation hinged upon it. A game of pine-cone soccer was lifting long, vigorous tunnels of dust toward the moon, and elsewhere the bacchanalia was proceeding with unabated fervor. It was here that the demon burned brightly. That was why John Dog had put in so many years here and that was why he was going to be so sad to leave.

There was Tink, for one. You could see the wild god in his eyes. And Bullseye Broomis. At times John Dog had spotted it in him, too, though only in spurts, by the season. Once the waterfalls froze and the ice shaped up, the Colorado boy seemed closer to wilderness than what passed for wilderness itself, certainly purer than this manmade amusement park called Yosemite. It wasn't the things Broomis said so much as what he did, sticking body, soul, and testicles onto those towering ribbons of cold, brittle glass where no one, not even in a dream, would think to go. Ice was his domain, winter his soul. But for sheer, unbridled heat, no one could beat Kresinski. He burned with the spirit. Not quite side by side, not quite like brothers, and with no love lost between them, John Dog and the King had grown strong in the Valley together. They were the same age, and even though they acted like old fishwives every time they met—certain to haggle if there was a bargain to be struck, to squabble when a few simple words needed exchanging—even though he would as soon kiss the man as climb with him, John Dog admired Kresinski's demon. Others were scared of it. Even Arthur—John Dog put an arm around the Austrian's slumping shoulders—even this hard-driving, ugly plug was afraid of Kresinski.

"Ah, but the mountains," Arthur repeated, swaying slightly.

"I know," said John Dog. The older man was liquored to his nose, plainly losing out against the night. Barely two o'clock and he was in a fast fade. It wouldn't be the first time he'd wake up in a pile of pine needles. Best that he not go pitching headfirst into the fire, thought John Dog as he steered his friend out toward the darkness.

"The walls," intoned Arthur, screwing himself up for a good cry. "It's just these fucking walls. They're everything." Typical, sloppy, drunk climber talk.

"I know," said John Dog. "You want your tent?"

"No," Arthur declared. "I'm going to find ..." He stopped in his tracks, and suddenly John Dog felt a catch in his throat. Arthur had nothing to find. It hit him, too. I have nothing to find here, he thought.

"Go look at the walls," John Dog advised, snapping Arthur's parka shut, readying him for sleep wherever he might drop.

"That's right," said Arthur. "The walls."

They parted, Arthur charting a lonely, black course in search of those beloved cliffs and John Dog returning to the boisterous circle. Blinded by firelight, he stumbled several times over tree roots, then a guy line, then a fire grate. He muttered to himself, shielded his eyes with a hand, and stumbled over another tree root. It was tempting just to give up and go find his tent, but he was thirsty still and wanted to see the party through. There was more than sufficient energy pulsing around the fire to get him through until dawn. At last he reached the outskirts of the crowd and plowed inward to one of the kegs. The gathering was considerably leaner now; most of the strangers had gone. It was obvious that the feds would have departed, too, but for devotion to duty and love of country. It was getting down to tribe now. The plastic cup of beer was good and chill, making him glad he'd returned. He rocked on his heels, Jesuit-style, waiting to get his social bearings again.

"Hey, you," he heard from the dark ring beyond. The guttural, feminine tone struck him slowly and distinctly. He peered into the surrounding shadows, looked twice, then lowered his gaze and found the owner hunched against a tree. "Liz?" he called above the noise, and approached.

"I need a beer," she answered back.

Squatting to one side, he courteously proffered his own beer. She took it with a sullen nod. After a minute of gauging her mood he sat down beside her. They passed the cup back and forth.

"You doing all right?"

"Great," she said. "Me and the fruitcups. Great." He had no idea what she was talking about.

"Matthew's three dollies. You haven't seen them?"

"Ah. Yeah." For a moment he wanted to be sober, then decided it would be better to be drunk.

"Well?" She was hurting, but damned if she'd beg for solace. He knew her just well enough to know that. If not for the alcohol, she wouldn't be talking at all. He opened his mouth, then shut it.

"Come on," she challenged. "Aren't you going to be embarrassed for me? Cozy up and try to get into my pants?"

He chewed at his lip. No wonder she wasn't smiling. Her boyfriend had announced his change of heart by showing up with three hookers, and tonight she'd probably heard their sex life trumpeted to all Camp 4. Normally, climbers would have taken the opportunity to console the Amazon, most of them with the best intentions. But pity was pity. Without really thinking, he reached down to take her hand and console her. Trying to keep his thoughts on track, he followed the gold stripe down the right leg of his warm-ups, then got derailed at the sight of her creased, worn cowboy boots. They pleased him.

"You going to try and fuck me, John Dog?" The question was barren of signals, one way or the other, and her hand was limp. He snuck a look at her face. The angles gleamed. She was beautiful, but then he'd thought that before. Her gaze was locked straight on the fire. Drunk, he knew. Heartbroken.

"No, ma'am," he said and started. Ma'am? Where had that come from? There was silence, and he was glad she hadn't been listening. Then her head twitched.

"Did you just call me 'ma'am'?" she asked. She pulled at his hand. He blushed and was further stupified by the fact that he'd blushed. "You did, didn't you?"

John Dog's mouth fell open with no good excuse available. Now it was her turn to look at him. Not for long, but boldly for him, he stared back at her eyes. Salty streaks had tracked down both cheeks, and yet she was smiling now, flushed by the fire or the booze. He looked down, at last. She brought to mind the packaged condom in his wallet, two years old and untouched. The fact that he bothered to carry it at all perplexed him; was it a symbol of his optimism or one more landmark of his ugliness? Either way, what he termed his singular state was a source of speechlessness.

She squeezed his hand. "You're okay, John," she said. "Timid as a mouse, just the way I thought. A nice change from. . . ." She searched, gestured toward the fire. At last she finished examining his face and sat back, her shoulder touching him. For a while they held hands and stared at the fire and the cavorting figures. There was enormous comfort in the palms of their hands. That's in the nature of touch, he cautioned himself. Come morning or whenever the hangover finished with her, Liz would either have forgotten this intimacy or banished it. Sort of like the Valley itself, he thought. Eleven of the best years of my life here, but when I'm gone it will be like I was part of a dream. He liked that and wandered with it, the notion that humans might be the conjurings of the forest or river or mountains.

"I'm leaving," she suddenly spoke. Later he would swear the firewater had him, because right then and there he'd have given a rib to have her complicating his existence. There'd been only one monumental woman in his life, a nurse he'd met in the Stockton Hospital emergency room. But she'd dumped him long since, unwilling to play widow to his matador in the mountains. Other females had streamed through, never staying for long. Something about the way Liz's hand fit his, though, or was it the cleanness of her solitude, her ability to get beneath all this pandemonium—something about her was more than simply enticing. Maybe it's just her cowboy boots, he allowed.

"You want . . ." he offered. "I'll walk you." The rangers had their own complex of cabins behind the post office.

"Leaving the park, I mean."

"No," he reacted and startled himself. Who was he talking to? Himself or her? "It'll blow over," he appended. "A shithead like him," he nodded at Kresinski, guessing. "He does it to everybody."

"Oh, Matthew," she sighed. "Screw him." She lowered their hands to her thigh, resting them there. "No, I've thought it all through. There're other parks. It's a rut here. A 3,000-foot rut. I want more than that." It had to be three o'clock, and suddenly John Dog wasn't so sure he could last until sunrise. How much nicer just to hold this woman and sleep and dream about the mountains dreaming about him. "What about you?" she asked. "You must have plans."

"Me?" The universe gaped at him. His plans? He'd never talked about his plans with anyone. Best to keep it finite and simple, he thought. "Well, Tink and me, we've got a new route planned on Half Dome. And something new up on . . . up higher. And, if we can ever get it together, maybe Cho Oyu or Pumori in Nepal next spring." He trailed off. It was a fine-sounding strategy, but hollow. Just more playtime in the mountains.

"No reason you can't get it together now," she stated with desultory conviction. "Thanks to me, you got your expedition bought and paid for. Yours and everybody else's."

She wasn't bitter, though she deserved to be. Everybody owed their fortunes to her indiscretion, and here she'd sat all night, armorless, stung by callow reminders that she was Kresinski's sloppy seconds. He opened his hand to take her fingers deeper and wondered if the federal agents had any inkling of her complicity. For all she knew, John Dog realized, jail hung next on her agenda. And all because she'd loved a man and gotten drunk with his tribe. A fine lesson in trust; she'd ended up with the dogs and wind.

As much to open himself as to break the chain of ugly thoughts, he suddenly pronounced, "Dry land."

"What?"

"You asked what I want. What my plans are. Dry land, that's what I'm looking for. An end to the amphibious life. I'm tired of the gulf. Of living in the interstices." He groped for the slippery sense of it. "I've become a master of finding the path of least resistance—in the cracks, between the Valley walls, halfway between the ground and the sky." He broke off, mildly embarrassed. It was all so vague, and he'd never talked about these matters, never even recorded them in his Fingerpaintings. But lately he'd sensed that, despite all the physical honesty and power and asceticism Valley life had given him, he'd grown weaker here. "Sometimes," he ventured, pushing himself to make an apple from the applesauce, "sometimes I think, damn, leave the Valley; go to school."

"School?" she prodded. The way she said it made the idea feel tailor-fit.

"Grad school," he fleshed it out. "History. I like history."

"Where?"

"I've applied to Harvard." That was a lie and came out sounding mousy and vulnerable. Well, why not vulnerable, he grumbled to himself. It was a pipe dream and precious. No need to lie, though. The Jesuits never had taught him to be brazen with a clear conscience.

"Boston," she ruminated, almost as if it had been an invitation. "Cambridge. I've never been there."

John Dog glanced up, but not over, letting his ears judge. She's lonely, he heard, and looking for a companion. He felt a rapid longing and wanted to wind in closer with other thoughts. He'd never been to Cambridge either. Long ago Harvard had quit being an institution and a Ph.D.; it had turned into an empty plateau on which ideas galloped down arroyos and beneath high mesas, and you just rode and rode, forever wandering and wondering. He'd stopped in New York City countless times on his way to the Eiger and Russia and Asia and could easily have visited Boston. By never going there, however, he'd implicitly erased it from the map. It had become so much a mystical province now that sending off a postcard requesting application information would have been like sailing for Atlantis. He wanted to saunter through the fantasy.

One minute they were alone, eclipsed by gyrating shadows. The next moment, an unsteady, very solemn, and familiar apparition was standing in front of them. It was Tinkerbell, and John Dog started to disengage his hand. Liz held on. She slid their joined hands into the crevice between their legs.

"John," Tink breathed with relief, "I've been looking for you." He seemed excited, almost aggressive. "These guys," he indicated Tavini and Bullseye, neither of them sober. "They won't believe me about the. . . ."

"Tink," snapped John Dog. But all too apparently, it had already been stated. Stated, argued, rebutted, and restated. The three went at it heatedly.

"Don't be mocking Jesus Christ," warned Tavini, barely able to stand on his feet. He was a born-again Bible thumper who garbled his scripture and had a zeal for blond hashish. John Dog normally enjoyed these martyred baitings, but the alarm bells were ringing in his head.

"Laughing Christ," corrected Bullseye, overjoyed to have the Christian in his clutches. "It's not mockery. It's heresy, the oldest one in the book. And, sinner, I've got a memory for heresies."

"Don't . . ." flared Tavini.

"You can't burn us *all* at the stake," Broomis lectured. He had three major passions that John Dog knew of: ice climbing, politics, and the destruction of God. College had given him birth. John Dog couldn't help but smile and felt Liz squeeze his hand with mutual delight.

"Let me tell you about your loving shepherd," Bullseye insisted, dressing his voice for the larger audience. "How He treats His flock. Well, once upon a time. . . ." He was hammered, which made him quick and lively. "You remember Peter?" The fire was diminishing beyond the three figures; night was taking over, if only for the hour or so before sunrise. "Well, the Romans crucified Peter, but with a difference . . . they did him upside-down. And while he was dying, slowly and badly, guess who decides to put in an appearance?" A rhetorical pause. "His old buddy, the Son of God." John Dog blinked, half remembering this story from his high-school days. Bullseye actually knew what he was talking about. "Now Peter's dying for this guy; he's upside-down, suffering, offering up his life. And here comes the Savior floating down from heaven. Maybe he's got an angel or two blowing horns behind him. And poor Peter's upside-down, watching. He knows his goose is cooked; even the Son of God can't pull him out of this one. That's okay, though, because here's his buddy all ready to welcome him up to heaven. But what does he see? His Savior opening His arms wide? Or weeping at all this pain? Nope. He sees Christ laughing. Laughing."

Tavini was puffing his cheeks in and out, outraged or ready to pass out or be sick or all three. Bullseye hooked his thumbs in his front pockets, evidence presented, case rested. Clarence Darrow couldn't have done it better.

"You want to dig on me, that's fine," Tavini burst out, bared for martyrdom. "Not Him, though."

"Down, boy. I'm just telling you what's written."

"No, it's not," wailed Tavini. Liz reined in a giggle; John Dog heard the grunt.

"But what's it got to do with drugs?" Tink inserted with stubborn awe.

"And guns. Drugs and guns and Jesus Christ. What's the deal?" He was as loud as he was mystified.

What it means, thought John Dog, is that there are smugglers in the world with an educated bent and a sense of the absurd. Laughing Christ, M16s, Uzi machine guns. And a planeload of top-quality weed. Heresy heaped on heresy. It's none of our business, that's what it means. Tink had promised not to expose the little address book. There was no telling who might be listening. Mafia, feds, smugglers. Luckily, no one was nearby now, but what about earlier?

Suddenly a bass yell issued from the forest, then sounds of pounding feet and breaking branches. John Dog froze, and Liz's grip tightened hard on his hand. Busted, he registered as he leaped to his feet. The same thought hit everyone else around the fire. Figures bolted away into the darkness; one of the stereo speakers tumbled into the fire and sent up sparks. A few prone bodies resurrected themselves and stumbled away. Someone appeared from the forest, pointed backward, and kept running. "Go!" John Dog yelled to Liz, but she had already vanished. Tink and Bullseye and the martyr were gone. It was John Dog alone, then, who saw a cinnamon-colored bear and her chubby yearling come ambling out from the trees. The party was over.

Chapter Seven

HIS WHITE PANTS FLECKED WITH DRIED BLOOD, sweatshirt tattered and stretched loose at every aperture, Tinkerbell balanced just beneath the summit. A thick, square roof of rock known as the Visor jutted overhead, seemingly a dead end. All the classic routes on the great face of Half Dome circumvented the Visor, passing to one side or the other. But Tinkerbell and John Dog had agreed to put an unusual finish to their unusual route.

Seven long days of strenuous ascent had taken them up the vast, fantastic landscape of Half Dome. The vertical surface was so forbidding and immense that until the pair actually traveled its full 2,000 feet, certain features of the wall had been completely unknown. Like sixteenth-century sailors they had struggled across places that could only have been found, prior to their effort, on wildly conjured maps.

On the first day all had gone normally. Difficult motions overcame gravity. The rock passed by smoothly. On the second day, with the morning shadows blue as plums, they had come upon a long tail of decayed granite. John Dog was too heavy to lead this rotten section, and even Tinkerbell's 145 pounds had almost been too much for the loose, broken flake. John Dog inserted his hand into a fist-size hole on the third afternoon, only to be bitten by a startled foxbat. Without a second thought he did the most intelligent, cold-blooded thing possible: he dipped his hand back into the hole, grabbed the bat by one dry wing, and brained it against the wall. Then he dropped the feather-light carcass to Tinkerbell, who gingerly stuffed it into the top of their red haul bag. That night, several hundred feet higher, the two climbers had scrutinized the brown creature and tried to decide if it might have been rabid. Finally, unable to decide, John Dog tossed the body away. A butterfly that had lost its color, it sailed crookedly into the night.

On the fifth day the pair had crept vertically across a sudden border onto enamel-white stone. Since beginning they'd been dwelling on black-and-gray monzonite. Now, suddenly, the world became a region of pure whiteness, utter virginity, which gave them the feeling of climbing on Carrara marble. They discussed what it would be like to climb the dome of St. Peter's, and that led to an anecdote about a wild Jewish-American climber who'd been shot by Israeli soldiers when he attempted a spontaneous ascent of the Wailing Wall. Tinkerbell had accepted the fiction. John Dog had accepted Tink's acceptance.

On the sixth day, shortly after completing their breakfast of M&M's, a stick of beef jerky each, and a pint of water between them, they had delicately ascended a harrowing 200-foot flake that was so loose in its scanty socket that an old bird's nest was dislodged when John Dog pulled too hard doing a lieback. At the top he found a crystal of transparent quartz embedded flush with the wall.

Each night, on ledges or in hammocks, John Dog had copied down in his notebook the landmarks of their passage up the middle of the northwest face of Half Dome. The route was an invention every bit as ingenious and laborious as the creation of poems Tinkerbell talked about writing. On the seventh day John Dog ran out of ink.

Now he stood on a narrow, sandy ledge eighty feet below his partner, calmly feeding out rope as it was needed. Beside him sat the haul bag, leaner and much lighter for all their days on the rock. As an act of faith, they had eaten their last oily chunk of salami and crumbled cheese and drunk the last of their water that morning. They'd squandered their last bit of sustenance believing they would be on top before another night fell. As a result, John Dog's lips were white with thirst. The week of short rations had dehydrated them beyond discomfort, and they were racked with pain. Unless he and Tink intercepted a hiker on the summit or on the crude cable-and-wood staircase that led down the back, it would be hours before they drank, maybe even another night. Water was not so foremost in John Dog's mind, however, that he couldn't appreciate Tinkerbell's confrontation with the Visor. The boy was a sorcerer.

Tinkerbell dipped his hand into the dusty nylon bag of gymnastic chalk that dangled from his harness. Hanging by his other arm, he extracted the hand smoking with white powder. When he opened and closed his fingers, chalk dust fluttered down toward the ground 2,000 feet below, disturbed here and there by soft eddies of breeze. John Dog breathed in the height. The trees were too small to pick out individually. People, if any were down there, were invisible. Mirror Lake was no bigger than a penny. More chalk dust drifted by; Tinkerbell had exchanged hands.

A thin, straight crack extended out under the Visor's ceiling, then turned perpendicularly up, following the twenty-foot, squared-off front to where, out of John Dog's view, the summit lay. Tinkerbell prodded the crack with his dry fingers, ferreting out a brief edge that might combine with an opposing knuckle to form a finger lock. Padding higher with his feet, he felt farther out beneath the roof. John Dog watched his calculations. He tried to guess where Tink would invent his next toehold. The boy committed himself, at last, to the ceiling. He moved his feet up and pushed his fingers into the crack by

his eyes. He was dead parallel to the ground, nearly half a mile below, glued to the flat roof. John Dog fed him a foot of rope.

Tinkerbell's sorcery continued. With taut confidence he explored the fissure, measured its possibilities, and squeezed the worn toe of his shoe into the crack. He was a pulsing, respiring fiber of muscle intent on the next moves. Not a motion, not even a glance was wasted. He reached the edge of the ceiling and locked his fingers into the new vertical crack that led up the front of the Visor. A few more moves, John Dog saw, and the boy would be on top. Then it would be his turn to try to copy Tinkerbell's movements out under the ceiling. He sensed the impossibility of that, licked his lips, tried not to think of water. He had to at least attempt the crack. If he failed, there were always the jumar ascenders to climb the rope with. Tinkerbell eased out from beneath the ceiling and pulled himself higher toward the summit lip. When he was in a more natural position again, he paused and leered down at John Dog.

"I'm amped," he chortled. Joy lit his green eyes. "That's the most . . . decent thing . . . in my whole life." It wasn't bragging. It was a very private admission.

"We'll celebrate," John Dog called up. "A beer. You'll drink a beer to this?" He wiped a hand across the rock. He had been saving something for the top, a reward for both of them. Once up, he was going to tell Tink about a secret climb he knew about in the high country.

"Yeah," shouted Tinkerbell, utterly liberated. He arched back. "Yeah." A slight wind lifted his exuberance across the wall.

"And some ice cream?"

"Swenson's."

"And more beer?"

"And more beer. Kathmandu, here I come!" Tinkerbell grinned like a lunatic chimp.

The wind slapped at the wall again, then was gone. John Dog stiffened, then relaxed. "Go plant the flag," he shouted playfully. "Then let's find some water."

"Yeah." The boy was already drunk with himself. He flowed up the remainder of the crack as fast as John Dog could pay out rope. At the top he threw a hand over the edge, kicked slightly with one toe, and disappeared onto the summit. John Dog felt the lead rope and the trail rope vibrate as Tinkerbell untied himself for the first time in a week and anchored the lines. The Apache busied himself with the haul bag, readying it for Tink to pull up. It was over. It was done.

But suddenly, horribly, Tinkerbell reappeared.

Somehow he'd slipped. He'd slipped headfirst, slightly to the left of the crack he'd just ascended.

His black hair flashed downward, then shivered. Violently, superhumanly, Tinkerbell managed to twist himself around so that he was clinging to the very lip of the Visor. With a wordless chill John Dog saw that the boy had indeed untied from the ropes. The homemade harness still looped his thighs and girdled his waist, but nothing was attached to it. The ropes lay against the rock to Tinkerbell's right, alongside the crack.

John Dog started to shout to the boy to work over to the ropes but saw, to his surprise, that Tinkerbell was talking to someone. He couldn't hear the words, though it seemed logical Tink was trying to coax some terrified tourist to his aid. The stranger would help; John Dog knew it. In a moment the terror would be over; Tink would be up.

And then he realized that Tinkerbell was arguing, not coaxing, as he clung to the edge. The motions of his head were angry ones, and at one point John Dog detected shrill cursing, Tink's. His horror mounted with his confusion. Tink never swore. His eyes involuntarily stabbed downward into the yawning pit of Yosemite Valley. A wild, penetrating vertigo punched him hard. He looked away, looked up, looked at the rock, but he was torn with visual echoes of the pit. His legs were buckling as he grabbed for the belay anchor.

He couldn't breathe. He choked. His knees smashed against the granite. Get the rope. It was nothing more than a coarse hope. "The rope!" he finally shouted. But Tinkerbell couldn't hear him. He was cursing, arguing as if with God Himself.

Something must have been communicated—or else Tinkerbell was sharing the same thought—for he suddenly scurried to the right, his hands fast and dextrous. Just as he reached the crack the haul rope began trembling like a reptile, then jerking as if it were being uprooted. Tinkerbell howled a fierce, incoherent curse. With his last syllable the rope slithered through the blank air, disembodied. It tugged at John Dog's waist, then went still. One more rope remained, but that too came alive, threaded free, and went dead at John Dog's anchor.

Now Tinkerbell's only hope was to lift himself over the edge and to safety, which, in John Dog's mind, should have been his partner's first action. It was an easy mantle; he'd seen Tink do it just two minutes earlier.

Instead, Tinkerbell started to climb, not up, but back down the crack, back down the front of the Visor. To John Dog it was complete madness. The wind rushed at the wall again, frightening the Apache with its hard, scaly tide. It moved on.

"Go up!" he yelled. But Tinkerbell continued down, inserting his feet into the crack and plunging his fingers in. His motions were ultimately sane and controlled; it was his direction that so dumfounded John Dog. "Up!" he yelled again. Half-healed scabs on John Dog's hands burst as he clenched at the belay anchor. A thin rivulet of blood ran across the tape on his right hand. He felt nauseated. His head was swinging narcotically, but his vision was crystal clear.

Tinkerbell was frenzied yet calm. There was a mute objectivity to his selection of holds. He descended to the corner of the Visor's ceiling and tried, insanely, to locate a foothold underneath. It was impossible. He didn't pause for a moment as he desperately reversed course and moved up again.

"My arms . . . " John Dog heard him groan. It was a soliloquy, a measurement of pain. There was fire in his arms, lactic acid. He lodged one hand deep in the crack and shook the opposite hand below his waist to force blood through the swollen muscle tissue. His legs were shuddering with fear and accumulated strain.

He attacked the crack again, then slowed near the top and threw a look between his arms at the lower portions of the crack and at John Dog and John Dog's ledge ninety feet below. He seemed almost to be considering a leap for the ledge, but that was geometrically impossible. He was simply too far removed from the main wall of Half Dome to have touched, much less landed upon, the thin ledge of sand. Go up, prayed John Dog.

Finally, in surrender, Tink did go up. He peeked hesitantly over the edge of the Visor, then ducked down in a tight ball as if a terrible monster was waiting. His whole being was quivering. At last he turned his attention to John Dog.

"This motherfucker!" he shouted. The wind swamped his curse, making it feeble and useless. He's scared, moaned John Dog. He's scared. Please, he whispered. Please.

It was Tinkerbell's last rite, that pathetic, banal curse. He extended himself high in resignation, threw a hand well over the top of the Visor's summit corner, and rose almost to a complete exit. He started to disappear from John Dog's field of view. Then, suddenly, definitely, Tinkerbell exploded backward from the Visor.

Someone had kicked him. There was no other explanation.

In animated torpor Tink grabbed for the crack—now five feet away from him—before starting his inevitable plummet to earth. His clothing rattled audibly, whipped in the descent. His hair waved upward. As he passed John Dog's ledge, Tinkerbell stared at the last human being on earth, reached for that fraternity with open hands. And was gone.

The northwest face of Yosemite's Half Dome.
STEVE ROPER.

David Roberts

ILLUSTRATIONS BY J. L. BENOIT

The Public Climber
A Reactionary Rumination

THE BROOKLYN DODGERS were my first heroes, and it was in books about baseball that I discovered the first adult world to which I yearned to belong. Like most boys, I believed everything I read. Rumors reached my ears that Babe Ruth had been a difficult fellow to play with. But then I read, in Paul Gallico's *Lou Gehrig: Pride of the Yankees*, "Would you like to know the true relationship between Ruth and Gehrig in those fine, glittering days? They loved one another." All doubt vanished.

A few years later I read *Annapurna*. Maurice Herzog recounted how Lionel Terray—the "strong Sahib," as the Sherpas called him—had relinquished his chance to go to the summit. "If only one party gets there," said Terray stoically, "it may be because of the load that I'm going to carry up."

"Terray's unselfishness did not surprise me," continued Herzog, who would reach the summit. It did not surprise me either. Of course the prize of Annapurna made brave, competitive men submerge their differences in a common effort. Of course in the bottom of the ninth a ballplayer would lay down a sacrifice to move his teammate into scoring position.

At seventeen I started climbing and three years later went on my first expedition, to Mount McKin-

ley. We were an amicable group of seven, but our teamwork was demonstrably less fluid than Herzog (and others) had led me to believe it would be. During storm days we nursed our annoyances with each other; we compared our efforts as Little Leaguers did their batting averages; and when it came one's turn to go first on the rope, naked ego rose to the fore.

Later the same summer I was an assistant instructor at the Colorado Outward Bound School. The legendary Paul Petzoldt was among our number, and no hours during that August were more magical than the ones I spent listening to the old man, with his great bushy white eyebrows, tell rascally gossip about expeditions of yore. About a certain team in the Karakoram that had divided into two groups and seceded from each other right on the glacier; about one Ivy League Brahmin who, in a particularly vexed moment in a tent in Alaska, flipped a forkful of butter into the beard of his equally well-bred colleague; about two famous alpinists who had actually come to blows over an argument about routes.

Iconoclasm like Petzoldt's intermingled with the politics of the 1960s; when I began to write about mountaineering, I was fired with a zeal to Tell It Like It Was. So were most of my coevals in mountain writing. We dismissed the homilies of perfect teamwork we found in earlier expedition books as the politesse of Oxbridge types, gentlemen climbers who believed dirty laundry should be kept in the closet. I remember an audience in New York in 1970 watching Chris Bonington's slide show of the magnificent ascent of the south face of Annapurna. Bonington had incorporated into the show actual tape recordings of intercamp radio dialogue. At a crucial juncture the crackly voice of Don Whillans burst into the parlay, roundly cursing his teammates below for not hauling more loads to various camps. We listened with glee and admiration. If one were tempted to conclude that Whillans and Dougal Haston had reached the summit because they had the strongest egos, well, that was simply Like It Was on most expeditions, were truth told.

Iconoclasm and candor have carried the day in recent mountaineering literature. Instead of the egoless cooperation found in Sir John Hunt's *The Ascent of Everest,* we have the let-it-all-hang-out intimacies of the recent American K2 books, Galen Rowell's *In the Throne Room of the Mountain Gods* and Rick Ridgeway's *The Last Step.* (And baseball fans know that Jim Bouton's *Ball Four,* with its vignettes of Mickey Mantle and Whitey Ford devoting extracurricular efforts to "beaver-shooting," is more accurate than anything Paul Gallico ever wrote.) In Rob Taylor's *The Breach,* we may be reading a book conceived in pure lust for revenge. It is not the sort of climbing narrative that would have been written in the 1950s.

One of the finest expeditions of the century—or so those of us who were born too late conclude—was the first ascent of Nanda Devi in 1936. A splendidly nostalgic impulse prompted H. Adams Carter, who had been on the original expedition, and Willi Unsoeld to lead another attempt on Nanda Devi, by a new route, in 1976. As is well known, the climb ended tragically with the death of Willi's daughter Nanda Devi Unsoeld at a high camp. After the expedition John Roskelley, who had almost single-handedly brought the team its success on a very hard route, wrote a book about it. As of this date, the book remains unpublished. In the course of researching an article about Roskelley, I recently read his manuscript.

It is an unhappy story, in which the foibles and vanities of all the team members are mercilessly scrutinized—including Roskelley's own. It is hard for me to imagine that any climber who read the text would not decide that he or she was glad to have missed Nanda Devi 1976, thanks all the same. Who, for that matter, would wish to have been along on the 1975 or 1978 K2 expeditions, after reading Rowell and Ridgeway?

This raises a question. Can Nanda Devi

1976—quite apart from Devi Unsoeld's death—have really been so much more divided, so much less congenial, an experience than Nanda Devi 1936? Conversely, if one could scratch the surface reticence of H. W. Tilman, would one find the "real" story of the classic first ascent? (What did Noel Odell really think of those young punks from Harvard? What was Charlie Houston's real problem, when he supposedly got sick from that can of bully beef?)

Or has the expedition experience itself changed—in part because of the very way climbers have chosen to write about it?

When I interviewed Reinhold Messner for an article recently, I was particularly interested in the serious rift that had developed in Messner's friendship with his long-time partner, Peter Habeler. It was my conclusion that, absurd as it seemed, the rift had been caused not by anything that had happened on a mountain, but because of remarks that had appeared in books and magazines: the quarrel was in-

Media star Reinhold Messner, epitome of the "public climber," is possibly the world's most remarkable and talented mountaineer. He has written extensively about his climbs, which include the spectacular solo ascents of the north face of Mount Everest and the Diamir flank of Nanga Parbat. Messner's writings, often pensive and poetic, nonetheless reveal a powerful ego, which he himself admits remains his driving force. Articles about him have appeared in numerous mountaineering journals as well as newspapers such as Paris-Match.

deed a "media event." In the brief time I spent with Messner, I found him strangely defensive, guarded, almost paranoid.

No wonder. Besides a credulous biography written by a British journalist with whom Messner had cooperated, he has had to suffer the innuendos of two sloppy, unauthorized "lives," as well as constant attention from magazines hungry for any morsel of gossip about the man's private life. In Europe, Messner is a media star.

There will be many in the climbing community who harbor precious little sympathy for Reinhold Messner and his troubles. In a sense, he has always sought the limelight, not least by means of the brash yet confessional narratives of his adventures that have made his books bestsellers. What Messner's defensiveness reflects may be nothing more than that climbing has finally (in Europe, at least) reached the level of popularity that baseball has had in this country for the last eighty years. To put it crudely, if Messner doesn't like being misquoted, he should shut up.

This is a course that athletes often take. Philadelphia Phillies pitcher Steve Carlton, for example, who for years has refused to be interviewed by reporters, lets his performance on the mound speak for him. Baseball stars learn early to avoid bad-mouthing teammates or even opponents when journalists are around. Fans like myself grew up on the story of New York Giants manager John McGraw, locked in a pennant race, coming into Brooklyn late in the season for a crucial series. "The Dodgers?" sneered McGraw. "Are they still in the league?" The lowly Bums knocked off the Giants in three straight and cost them the pennant.

The reticence of earlier generations of climbers, then, far from reflecting merely prudish decorum, may have sprung from a well-considered sense of ethics. Old-time expedition veterans knew that the strains of being tent-bound could produce absurd petulance, and they took for granted that danger could elicit behavior about which one might feel embarrassed later. The smooth operation of the team depended, they knew, on all that bother being the expedition members' own business.

Consider, for example, the reaction of Hudson Stuck, who led the first ascent of Mount McKinley, to Frederick Cook, who faked the first ascent. According to Stuck, when Cook's bogus narrative *To the Top of the Continent* appeared in 1908, the miners in Fairbanks eagerly seized upon it and found without much trouble the very page on which the account ceased to be genuine and the "fine writing" of Cook's spurious ascent took over. A year earlier, Robert Dunn had published *The Shameless Diary of an Explorer,* a muckraking, candid, and thoroughly unflattering narrative of Cook's first (1903) attempt

on McKinley. Stuck was quite convinced that Cook was a phony; yet his reaction to Dunn's *Diary* is mixed: "The book," he wrote, "has a curious, undeniable power, despite its brutal frankness, and its striving after 'the poor renown of being smart,' and it may live. One is thankful, however, that it is unique in the literature of travel." Thankful, one presumes, because Stuck knew that few expeditioneers of any stripe would emerge unscathed from the kind of tell-all treatment Dunn dealt out.

It is, in short, vital that climbers, while they are climbing, not have to worry about how they will look in print. I remember a day in September 1966, on Kichatna Spire in Alaska, when I engaged in an extended debate with one of my teammates. We had discovered a steep, 1,600-foot couloir that we called the Secret Passage, which turned out to be the key to our ascent. To get our loads up the mountain, we had to climb up and down the Secret Passage quite a few times. On this particular day, shortly after a

John Harlin was one of the first American climbers to seek public recognition. In the mid-1950's he falsely claimed to have scaled the fearsome north face of the Matterhorn, presumably to impress his Stanford Alpine Club friends. He was probably the first American climber to perform on live television, doing a short route in Yosemite Valley for "Wide, Wide World" in 1957. Harlin later established a reputation in Europe with several fine climbs, including the North Face of the Eiger. He lost his life on this notorious wall in 1966 while attempting a direct winter ascent.

heavy snowfall, I was not at all sure the whole couloir wasn't ready to avalanche. My partner didn't think it would. I harbored doubts about the way he approached flip-of-the-coin uncertainties; he probably wondered if I was feeling psyched out that day; and each of us knew enough about the other's private life to speculate damningly about the possible sources of our avalanche thoughts.

But at least there was nothing but the snow underfoot to ponder. We went ahead and climbed the Passage, and it didn't avalanche—not that day. Suppose, however, that I were in the middle of an expedition in 1985, with a latter-day Ridgeway or Rowell on the other end of the rope, who I knew had signed a book contract before he left the States and was taking notes nightly on our personality conflicts. And suppose we were about to cross one of those maddening slopes that might or might not avalanche. I am quite sure that I would be loath to confess my fears and doubts, and I would be especially careful not to give voice to those freaked-out whimperings and snivelings that somehow, sometimes, add up to that elusive mountain sense called "judgment."

If Steve Carlton lets the media get to him, he may give up a home run and lose the game. At worst, he might blow the World Series and leave vast populations of kids and fans desolate. But if a climber lets the media influence him in the wrong way, he might actually get himself—and others—killed. One wonders, in fact, if there has yet been a true media-provoked climbing death. I know of at least one close call.

A few years ago, for the television show "American Sportsman," Henry Barber soloed a famous British sea-cliff climb, A Dream of White Horses. High on the route he was being filmed by John Cleare, who was dangling from a nearby rope. Cleare suddenly shifted his position. As Barber related to his biographer, Chip Lee:

It caught me the wrong way. I could feel that somebody was there, that somebody was filming me, and it was crucial to that moment. My inner and outer balance were thrown off when I started paying attention to the foreign presence of Cleare.

I went up into the groove, and was doing some stemming moves, pushing with both hands against the sides of the groove. I pushed just a little too hard and my left shoulder bumped the wall, so that I started to fall. Adrenaline shot from my toes right up to my head. My mind came back instantly. In the movie, you can't actually tell I flinched at all. You can see my shoulder hit the wall, but you can't see me push with my fingers to keep myself in the groove, or sense that I had started to fall, that I was off and headed down. But the balance and flow of all the movement that had gone on until that point carried me through, keeping me on the rock and still moving.

Barber's near fall is the extreme case, and there will be those who have little more sympathy for his dilemma than for Messner's. After all, if fame and glory and ABC seduced the well-paid Barber into taking chances he wouldn't otherwise, that's his problem. High-risk sports such as race-car driving and bullfighting would not exist without an audience, and top competitors learn to deal with the pressures a bloodthirsty crowd creates.

More important than unnecessary risk, I think, is the question of what publicity costs the climber in terms of what could be called innocence. In the early 1960s I was lucky enough to climb at the Shawangunks with a group that hovered on the fringes of the Vulgarians. Today, Vulgarian lore is an eastern climbing legend, but in those days the scruffy, bohemian gang was simply the core of a homegrown social scene at a local crag. For a twenty-year-old just leading his first 5.8s, the height of ambition was to converse with Art Gran or Jim McCarthy. Heroes they might be, but not beyond the society of our own kind. It would have been preposterous to imagine a national magazine or a television station coming to the cliff to do a profile on Art Gran.

The wild stunts for which the Vulgarians were famous were, in this sense, innocent. They were concocted merely to impress one another, or to have a high old time, or, at their most satiric, as in the nude ascent of Shockley's Ceiling, to gross out the gawkers who had parked their cars at the hairpin turn below. By the late 1960s, as climbing in this country became more chic, a different tone had crept in. The Henry Barber ritual of downing a few beers at the foot of a desperate climb is an attempt at Vulgarian nonchalance, but it has a mannered quality that pissing off the roof at Emil's never did.

In Great Britain the antics of the Creagh Dhu and the Rock and Ice clubs played the same role as did those of the Vulgarians in the East. The wry lampooning found in Tom Patey's finest ballads and articles, such as "Onward Christian Bonington," "The Professionals," and "Apes or Ballerinas," has its sting in the rebuke directed against such former hard men as Chris Bonington and Gaston Rébuffat, who had perhaps lost touch with their origins as they succumbed to publicity. Patey could even turn that satire against himself, as he did in the hilarious "The Greatest Show on Earth," his memoir about the BBC extravaganza in which he took part on a sea stack in Anglesey.

First-rate climbing can no doubt be accomplished with a mike taped to one's chest and a national audience tuned in. But it is somehow not the real thing. Television executives may salivate over the prospect of a live broadcast from the summit of Everest, but I don't know many climbers who would miss a good party to catch the show. For much the same reason, I suspect, climbers as a group have for the most part remained unmoved by the space shuttle and the moon shots. The premeditated self-consciousness of Neil Armstrong's announcing his Giant Step for Mankind at the moment he performed it prevents our belief in it.

In 1513, however, Vasco Núñez de Balboa waded into the Pacific Ocean, unfurled a flag, drew his sword, and delivered himself of a single bombastic

---

Gaston Rébuffat, of an earlier generation than Reinhold Messner but driven by similar forces, began as a powerful amateur climber in Chamonix and guided in that region for many years. He was a member of the 1950 French expedition to Annapurna but later eschewed the realm of 8000-meter peaks for a more sedentary life of writing books about his beloved French mountains and assisting in the production of mountain films. In his famous book, On Snow and Rock, *published in 1963, Rébuffat appears in more than two-hundred-and-fifty photographs demonstrating mountaineering techniques. In his foreword to the book, Everest climber Sir John Hunt wondered whether Rébuffat, "with his growing reputation, enhanced by mass media publicity . . . might not have fallen a prey to the snare of flattery," but concluded, "I need not have worried."*

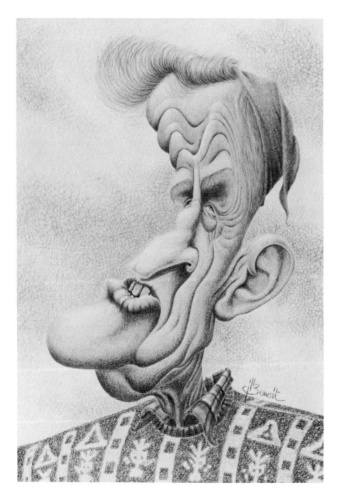

sentence 202 words long. Its purport was to claim for Spain all the land and peoples therein in any way contiguous to this new sea, from the Arctic to the Antarctic, "both now and in all times, as long as the world endures, and unto the final day of judgment of all mankind." Balboa had his notary write down the sentence, and his men signed the document on the spot.

Most climbers, I think, the same ones who abhor the pretensions of the astronauts, find something of a kindred spirit in the sixteenth-century conquistadors (Terray's autobiography was titled, in English, *Conquistadors of the Useless*). What is the difference between Balboa and Armstrong? To put the Spaniard into perspective, it is worth recalling that he (like Pizarro and Cortés) commanded a tiny band of drop-out adventurers, as scruffy a crew as ever the Vulgarians were. The vainglory of his Pacific pronouncement was thus a hedge against the obscurity of his deed. Having his notary write it down was like sending out a message in a bottle: a strong likelihood existed that word of his great discovery might never trickle back to the people who mattered, in Spain.

The life-giving impulse behind our climbing has always been escapist, anarchistic, "useless," in Terray's phrase. And one of the most deeply satisfying rewards of going off to climb is the opportunity it affords to shuck off the postures and personae that one carries through the "civilized" world. On expeditions there always used to be an absolute distinction between "out" and "in." During the first days of each of my own Alaskan expeditions, I would have terrible dreams: things had gone wrong logistically, and I was back "out" in Fairbanks or Anchorage, running around trying to find rope or water bottles. My psyche would eventually adjust: I would settle into "in"-ness, and my dreams were troubled by nothing worse than bottomless crevasses and endless storms.

The "in"-ness of climbing—its temporary establishment of an anarchistic utopia of common purpose—is our link to the great voyages of the past, when a ship might sail from Bristol, drop off final messages in Newfoundland, then be out of touch in the Arctic for three long years. In the twentieth century, nothing has eroded the clear boundary between "in" and "out" like the radio and the airplane. It was, no doubt, easier in previous centuries to sail into the unknown, knowing that beyond a certain point a party was utterly dependent upon its own resources. Today, to capture this feeling, we must deliberately eschew the radio and the airplane, like Faulkner's Ike McCaslin discarding his compass and his watch before he is able to find Old Ben, the bear. In my experience, doing without radio and airplane bestows an immense gift of psychic wholeness, whatever it costs in safety.

Even on a half-day rock climb, one normally ignores the complicated world we call "out" and instead penetrates the mysteries of self-reliance. On the climb, all that should matter is oneself, one's partner, the rock, and the weather. Climbing is not an act that can be carried on publicly without considerable compromise. It is a deep experience precisely because it tends to pare the superficial. On one's best climbs, one goes through long, squirmy moments of fear and doubt. Only a narcissist could enjoy a movie of himself at such moments or could wish a journalist there to take notes.

An expedition, then, is in a sense an experiment in Rousseauvian primitivism. In a soggy sleeping bag in a drooping tent on the fourth straight storm day, a certain naive, instinctual self comes to the fore. This is quintessentially the place to hold forth for hours about favorite desserts, unfavorite people, objects of long-hidden lust on whom one hopes to perform the following unmentionable acts. But such storm-sitting banter belongs only to one's tentmates. It is of such stuff that trust and the peculiar intimacy of climbing are built, and it depends on being private. To rope up with another climber, when all is said and done, remains a profoundly trustful act. The difference between private and public climbing is like the difference between the act of love and a pornographic film.

Yet, one might well demur, climbing is a supremely interesting business, and thus it is worth examining in depth, by means of writing, filming, and photography. It is hard to dismiss this self-evident proposition. One might say that the proper place for depth of insight is fiction; that what Melville could not put into the travelogues of *Typee* and *Omoo*, he put into *Moby Dick*. Alternatively, one could argue, as Fritz Wiessner did a decade ago, that a climber should restrict his self-advertising to the audience of his peers via the relatively modest genres of slide show and journal article. It is no accident, I think, that even the finest films ever made on climbing lack the integrity of a good slide show, or that the journal article, not the autobiography or expedition book, remains the embodiment of the truest written expressions of our craft.

There also may be a kind of anthropological irreversibility about climbing's drift toward entertainment. Just as the snowmobiling Eskimo can never revert to the dog sled, so today's Everest expedition can never again be carried out with quite the unself-conscious zest exemplified by the 1924 expedition. Deliberate self-limitation, as in clean climbers' refusal to use pitons and bolts, is in a sense the most self-conscious of acts; similarly, refusing to depend on radio and airplane can be mere romantic atavism. Still, I remain heartily grateful that when I went off for a weekend at the Gunks, my nonclimbing college roommates thought I was simply a weirdo, and that during our months of immersion in the Alaska Range we knew that our families would worry about us and some of our friends miss us, but that our arcane deeds we had dreamed so obsessively about all winter would, once performed, not even make the pages of our home-town newspapers.

Hank Levine

A Bouldering Gallery

This and facing pages: Stony Point, Chatsworth, California.

Opening page: Castle Rock, near Palo Alto, California.

Above and right: Stony Point.

Above and left: Buttermilk Country, near Bishop, California.

Buttermilk Country.

Left and facing page: Panther Beach, near Santa Cruz, California.

Stony Point.

Ed Webster

Cold Shadows and Rushing Water

Rockclimbing in the Black Canyon of the Gunnison

DAWN. Chirping birds welcome the first rays of sun filtering through the canopy of piñons and junipers. Climbing gear clanks and jangles as we throw it over our shoulders in haste. Joe Kaelin grabs two ropes; we know there's not a moment to lose. Even at this early hour, our energy is palpable; it vibrates in the air, mingles with the morning breeze, and sends us jogging down the dirt road, wolfing sandwiches on the run. Stepping carefully across a cattle guard, we turn into the woods, reach the canyon rim, and begin stumbling and sliding into a cold, claustrophobic chasm.

It is perhaps the twelfth time in my climbing career I have plunged over the rim of the Black Canyon, and each time I marvel at the paradox of doing the descent before the ascent. And on each occasion I also marvel at the geology, the relative lack of climbers, and the fact that no climbing routes even existed here a quarter-century ago.

Few of America's natural wonders are quite as overpowering as the Black Canyon of the Gunnison River, a fearsome-looking gorge in western Colorado. The canyon's great depth, nearly 3,000 feet at one point, contrasts dramatically with the narrowness of the gorge; at Chasm View a scant quarter of a mile separates rock walls almost 2,000 feet high. While many first-time visitors regard the Black Canyon as a more startling sight than the Grand Canyon, its name is hardly a household word. But to rockclimbers, this slot, one of the narrowest and most precipitous on earth, is renowned for the dozens of challenging routes that ascend dead-vertical walls of Precambrian stone interlaced with crumbling bands of pinkish-colored pegmatite.

The very fact of the Black Canyon's existence is hard to grasp. How was it formed? Why are the walls so steep, and the edge so abrupt? The mind refuses to admit that the Gunnison River, a seemingly insignificant stream when viewed from the canyon rim, could have carved such a mighty trench. But it's true. During the past two million years the Gunnison has succeeded in carving this grand chasm from some of the most unlikely of rocks: the erosion-resistant, two-billion-year-old Precambrian basement rocks of the Colorado Plateau.

The interplay of four primary factors has caused the Black Canyon's unique narrowness and depth. Initially, successive deposits of volcanic debris originating from the nearby West Elk Mountains trapped the Gunnison in its course on Vernal Mesa. When this tableland began to rise, the river was already well entrenched and thus had nowhere to go

but down. And down it cut, at roughly one inch per century. An exceptionally steep average gradient, falling more than 180 feet in half a mile at one location, then gave the Gunnison an exceptional cutting ability. The lack of major tributaries also kept the canyon steep-walled and confined. Lastly, the dense, crystalline core, a blend of metamorphic and igneous rocks, was more easily eroded downward than outward. The end result is an unobstructed view of the earth's geologic foundations: the Precambrian schists, gneisses, granites, and pegmatites.

Understandably, few people completely comprehend this geologic chain of events during the course of a brief stay, and the majority of visitors, sightseeing by car along either the north or south rims, drive away with a superficial grasp of what they must regard as only a sinister gash in the earth's crust.

The number of curious and intrepid explorers who venture down into the canyon's barely accessible interior are, not surprisingly, and perhaps thankfully, few. Most are fishermen, lured down SOB Gully by tales of enormous, man-eating trout. Certainly only a handful of adventurous souls have ever followed the path of Will Torrence and A. L. Fellows, who, in 1909, hiked, floated, and swam thirty tortuous miles through the Black Canyon's inner gorge. These two men thus became the first ever to pass through the Narrows, where the full force of the Gunnison River rages through a forty-foot-wide channel, and to gaze upward at the towering sweep of the Painted Wall, Colorado's tallest cliff. They also disproved the persistent legend that those who descended into the canyon would never be seen again.

Due primarily to the unflagging lobbying of the Reverend Mark Warner, the Black Canyon remains today as one of the West's last truly wild canyons, home to bobcats, mountain lions, golden eagles, and herds of mule deer and wintering elk. During the 1920s, Warner, of nearby Montrose, saw the Black Canyon as a one-of-a-kind wonder that had to be saved from exploitation. President Hoover signed legislation creating the Black Canyon of the Gunnison National Monument in 1933. More recently, the status of the inner gorge was upgraded to that of a Wilderness Area.

My first visit to the Black Canyon was in the autumn of 1976, under the tutelage of two canyon veterans, Jim Dunn and Earl Wiggens. Six months earlier, Jim had burst into my dorm room at Colorado College brimming over with enthusiasm. He and Earl had just succeeded in free climbing a Grade

V of Layton Kor's in the Black Canyon. I'd read accounts of some of the canyon climbs—who hadn't heard of the Painted Wall?—but would have been hard pressed to locate the gorge on a map. It was somewhere on the western slope, wasn't it? Jim, quite beside himself, insisted that I had to visit the place. What's more, he would take me there.

Gazing at the precipitous rift for the first time, I felt some of the same possessive energy that had captivated Jim. Earl firmly clasped my legs as I lay prone on the canyon's north rim, peering into the depths. The continuous roar of the river pounded in my ears like primitive drumbeats, and a strong updraft brought tears to my eyes. My senses thus overpowered and vulnerable, the canyon began to whirl like a vortex in front of my clouded vision, drawing me in against my will. Only with a sudden, determined effort did I slide back from the brink of the fathomless void, gasping for breath.

People actually climbed here? Or, more to the point, *we* were going to climb here? Tomorrow? Maybe I'd just watch, I decided, though in the company of Earl, Jim, and Bryan Becker, I should have known I'd never get off the hook that easily.

Earl and Jim were so supercharged with energy that their feet barely touched the ground. I'd often wondered if they were somehow immune to the forces of gravity when they climbed together. Their plan, to free climb a Grade VI of Kor's in a single day, with one rope and a rack of chocks, was typically audacious, but by the electric look in their eyes, I had little doubt they'd pull it off.

Bryan and I, on the other hand, felt like a couple of sacrificial lambs. Phenomenally limber from years of gymnastic training, Bryan was equally adept on steep rock, ice, or alpine climbing, but he too had never climbed in the Black Canyon. Jim was insistent that Bryan and I repeat his and Earl's free ascent of the Cruise, their free version of Kor and Dalke's 1964 first ascent of North Chasm View Wall. Although Bryan and I had climbed together extensively for two years, an 1,800-foot, 5.10 free climb was a step or two beyond our usual fare. And to climb it in one day? It just didn't seem possible.

"Aren't there any slightly easier routes in the canyon?" I asked of Jim, "something we can break ourselves in on more gently?" Unswervingly, he replied that we absolutely had to climb the Cruise; it was one of the finest free climbs in Colorado.

To add to the challenge, Bryan had suffered a spectacular accident several days earlier. On a dare from his younger brother, a state rodeo champion, Bryan had agreed to ride a rodeo bull if his brother consented to go rockclimbing in return. The bull shot out of the chute, bucked once, and sent Bryan into orbit. When he crash-landed, the bull turned and trampled him, resulting in a badly bruised right

A climber jumars an overhang on Hallucinogen Wall.
ED WEBSTER.

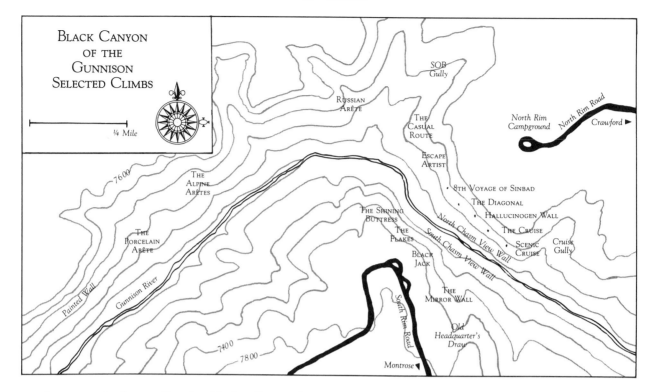

The Black Canyon of the Gunnison, with topographic contours and selected climbs depicted.

arm. As we racked gear for the Cruise, I saw that Bryan could hardly move his arm; what had we gotten ourselves into this time?

The four of us left the north rim campground at first light, racing down a nearby gully into the shadow-cloaked depths. The rapids of the Gunnison River grew louder by the minute as we descended tricky cliff bands, hurtled down loose scree, and crashed through annoying bushes. At one point, while wading through waist-deep poison ivy—a trifling inconvenience we hadn't been warned about —I glanced up to see Jim and Earl waiting impatiently.

"This is the start of the Cruise," Jim said hurriedly, pointing to an obvious crack system. "Good luck!"

We'd need it. Having no written description, we were depending on Jim and Earl's few words of wisdom regarding the two 5.10 cruxes.

"See you back in camp," Earl added before chasing after Jim. A moment later they had vanished, consumed by the cold, deafening depths, eager to embark on their own vertical journey back to the warm world above.

Our rendezvous was not to be. They made it; we didn't. While they celebrated around a blazing campfire, we nearly froze to death several hundred feet below the rim. Bivouacking in T-shirts, sweaters, and balaclavas, we listened to the unearthly drone of the river, huddled together for warmth, and prayed for the orange glow of dawn.

The long October night gave us more than enough time to reflect on what we'd done wrong, where we had lost precious time—in short, everything that had led up to the misery of the bivouac. Black Canyon climbing, we had learned, was a trial of fire and ice: during the day the searing heat had sapped our strength; during the predawn hours, as the sun refused to rise, a brief snow flurry whipped around us, and I could have cried. Suffering had been elevated to a new degree.

We struggled over the rim a few hours later to be greeted by the lighthearted ribbings of our cohorts and cans of ice-cold beer. The canyon had demanded our best and we had given it. We really hadn't had any choice. To retreat once we'd realized we'd have to bivouac unprepared would have been ridiculous. Slowly I began to realize that although I hadn't felt so at the time, we'd been committed to completing the venture right from the start.

A hot wind, heavy with the aroma of sage, blew in my face. Sitting cross-legged on the canyon rim, I felt the warm sun bore into my bones. I was drained and empty, yet idly content, and the chill of the bivouac had finally fled. Remembering my initial fearful reaction to the canyon two days earlier, I shook my head in disbelief. What had happened in the interim to cause me to feel so positive about the place? I felt at that moment a basic change in my attitude toward climbing and saw a powerful new

Looking east up the Black Canyon of the Gunnison River. ED COOPER.

vision of free climbing's true potential: one-day free ascents of big walls. Jim and Earl had shown the way.

I had a hunch I'd soon be back to climb again in the Black Canyon, but how often, I hadn't a clue. Meanwhile, I would learn what I could of the routes and their histories.

Although tentative explorations of the Black Canyon's walls were made in the 1930s, it wasn't until the late date of 1961 that the first significant climbs were done. Carrying the torch was Colorado's most talented and respected climber of that era, Layton Kor. During a seven-year period, he made first ascents on nearly every major wall, pillar, and arête in the canyon. Bob Culp, another noteworthy climber of the period, described for me the first Black Canyon climbs:

Kor was just beside himself with expectation. Bob LaGrange had returned from an outing to the canyon with a collection of snapshots. He showed them to Layton. . . . We were astounded to find a place like the Black Canyon so near to Boulder, yet hardly touched by climbers. It was like finding Yosemite in our own backyard.

LaGrange and Layton returned to the canyon the very next weekend and completed a two-day ascent up the south side. Upon their return to Boulder, Layton was frantic: he had seen a large pillar on the opposite side of the river and was determined to do it. LaGrange was too tired to return right away, so I went along. As I recall, we went right back the very next day.

It turned out that we did the pillar pretty easily, though we'd been expecting a hard climb. We even poured out a gallon of water near the summit. We'd been prepared for anything. That was my first climb in the Black Canyon, and since it was Layton's idea, I've always referred to it as Kor's Pillar. I've repeated it many times since, introducing others to the canyon. It's a pleasant 5.9.

Between 1961 and 1967, Kor unlocked most of the Black Canyon's innermost secrets, scaling more than twenty known routes, including the Porcelain Arête, the Alpine Arête, the North Chasm View Wall (now the free climb known as the Cruise), and the Russian Arête ("like Russian Roulette," Layton told me). In addition to this impressive list, Kor also ascended a host of routes now forgotten both by their creator and by present-day climbers. In short, Kor was as productive in the Black Canyon as he was elsewhere in Colorado, and he managed to persuade many of the best climbers of the era—Pat Ament, Culp, Larry Dalke, Wayne Goss, Huntley Ingalls, and Jim McCarthy—into accompanying him on various new undertakings.

Every climbing area has its own heritage of epic tales, and the Black Canyon is certainly no exception. From Kor and Ingalls's near tragedy during the first ascent of the Shining Buttress, when a large pegmatite flake broke loose with Kor holding onto it, to modern ordeals such as Harvey Miller's T-shirt bivouac only fifty feet short of the north rim on the first ascent of Air City, or Earl Wiggens's desperate use of lip balm to lubricate his parched mouth during the first ascent of High & Dry, the Black Canyon has exacted a toll on nearly all of its suitors. For some climbers, one Black Canyon route is one too many, as a chuckling Kor related to me one day:

I had this great line picked out on South Chasm View Wall, but I was having trouble finding a partner for it. Brian Marts had never been to the canyon, so I figured if I talked it up real big, he'd come along. I remember saying that it never rained in the Black Canyon, that the weather was always real nice, that kind of thing. Finally he said, okay, I'll go. We descended a gully I'd never been down and had to rappel over a huge chockstone. Now we weren't sure if we could get back out. We crossed the river a couple of times and started up the wall. Well, wouldn't you know it: about midday it started raining! We bivouacked in hammocks—what a miserable night!

After the river rose from all the rain, we knew we couldn't retreat. Brian wasn't feeling too well, so I led the rest of the way to the top. I used some rurps and knifeblades, a few bolts. I even fell twenty or thirty feet, pulling out some pins.

We made it all right, but I'm pretty sure that was the last climb Brian ever made in the Black Canyon.

Of all the partnerships in Colorado rockclimbing during the 1960s, Layton Kor and Bob Culp's was undoubtedly the most enduring and influential. "Layton and I were both stunned by the Black Canyon," Culp remembers today, "but we always felt at home there." The pair did several classic Black Canyon routes together, including a first ascent on South Chasm View Wall that turned out to be Kor's last big route before his "retirement" in 1968. "We had plans for a lot more climbing trips," says Culp wistfully, "but at least we got in a few."

In the late 1960s and early 1970s the unconquered central portion of the 3,000-foot Painted Wall was recognized as the "last great problem" in the Black Canyon. Kor had climbed both of the arêtes that flank the wall, but the midsection proved much more elusive. Kor tried twice—once, with Dalke, up the eventual line of the Dragon Route and, again, with Dalke and Culp, somewhat to the left—but uncharacteristically failed.

Rusty Baille was the next to try the wall, concentrating his efforts on the line destined to become the Dragon Route. Frustrated by poison ivy, river

Typical Black Canyon buttresses, airy and challenging.
ED COOPER.

flooding, and hard aid climbing, Baille met with repeated defeats. Karl Karlstrom, one of Baille's partners, wrote:

The Painted Wall presented problems other than those of route finding and climbing. The wall has an aura of strangeness about it that created another sort of obstacle. I experienced a feeling of anxiety, an empty sensation in my stomach, as if I were out of place and in a forbidden world. I think we all experienced this sort of feeling on our first attempt, and, perhaps as on any new type of rock, this initial strangeness needed to be worked out before a successful ascent could be made.

Colorado's tallest cliff was finally scaled by Bill Forrest and Kris Walker in May 1972, after a grueling five-day climb up a previously untried crack system, one that contained a dangerous amount of loose rock. Forrest later wrote about one particularly harrowing rockfall experience: "On pitch thirteen, Kris shoved off a 75 lb. block, hoping to direct it, but the block took a bad bounce and plummeted directly for me, blotting out the sun. I was tied to my belay anchors and couldn't move. It looked like death and then the sun reappeared. . . ."

As might be expected, Baille was disheartened upon hearing that the Painted Wall had at long last been scaled. But the Rhodesian climber was not to be deterred; his nearby route, named for two bands of pegmatite resembling Oriental dragons, lay ready and waiting, still unclimbed.

Only a month after the Forrest-Walker ascent, Baille, Karlstrom, Scott Baxter, and David Lovejoy completed the Dragon Route. The foursome found few ledges on this gutsy ascent, spending six of their eight nights in hammocks. "All of us," Karlstrom wrote, "experienced some difficulty in making the shift back to the horizontal environment—those first steps after nine days were surprisingly unsteady. . . . We all decided long ago that if ever there was a second ascent of our route we would all get some lounge chairs and a couple of cases of beer, sit on the South Rim, and watch."

Of the two Grade VI routes on the Painted Wall, the Dragon Route is the more popular, having been ascended some half dozen times. It was also the first—and to date, only—Grade VI in Colorado to have been soloed: Bryan Becker spent six lonely days on the route in 1978. While the recent and spectacular first free ascent of the Forrest-Walker Route by Leonard Coyne and Randy Leavitt may lead to increased traffic on that route, the rockfall danger so vividly portrayed by Forrest is still extreme. Coyne and Leavitt's eighteen-hour ascent, described in more detail later, was a landmark climb: the first free Grade VI in the state.

Jim Dunn, the first climber to solo a new route

Chester Dreiman leading a 5.11 pitch during the first ascent of Escape Artist. ED WEBSTER.

on El Capitan, has always sought unusual challenges. One of the preeminent Black Canyon climbers of the mid-1970s, he had already accomplished some fine routes there when, in May 1976, he and Earl Wiggens made a radical break with tradition. Most of the major Black Canyon climbs done before this time were of the multiday, mixed free-and-aid variety. But in an amazing six hours, the pair free climbed the fifteen-pitch route put up a decade earlier by Kor and Dalke on North Chasm View Wall. Dunn and Wiggens, dumfounded by the ease at which they had dispatched the route, christened their superb effort the Cruise.

This excellent climb marked the beginning of an exciting and bold new era in Black Canyon climbing. All the canyon's biggest walls soon began to be climbed free in a single day, with, as the motto of the times proclaimed, only a rope, a rack, and the shirt on your back. The process of mentally sizing up a climb had been irrevocably altered, and the rate of success since 1976 has been astonishing: virtually

Bryan Becker skyhooking an A4 pitch on Hallucinogen Wall. ED WEBSTER.

every one of the Black Canyon's major walls and arêtes have seen rapid, free ascents.

Many noteworthy routes have been established during the past eight years. In 1977 Scott Gilbert and John Rosholt free climbed Kor's classic Southern Arête of the Painted Wall, a recommended and comparatively safe Grade V, 5.10 route. Another popular route, the Grade IV, 5.10 Journey Home, on North Chasm View Wall, was put up by Ed Webster and Bryan Becker in 1977. South Chasm View Wall was also climbed free the same year in a fifteen-hour effort by Webster and Steve Hong. Leonard Coyne and Ed Russell made a notable first free ascent of the Goss-Logan Route (Grade V, 5.10) on North Chasm View Wall. Not all the modern-day routes are free: the Black Canyon's most difficult climb to date, the Hallucinogen Wall, involves A5 climbing as well as 5.11 free climbing. This intimidating route, which took eight days to complete on the final push, was climbed by Webster, Becker, Bruce Lella, and Jimmy Newberry in May 1980.

Leonard Coyne has been the driving force behind several recent, major Black Canyon climbs. Success on each of these ventures came at a high price, as repeated failures, forced bivouacs, and endless rappels into the canyon bottom tested Coyne and his partners to the utmost. The first free ascent of the Forrest-Walker Route on the Painted Wall was perhaps his biggest coup. The route had been done mostly free in 1979, when Stan Mish and Dan Langmadz made the third ascent under a sun so fierce they had to seek shelter beneath their bivy sack at midday. But from that point on, Coyne was the driving force behind all future efforts.

One of these attempts proved especially memorable, as Coyne related it to me along with his account of the final climb:

We arrive at the Black Canyon about 4:00 A.M. Despite all common sense, we head down SOB Gully immediately. It's 6:00 A.M. when we arrive at the base of the wall. Chris Wayne has come along to jug a fixed line and carry a pack but decides this is unreasonable since he has a broken arm—in a cast. He descends and Randy Leavitt and I proceed with a minimum of provisions. We reach midheight, the start of Death Valley [a rock-fall-prone groove], by noon.

Death Valley is hard but uneventful for several hundred feet. Around 3:00 P.M. we arrive at the base of a large pegmatite band. The belay is manky, and the next pitch is extremely loose with no protection. . . . This puts us a few hundred feet below the top.

The overhangs above are impossible to free climb or nut. We resolve to try to find a bivy site. Randy finds a ledge one hundred feet down. We rappel and find it covered with ropes from the first ascent. Clouds, which have been gathering all day, erupt into one of the most violent storms of the year. We both get soaked and become fairly hypothermic. Lightning strikes the pegmatite above us on occasion, sending down some rockfall.

The next morning we try the overhangs to no avail. Twenty-three rappels land us on the ground. . . . I'm delirious on the hike out. By the time we get back to Boulder we've gone well over fifty hours without sleep. Fear and Loathing in Colorado. . . .

The final attempt takes place in May 1982. This time it's Leavitt and me alone. We bivy at the base and are on the wall at 6:00 A.M. We carry a pack with minimal survival gear (tube tent, stimulants, etc.). We hit our high point around 4:00 P.M., then head right for several pitches, angling toward the exit pitches on the Dragon Route. This area has some of the most amazing free climbing I've ever done on a wall: 5.11+ face climbing protected by knifeblades and copperheads. It's well past night by the time we hit the Dragon exit chimney. Three pitches of 5.10 off-width, climbed with headlamps, land us on top at midnight, eighteen hours after we began.

This place is brimming with history, I think, as Joe Kaelin and I make our way down into the chill depths. And we're going to make a little ourselves today, if all goes well. Leonard Coyne unselfishly suggested, last night, that Joe and I try a new route to the right of the Cruise. Actually, it will be only a variation, since it follows the old classic for a few pitches near the bottom, and joins it again at midheight.

In no time flat we are three pitches up the Cruise, at the point where our variation diverges right, up a diagonal crack. I lead the next pitch free at 5.9; it's part of a big-wall climb called the Dylan Wall. (I recall asking Bryan Teale which Dylan he had named his new route for. "Both of them," he replied enigmatically.) Nuts drop easily into perfect keyhole slots, and handholds are sharp-edged and secure. Methodically, I gain height, rising out of the dark chasm into the blazing morning sun.

The poetic beauty of the canyon is in stark contrast today; the sun is so bright I must squint. Even the north-facing walls opposite us are enjoying a brief respite from their bleak, shadow-clad incarceration. Already, though, the shadows grow longer and blacker as the sun tracks across the bleached sky.

"Joe, you're gonna love this!" I yell down. We shout back and forth to make ourselves understood above the river's clamor. When he reaches my small but comfortable stance, his broad grin says it all.

"Are you sure nobody's ever done this before?" he asks.

North Chasm View Wall. The obvious slanting crack system at right center is called The Diagonal. Many other routes have been accomplished on this vertical, 1,800-foot face. ED COOPER.

"That last pitch has been done, but where we're going, up there," I reply, pointing, "that's new. I probably would have heard about it if it had been done already."

Joe leans back on the anchors for a better look, uttering a few reverent words in agreement with my pronouncement.

"Why don't you keep leading, just the same," he says. "I'm having fun seconding. Okay?"

I'm only too happy to oblige. Another 5.9 crack brings us to one of several small stances beneath a vertical finger-and-hand crack, a fissure so perfectly sculpted it seems like a fantasy come to life. Nirvana? Probably as close as I'll ever get.

Scoured by the river eons ago, and later polished to a sheen by the elements, the salt-and-pepper granite sparkles in the sun. I begin jamming upward, absorbed in the repetitive, athletic movements of slotting fingers, hands, and toes into the crack. The climb is an illusion; it's gemlike, too perfect to be true. We haven't even struggled through a single pricker bush or met any loose pegmatite yet! Quite unwittingly, we appear to have found a classic.

Placed conveniently on both sides of the crack, in-cut holds allow for leisurely rests. I toy with a small overhang, strain to place a wired nut as high as possible, then muster the necessary momentum to reach easier ground. The effort registers as 5.10. Soaking up the sun, I belay on a sloping ramp. It's Joe's turn.

Quite simply, the rock is some of the best I've run across in the Black Canyon, and the climbing has been aesthetic and well protected. The pitches have been even easier than the neighboring ones on the Cruise, an extra bonus.

A thought springs to mind: what shall we name the route? My mind clicks and whirs on the problem as I watch Joe dispatch the crack with ease. He's climbing effortlessly. Will the overhang slow him down? Nope, not for a moment.

The Cruise. Luxury Liner. Clear Sailing. Ocean Voyage. The names filter through my mind. I've always thought that christening a new route was an important event. A good name bestows a distinctive, lasting quality on a climb; it gives it body and soul, bringing an otherwise inanimate piece of stone to life. Well-known names, such as the Central Pillar of Frenzy, the Naked Edge, or A Farewell to Arms, possess that elusive quality that makes one want to do the route, regardless of the type of climbing entailed. Coming up with a good name can be sheer torture, or it can flash on you like a thunderclap.

Today it's easy. This climb, this small acreage of rock, can have but one name: the Scenic Cruise. We shake on it and continue our relaxed vertical ramble.

Above, the climbing becomes more intricate. But after 300 feet of crack climbing, it's a pleasant change of pace. I lieback the edge of a hollow-sounding flake, then face climb to the base of a right-facing dihedral capped with a small roof. Now where? Fingers grope blindly around the corner and discover a secure finger jam. With less control than I would like, I swing around onto a steep, blank face.

A dead end? Not quite. Two serpentine bands of pegmatite snake across the vertical expanse. Composed of mica, quartz, and feldspar, most intrusions of this type are softer than the parent rock. Eroding at a faster rate, they end up slightly concave and covered with a patina of friable crystals—a climber's nightmare. Luckily for us, these two dikes are flukes. Harder than usual, they protrude half an inch or more, forming a convenient, if airy, railing across the impasse.

"Joe! Keep a good watch here!"

I lunge for the nearest dike, reach it, and launch across the traverse, feet scrambling for purchase, scraping brittle flakes off the rock's weathered surface. I can't possibly reverse the moves I have just made. Nervously, I hang from a sharp hold, trying to rest. It's no good. Swinging my right foot up onto the sharp upper lip of the pegmatite band, I ease my weight over onto my leg, strain for an extra inch of reach, and slot two fingers into a crack. Soon I'm back onto familiar ground: I have rejoined the Cruise. And how very scenic our new cruise has been!

We are, however, only halfway up the 1,800-foot wall. Since I've done the Cruise twice previously, I handle the next two 5.10 leads to speed up the show. Afterward, we swing leads to the top, scaling pitch after pitch of beautiful, varied 5.9, weaving this way and that up improbable oceans of vertical rock.

We arrive on the north rim tired and thirsty, but it has been a memorable day. Our best climbing experiences, I reflect as I walk back to camp, are spontaneous and uncalculated. Like love affairs, they can't be planned in advance; they just happen. I know that if I keep coming back to the Black Canyon, I will broil in the sun, shiver in the cold, encounter more loose pegmatite. . . . But I also know it's all worth it, perhaps just to get the chance to name a few more classic climbs.

Joe Kaelin follows a pitch during the first ascent of Scenic Cruise. ED WEBSTER.

Chris Noble
ILLUSTRATIONS BY DEBRA SMITH

Slater's Tale

SLATER IS DEAD NOW. He was killed by a deadfall fir during a coastal storm on Gilford Island, British Columbia.

At least that's what the reports and death certificate say. That's what most people living in that country think. But there are some, and they are mostly Indians, who say he isn't dead, that he has gone to the North again, gone to answer the voice in his head.

As for me, I don't know. I was many months gone from the island when it happened. They say the body under the tree was crushed beyond easy recognition, but I heard from the constable who investigated the accident that the man had the same coloring as Slater and was wearing the same faded shirt Slater always wore.

When I first met Slater, I had been on Gilford for nearly three months studying the folklore of the coastal Indians. Several times when I discussed certain topics with the old men of the tribe they would mention Slater and his tale. They said if I truly wished to learn about such things I should talk with him.

So I sought him out one night, this white man who the Indians said knew more about the dark heart of wilderness than they.

Even now, looking back, I can't say for sure why the story took such a powerful hold on me. I had heard many similar stories before, so many myths and folktales and outright, bald-faced lies. I have heard the simple bragging of men when they drink, when you know it's the liquor talking and not the man himself. God knows, this man drank. I have no way of knowing, but I would guess nearly a bottle of whiskey every day. How much simpler it would have been to dismiss the tale, to write it off as just another story and leave it at that, a broken-down climber's fantasy.

But that was not to be. No, in spite of all these things, perhaps because of them, because of the man himself, and the chain of events that fell into place like bones thrown by a shaman—and that hint at things about which, even now, I dare not guess—the tale remains with me. It was like a stretch of wild country that you catch just a glimpse of as you drive through, but it gets inside you, and it won't let you rest, or forget.

Not the least of the factors was that I had heard of a climber named Slater before. It had been years ago, on one of my first trips to Yosemite. There, one evening in the Valley of Light, as the stars flowed like a river above the dark walls, I listened to climbing stories at a campfire. One of them concerned a man named Slater who, the speaker said, would appear from time to time to float up the test-piece routes, then fade off, bound for higher ranges, not to reappear for months or years.

"One of the strongest, boldest climbers I've ever

seen," a local "hard man" once told me, and I took those as strong words from one whose own accomplishments were nearly beyond my comprehension.

Finally, there was the telling. I have found that when a man speaks what he thinks is the truth—and there are all kinds of truth—you can read the pain or the joy of it in his face as he speaks. A liar speaks right to you, because he is always measuring the weight of his words as he goes, but a man telling what he believes looks through you because he is seeing the thing itself and not merely its effect upon his audience.

Slater's cabin was set back in the forest on a promontory rising above the ocean. The night he told me his tale the sound of the wind outside was loud, rushing through the dark branches of the firs, mingling with the voice of the ocean.

I no longer remember Slater's exact words, nor how he wove his story. All that remains is the tale itself, and I doubt if it will ever fade.

"It is there, in his eyes," an Indian had told me, "as sure as I see you now. When you look deep into Slater's eyes, you can see her."

From the high eaves of the mountain, Slater watched the sky. It had been a day of storm. Clouds hung broad and heavy, like a thick, gray-black quilt stretching out to the horizon. Occasionally, lightning glowed within, and thunder, deep-throated, would call after it.

The storm had found him the day before, as he reached the end of a long icefield. There, perched on his crampons above the swell of milky, blue-gray ice, he had first seen the clouds appear above a high shoulder. Even as he watched, they had moved down, masking the face of the mountain, smothering the sun.

Below a nearby rock band he had found a place to carve a snow cave, and now, twenty-four hours later, full of food, he stood at the mouth of his cave sipping black herbal tea, watching the sky.

Slater was a large man, with a month-long growth of black beard flecked with gray. His hands, which held the steaming cup, were flattened, rough, crossed by a net of scars. With gray eyes he searched the western sky in an attempt to read the weather.

There was no sign of clearing.

Slater shrugged. It was to be expected. He had crossed the Arctic Circle a week earlier. In the southern countries it was high summer, and somewhere grain rippled in sunlight; but here, in the north, winter held the land.

It began to snow, hard and thick. The man mused over his position. He had food enough for another four days if he stretched it, but he could go for three more without any food at all if he had to. The upper reaches of the mountain loomed dimly above him. Rock, which yesterday had looked straightforward, gleamed thinly now, lacquered by ice. If necessary, he could afford to wait one more day. It would be good to wait out the storm.

Pitching the dregs of his tea out into the swirling curtain of snow, Slater turned and retreated into the darkness of his cave.

The dreams began hours later in the cold, damp night of the snow cave. In the midst of a restless sleep Slater heard a voice, which came and sang to him.

It sang of many things, of mountains and country he had seen. It spoke of cold and winter unending.

Terns. Arctic terns, white with black, sweeping above the snow. The voice chanted, called them up, and he saw them clearly as they flashed across a glacial plain on a brilliantly cold morning in Alaska. Slater stood and watched them go, fleeing north.

"Follow them," he heard the voice urge him, like the faintest breeze.

Then the scene changed. Far off, he heard the call of hunting wolves, then saw the gray-black and blond shapes hurtling through the forest. Taiga—the word sang in his ear. He saw that archaic world where the aurora shimmers above the pines. Wolves and ravens hunting caribou together.

The voice rose and fell with the wind, the same wind that had carved immense hanging cornices above him and his partner on Foraker, that had torn his tent to ribbons on the Grand. The voice was within a mountain spring, and he drank from it.

The voice chanted in the cold, wet dark of the cave. It sang of a wide glacial valley, and he was there. At his feet, half buried in the gritty soil, lay a bear's skull. He stooped, dug it from its resting place. And the voice sang to him from out of the skull.

Slater shuddered, tossing on the low bench he had carved for himself in the wall of his cave. He was held in sleep, trapped in his dream by the gaze of those long-empty eye sockets, held against his will by the voice that sang to him. Now it sang of immense forms waiting over the rim of the world. It spoke of things too dark, too strong, for even that powerful bone to contain.

It was a woman's voice.

Trapped in the dream, Slater dropped the skull. He turned away and tried to flee. Tripping, he began to fall down and down, end over end, out of control.

Only then did he awake, jerking upright so quickly that he drove his forehead against the sagging roof of the snow cave.

"Damn!" The man rubbed at his brow where it had split against the ice. His fingers came away wet with blood and sweat.

He daubed at the blood with the back of a ragged glove and lay back, easing into the warm cocoon of his sleeping bag and bivouac sack. Judging by the soft glow of light at the entry, it was near dawn. He had slept nearly all night.

A shadow passed over the entry of the cave.

Slater twisted beneath the low ceiling, staring at the doorway, where the dawn light slowly grew.

The shadow passed once more.

He tore at the zipper of his sleeping bag. It jammed. He heaved, and it popped open with a muffled tearing of nylon. He ripped open the closure of his bivouac sack, wrenched his shoulders and waist free, then his legs, and lunged for the door.

Outside, the mist was thicker than ever. Snow fell heavily; already more than a foot had accumulated since evening, when he had cleared the entry. A drift was forming. There was nothing else.

What could there be?

He rubbed at the swelling lump on his forehead. What was happening to him?

"There's no room for this," he whispered to himself, and he fought the dull ache that was growing deep inside him. Mountaineering was a discipline. Visions didn't fit.

The snow fell softly on his shoulders, in his hair; it brushed faintly over his cheeks and the bridge of his nose.

"What a dream." He said it aloud in the muted hiss of snowfall. The bark of his own voice was reassuring in this world of fog and twilight.

"I said . . . what a dream!" He shouted this time, out into the long corridors of air that surrounded him, and the sound was strong and good.

He looked at his hands, he looked up at the mountain, then he looked down where the slope fell steep and fast away into the clouds. These things—height and distance—were more powerful than dreams or shadows. He smiled to himself. Then, with a shrug, he turned and entered the cave.

Outside, somewhere to the left and above, there was the clatter of stonefall.

The next day the storm had passed, and Slater climbed. He climbed as if a wolf snapped at his heels. He climbed until the thin Arctic air tore at his throat, until his temples and his thighs throbbed with the exertion; yet still he did not rest or pause.

Each bite of his twin axes sent a spray of ice into the blue of the sky. Each thrust of his legs sent his front points biting deeply, propelling him upward.

A steamy river of spindrift hissed over him. He watched as the stream broke around his arms and legs before flowing away into the gulf.

Tying a red bandana around his temples to keep the sweat from his eyes, he felt the cut on his forehead sting. There was a certain revelation in this, and in the strength of his arms and the sharp pumping of his legs. At times he balanced precariously on rock edges, his crampons grating sharply over the granite, a mitten clamped in his teeth, one hand wedged in a crack lined with ice. These things were substantial and concrete; he welcomed them. Here there was no questioning. Nothing was between him and a fall but his own skill, experience, and luck. This was his element; for this he had been trained. He was climbing as always before. And here, now, in the sharp sunlight, the memory of the nightmare and that small moment of doubt began to fade like morning fog along a riverbank.

He breathed deeply. He moved first one axe, then the other, felt and heard and saw all at once the solid *thuuunk* as the axe sank into the ice. He lifted one foot, then the other, in a strong flurry. Then one axe . . . then the other. . . .

Laughter, sparkling in the mountain air.

He jerked his head up. Fifty feet up the slope something shimmered above the ice.

He rubbed at glare-reddened eyes. The vision remained.

It was a woman, a beautiful woman, naked save for a veil that blew and shimmered about her in the biting wind, recalling for Slater fields of snow under moonlight.

Cold slammed in Slater's bowels. The nightmare returned, a cold weight that forced the wind from his lungs, making him gasp. He felt the sweat pop out on his brow and beneath his arms. The world had suddenly gone cold, as if something huge had passed before the face of the sun.

Above him, in the blue sky, the laughter rang out, cold and taunting. He heard the voice once more, the voice of the dream, first low and strong, then floating like a breeze, swinging suddenly into higher tones, the tones of a temple bell. They were not words in any language Slater had ever heard; yet their meaning was plain.

"Slater!" she seemed to say. "Why do you fear? Why are you all so frail and shy? I want you, Slater. How long must I call?"

Then something took him. He cried out in that lonely place, high on the mountain of cold stone. He cried out in shock and outrage and in a wave of tidal longing stronger than any he had ever known.

"This can't be!" The mind screamed it, but she was as real before him as the ice, the rock, the mountains. He had never wanted anything so badly. He planted his axe, very high, and surged upward.

Above him there was laughter and a sudden swirl of ravens. She was off.

Two axes were too slow. He threw one off and it dropped into the void. The remaining axe pricked at the ice, barely seated. Slater heaved his way upward, not caring, crampons flashing below.

Above him the figure dwindled until it was like a small doll, then merely a dark point floating upward, always gaining.

Slater ground his teeth; twice he nearly lost his balance. She knew. He could hear her laughter drift down to him.

The sound drove him mad. He thrust upward with no other thought than to crush her beneath him. His lungs strained as though they would burst. Blood roared in his ears, clouded his eyes. Slater ignored it, and, gradually, as the day drew on, the angle of the slope lessened. Ice and rock gave way until he stood at the base of a long ribbon of snow that swept upward to the summit of the mountain. There, far above him, a snow plume beckoned in the wind.

With a growl he tore at the straps of his pack, letting it drop. Not more than a thousand feet away, she sat in a scatter of boulders, her back to him.

A fire burned in Slater's eyes. He started forward, his boots crunching on the firm bed of wind-packed snow.

She heard him and turned. This time there was no laughter, and for the first time the smile left her cold lips. Something flashed across her features, brightening her eyes. She leaped up and skimmed over the snow, barely touching it.

He lumbered after her, his breath rasping, and this time she did not gain—not here where the hard névé supported him.

The gap between them dwindled; he could see her look back over her shoulder. Then, with a frozen grin of exertion on his face, he was upon her, crushing her in his arms, bearing her into the cold sting of snow. He tore the veil from her body, gasping at her beauty. He clutched her long hair in his fists.

Suddenly his hands held not hair but feathers. A hawk screeched in his embrace, its talons raking long furrows down his cheeks, barely missing his eyes. He crushed it down into the snow.

A she-wolf, the largest he had ever seen, twisted beneath him. Golden-furred paws tore open his clothing and grated against the buckle of his harness. The wolf wrenched her head from his grip and caught his forearm in her jaws. Slater shouted as the teeth clamped down, shuddered off bone.

Slowly, though the pain tore the breath from his body, he forced the animal back with his bleeding arm. Then he fastened his hand, strengthened from years of climbing, onto her windpipe and began to squeeze.

The wolf released her grip. Once more, for a moment, Slater looked into the deep green eyes of the beautiful woman he had first heard, then saw, then hunted over the steep face of the mountain. Once more he bent down, seeking her lips. As he did, the eyes shifted and became cold, empty, obsidian. The parted mouth, awaiting his kiss, was smiling now.

He felt himself lifted up, borne out of the snow; still the eyes held his. He felt huge arms, arms of unbelievable bulk and strength, return his embrace. Then the mountain, the sun, the sky, all were gone, hidden behind the immense form that swelled above him, pinning him to her body.

Power held him—power beyond that of humans or animals, something wholly primal. The strength of Fimbulvetr, that long winter Norsemen say will arrive at the end of the world, the whisperings of which can be heard even now in the groaning call of a glacier at dawn.

The thing bent over him and the arms drew him upward.

Slater grasped for the axe still hanging from his wrist loop. He swung with all his strength, and the curved pick with its cruel teeth sank deep into a massive shoulder.

He fell for a long time, thrown out and downward in an explosion of pain and rage.

It has been years since the stormy night Slater told me his tale. Thousands of miles now separate me from the coast of British Columbia. New projects called, and months would pass between the times I thought back to what Slater had told me. Eventually, the news reached me of the accident on Gilford, and I thought that would prove to be the last chapter in Slater's story.

But one night, in an eastern city, I made a startling discovery. It was late, and I was tired, committed to drinking too much coffee. I was leafing through a dog-eared collection of climbing journals laid out before me on my desk, researching material for an upcoming trip to Europe.

Sometime past midnight, I became engrossed in reading an article in *La Montagne*. It described an expedition to the northern sectors of Baffin Island in 1977.

I was nearly exhausted. My eyes burned and my mouth was bitter, yet something drew me on. Near the end of the article I found the following paragraph, which I have roughly translated from the French:

. . . and on the thirtieth of June, as we made our way over the interminable swath of gravel left by the glacier, we came upon a man crawling on his hands and knees below a gigantic bergschrund on the flanks of a large, but unnamed peak. He was in severe condition, apparently having sustained a bad fall somewhere on the mountain above. As to the nature, the existence, or the whereabouts of other members of his party, we had not the slightest clue, for there was no trace of other survivors, and the man himself was incoherent and suffering from exposure. Our team physician, François Jovin, upon examining the man, found a tag in his clothing with the name John Slater. From that, together with his clothing and equipment, we took him to be an American.

My hands trembled as I read. An inexplicable feeling of awe, almost dread, overcame me. Slater had been there. He had been in the Arctic during the summer he had claimed.

Following this discovery, more time passed and my work took me to Europe. For months I had little time to ponder Slater or his encounter on the mountain. I found that the Alps held many charms of their own.

Then, one evening, more than two years after I first heard Slater's tale, I was introduced to a doctor in a mountain hut above Chamonix. He was a well-known mountaineer, I was told. Had I heard of him? His name was Jovin.

Later, when the stars were out and the others had retired, we sat before an apple-wood fire with wine. I asked him about the 1977 Baffin Island Expedition.

He remembered Slater quite well.

At first Jovin thought his patient had little chance to live. His face had been raked during his fall. Deep lacerations ran from one eye down to his jawline. One arm was punctured and bruised, caused, the doctor theorized, by whipping against sharp rocks when the man fell, perhaps down a steep gully. As if to substantiate that theory, the climber's clothing had been shredded from collar to groin. Slater's lips were so mashed and blistered that on the rare occasions when words came, they were largely incomprehensible. To add to the gravity of the situation, he was suffering from dehydration. When Jovin removed Slater's boots, he found that several toes were severely frostbitten.

"Did nothing strike you as especially strange about this Slater? Were you never able to communicate at all with him, about his climb, about what happened?" I blurted out the questions with such force that the doctor glanced up with surprise.

"No," Jovin said. "Even later, after his enormous vitality pulled him through—and that was what saved him—he said very little. He spoke superficially of his experiences, even to the authorities in Paingertung Fiord, after he was airlifted out.

"Mostly he left us to our own theories, merely nodding yes or no to our guesses about his situation. 'Were you soloing?' 'Yes.' 'Did you fall?' 'Yes.' And so on.

"But it surprises me that you should ask about

his strangeness, for there was one curious circumstance that I have pondered many nights since. I didn't think much about it at the time, and I never spoke of it to anyone else, not even to Slater himself.

"You see, after we set up the tents and I got Slater packed into mine to begin the examination, the first thing I did was to pull off his mittens. His fingers were black with frostbite, but—and this is the interesting thing—intertwined and wrapped about them were several long and fine golden hairs. Slater, you see, had dark hair." Jovin paused, taking a long sip of wine before continuing.

"At first this didn't strike me as odd. I suppose I simply tossed the strands out the tent door because I was worried they might have made the frostbite worse by closing the circulation. It was only later that I began wondering where they could have come from. But when I looked, they were gone.

"The wind took them, of course. The wind was always whispering about the tents. We all noticed it; I remember some of the men actually thought they heard voices."

But he didn't have to tell me. I could see it as if I had been there: the long threads of gold, shimmering, thrown out to settle upon the ice, and the wind coming then, clutching them, carrying them away into the night.

Joe Kelsey

Confessions
of a Guidebook Writer

I WAS LOST. Worse yet, I was lost in a swamp and couldn't even resort to the survival-manual expedient of heading downstream.

Having entered Wyoming's Wind River Mountains by a trail up the Popo Agie River's Middle Fork and wanting to leave by a different route, I had headed for Stough Creek. The Forest Service map showed a trail down the creek—even if the topographic map did not—and while hiking up the Middle Fork Trail I had passed a junction with a sign indicating a Stough Creek Trail.

The promised trail began innocently, but fallen logs soon necessitated detours and made me uneasy: such obstacles had been diligently pruned from the Middle Fork Trail. Then I was in the swamp, hopping from hummock to hummock in a futile effort to keep my feet dry. Finally, adrift in a maze of meandering channels, I pointed my soggy boots toward the nearest high ground. This slope lay beneath a lattice of logs so thick that I walked on them rather than between them, but suddenly a trail materialized from under the deadfall; it took me eventually to the signed junction.

Warbonnet, a striking peak in the Cirque of the Towers, Wind River Range, Wyoming. JEB SCHENCK.

The Middle Fork Trail led to my car, but I had read of a shorter trail that would meet the highway at Frye Lake. Though I'd have to hitchhike to my car, I couldn't resist walking somewhere new.

Trouble reappeared strangely and subtly. Two miles from Frye Lake the trail became a road, then a network of roads, but with junctions unmarked by signs. Taking, at each intersection, the road most traveled by, I came to an affirmation of my common sense—two parked cars. I continued more confidently, until my road became less traveled by, became a trail, and ended on the banks of Roaring Fork Creek. Since this stream flows to Frye Lake, I followed it until an old but inexplicable footbridge lured me onto a road that promptly curved back upstream. I then swore off trails and roads and tramped cross-country to the highway.

These misadventures would have been a typical backcountry day—the stuff of fond winter memories—had I not just sent the Sierra Club the manuscript for a book to be titled *Climbing and Hiking in the Wind River Mountains.*

I managed to dash off a correction to San Francisco, feeling only slightly embarrassed, for I realized that a guidebook writer is distinguished from a guide by his enthusiasm for becoming lost. A guide cannot lose his way without jeopardizing the confidence of his clients. However, a guidebook writer's

function is to get lost, to climb and hike where he is most confused by the geography or by ambiguous accounts. Uneventful success is disappointing, for nothing is learned. To be surprised is to obtain information. To be unpleasantly surprised—to suffer from mistakes—is to obtain useful information.

I once thought I had turned, at an unmarked junction in a vast meadow, onto the trail to Raft Lake. At dusk, when the lake—and water for dinner—failed to materialize, I realized the trail had been rerouted since the ancient topographic map had been published. I bivouacked on another trail that diverged in the same meadow: a misdemeanor for a guide entrusted with his clients' welfare, but only a thirsty night in the life of an information gatherer.

My guidebook evolved from a climbing guide to a climbing-and-hiking guide because of climbers' propensity for losing their way when walking into the mountains. Checking trails led to more misadventures—the Stough Creek and Raft Lake fiascos were but two—than climbing did. Yet proving a map wrong was exhilarating; I discovered, literally, the pleasure of pathfinding. In the most remote, least visited corner of the range I once followed a trail

North from the top of Warbonnet; in the center, displaying a wide expanse of granite, is Wolf's Head. Pingora is the sunlit monolith on the right. JOE KELSEY.

from Camp Lake to a pond just downstream. The map showed the trail ending at this point, but as rumor had it continuing for several miles into the high country, I explored. I eventually found a bridge, hidden behind a clump of trees and apparently missed also by the mapmaker, that crossed the Camp Lake outlet stream. A well-constructed trail led from the bridge up into the mountains. Later, I passed a pair of lakes whose drainages are incorrectly connected on the map; I was proud of the Wind Rivers for this slight assertion of wildness, of obstinacy, of resisting our efforts to know the mountains.

The most intimidating aspect of writing a guidebook to a large, remote range is knowing that many readers—even experienced mountaineers—will believe that the author has firsthand knowledge of every mile of trail and foot of rock. More than 600 climbs reach Wind River summits that lie from five to twenty miles from the nearest road. Climbing

600-odd routes during the short mountain summers would be difficult enough; finding a partner for the most remote or least attractive routes would be impossible.

On my first few trips I took along the section of Orrin and Lorraine Bonney's *Guide to the Wyoming Mountains and Wilderness Areas* devoted to the Wind Rivers. But much had happened to our sport's techniques, terminology, and equipment since Orrin Bonney found, climbed, and named Pingora in 1940. Making sense of some of the accounts in the Bonneys' book proved difficult. After puzzling over upward tension traverses, hardware lists that included "boo-boos," and Route 1/2 on the Plume, which reached the summit of Sundance Pinnacle, a mile away, I began collecting accounts of first ascents from publications such as the *American Alpine Journal*. In addition, friends and I traded descriptions of routes we had done. I assembled this information in a notebook—an embryonic guidebook. My project evolved not because I had climbed every route, but because I hadn't; not because I never got lost, but because I did. Later, after I brashly decided to write a bona fide Wind River guidebook, I sought out information from a variety of sources; this detective work often revealed more than just route recipes.

The ostensible purposes of reporting a climb in the *AAJ* are to provide information and, in the longer accounts, share an experience. The real motivation for many reports, I soon suspected, is to claim credit. Sometimes the wording seemed intended to stake out as much territory as possible, as explorers once did when they entered the mouth of a river and claimed the river, its tributaries, the lands drained by it, and the hills beyond it in the name of some most exalted Christian majesty. Why else would the writer of an account announce, "We climbed a new route on the mile-wide west face of Fremont Peak," without further locating the route? Other accounts emphasized difficulty: "We climbed a route harder than any of the other fourteen on Squaretop. On the eighth pitch we encountered unspeakable horrors." Never mind where the route lies or how to reach the eighth pitch; the point is that the climbers were skilled and bold.

Summit registers often mentioned ascents unreported elsewhere. The details were sometimes extravagant, but waterproof canisters and leaky peanut butter jars alike proved to be dubious sources of information. The first-ascent party had arrived suffused with savage exaltation and, before the brisk summit wind had chilled their sweat, proclaimed their new route "classic" and "very direct." Verbosity further dulled the inch-long pencil stub, and the signatures would be illegible. I copied what I could read and later would look for the route from below; typically, from no vantage point would the description make sense.

Summit registers occasionally contained childish scrawls announcing inconceivably rapid first ascents of walls I would expect to take days to climb. But since youth is accomplishing feats we graybeards have declared impossible, I was hesitant to doubt the authenticity of a claim.

Dubious information was also available in Jackson Hole bars. More than once I was accosted by a stranger who had heard of my project and had a route I should know about. I would encourage him to send me a written description, but his need to tell me right then would be compelling. He would spill out details of the Wind River's most amazing climb, while I concentrated on his face in hopes of recognizing him if our paths crossed when we were sober. Never did I get a written description; never did I remember a face. I don't know how many routes were thus lost. Perhaps it was always the same stranger telling me of his same moment of glory.

A carefully detailed route description, accompanied by a neatly drawn "topo"—climbers' jargon for a schematic diagram of a route—once surfaced at a local climbing shop and was passed on to me. Only two pieces of information were lacking: the name of the peak and the names of whoever had done the route. Reluctant to omit what appeared to be an excellent route, I considered including it in an appendix and inviting readers to locate it. I was spared this unusual tactic by chance: a route description on my desk had similar calligraphy. I checked with its author, and, indeed, it was his work. But the route was in the Tetons, not the Wind Rivers!

Writing letters to solicit information proved both fruitful and enjoyable. Correspondents, whether asked to resolve ambiguities in journal accounts or to confirm rumors of unreported ascents, responded enthusiastically. Strangers entrusted me with invaluable photos and slides. Freed from the constraints of journal prose, letter writers provided many a quotable characterization of their routes. Jeff Lowe described one of his routes as "stupid but beautiful" and, specifying the hardware for a three-day climb, suggested taking "all the ticks and tacks and crackerjacks you can think of."

The most enjoyable letters were from old-timers, who were tickled to reminisce and to find their knowledge still valued in a world of EBs, off-widths, and bat-hooks. My pleasure at personally confirming that the mountaineering spirit spanned several generations was diminished only by the frustrations caused by the sport's changing vocabulary. Climbers who "retired" decades ago could hardly be expected to know the difference between 5.7 and 5.8, for instance, since the decimal system is but thirty years old. A letter from Kenneth Henderson, pioneer climber of the 1920s and 1930s and author of the first Wind River guidebook—in the form of a pair of articles published in *Appalachia* during the 1930s—made my heart skip a few beats. He informed me that he had used "left" and "right" in the "orographical" sense, which, I soon learned, means facing downstream—*away* from the mountain. Today's climbers, plastered to vertical walls, naturally visualize directions while *facing* the rock. I revived when I noted that in practice Henderson used compass directions—"west side of the south ridge"—thus avoiding ambiguity.

Climbers take more pride in their prowess on rock than in their accuracy as reporters, so I did as many routes as I could. I wanted to make sure that a reported "traverse left" did not mean "traverse right" and that "5.6" was not a typographical error for "5.9." By doing enough routes I hoped to introduce some consistency into the ratings. I selected climbs by the self-serving assumption that what I wanted to climb was what others would want to climb, so that information about these routes would be most valuable.

If the first stage of writing a guidebook—gathering information—proves interesting, amusing, and ultimately rewarding, the next step, choosing how to deal with the information, can be a solitary and depressing business, for one is constantly aware of various options. Should topos be included? How much detail should go into a description? What style should be used? Climbers have historically held diverse opinions about what a guidebook should contain, and a writer should be sensitive to various viewpoints, finally choosing an approach he or she feels is best suited to the particular mountains.

A concise, precise numerical rating system would seem to be especially welcome to guidebook writers, for it would spare them having to use such vague phrases as "moderately difficult." But while the numbers of the decimal system may be concise, they are precise only to a hypothetical climber kept under a bell jar at sea level by the National Bureau of Standards. Real climbers argue interminably about ratings. If enough arguing is done by enough climbers, a consensus emerges and can be used in a guidebook. Thus, the author of a guidebook to a popular area such as Yosemite or New York's Shawangunks easily obtains a generally accepted measure of a route's difficulty. But in remote ranges such as the Wind Rivers the writer must often rely solely on the assessment of the first-ascent party, who may have been overly modest, overly vain, or influenced by storms and routefinding dilemmas.

The problem with rating Wind River routes is further compounded by the diverse backgrounds of the people who climb there. Most routes are climbed—and rated—by out-of-state visitors. Ratings are not applied consistently throughout the country, as travelers to faraway outcrops commonly observe. Visitors to the Wind Rivers naturally apply the standards of their home crags when reporting ascents—and complain about the numbers assigned by others.

Rating the difficulty of routes I hadn't done meant relying on the assessments of others, and I wished I could specify uncertainty as physicists do, stating that a route was, say, 5.5 ± 0.2. I also was tempted to write such phrases as "5.7, according to a climber who consistently overrates routes." But in the end I indicated difficulty by a simple, vulnerable number.

Another dilemma concerned topos. The current guidebook trend, which could be associated with declining literacy, is to present route descriptions as topos or marked photographs. To me, pictorial representations seem most appropriate in areas featuring short, difficult, closely spaced routes that encounter heavy traffic. Climbers don't seek routefinding challenges on a one-pitch jamcrack; they want an accurate assessment of the difficulty and a detailed equipment list. In an area like the Shawangunks, where the climbs lie so thick that one must keep the elbows in close to avoid a neighboring route, marked photos are a necessity.

The virtues of prose descriptions are most apparent on middle-length and longer routes. The written word can evoke the ambiance of colorful or historical routes; the topo is merely a sterile diagram. The adjectives "famous" and "precarious" describe the Royal Arches' Rotten Log far better than do the words "Rotten Log" pointing to a topo's minuscule pair of parallel lines. Nor do I want to learn from a topo that the pitch above the log ascends to a block on a ledge and is 5.5, and that the one after it is 5.6 and ends at a tree. I'm content to read: "Work up several moderate pitches until forced up and left." I prefer looking over my shoulder while belaying, trying to guess where a route goes next, to taking out a topo and matching diagram to cliff.

Most topos and some prose descriptions rate each pitch of a route, and this information is sometimes useful: if I am going to try a three-pitch route with the pitches rated, respectively, 5.10, 5.8, and 5.9, I quickly volunteer to lead the even-numbered pitches. But on longer climbs, knowing each pitch's difficulty drastically alters the mood of the ascent and provides perhaps the best argument against topos. What a pleasure simply to know that a 1,000-foot wall is rated 5.9, and, not knowing where this crux lies (or cruxes lie), to study the face from below. Could it be that overhanging corner near the midpoint? Could there be more 5.9 climbing high on the route? Not being able to relax until the top is reached prolongs the adventure and makes an ascent more rewarding.

I feel that routes in a range like the High Sierra or the Rockies should be described in prose. And there is a more compelling reason to use prose descriptions in the Wind Rivers. The lines on topos and photos are narrow and authoritative; implying well-defined routes, they discourage exploration. A majority of Wind River routes have been climbed no more than two or three times, many but once. There are a number of Yosemite routes where the now-standard line is no longer the original one; the list includes the east buttresses of Middle Cathedral Rock and El Capitan, the Steck-Salathé Route on Sentinel Rock, and the Salathé Wall. To represent Wind River routes as distinct, unalterable lines would be presumptuous.

Concerned about how much detail to include in a route description, I narrowed the spectrum from each end by ignoring both the purists, who believe a guidebook is an invasion of wilderness sanctity, and the gymnasts, who view climbing as the execution of precisely defined moves. I reasoned that purists, unless hypocritical, never use a guidebook, and gymnasts rarely practice their competitive sport in the hostile solitude of the backcountry. I concentrated instead on the "normal" alpinist whose wants are expressed by Thoreau's words: "At the same time that we are earnest to explore and learn all things, we require that all things be mysterious and unexplorable, that land and sea be infinitely wild, unsurveyed and unfathomed." We—I include myself—want information without a diminution of adventure.

I turned this impossible mandate into a precept of sorts to govern my writing of route descriptions: I would attempt to help climbers locate adventure by characterizing a route's challenges without lessening those challenges, and I would try to assess the difficulty without diminishing the difficulty or improving the chances of success. I also felt constrained to blend the description with the landscape as inconspicuously as possible, for a guidebook, like rock and weather, is unavoidably part of the environment. In mountains far from civilization and rarely patrolled by rangers, a book should encourage self-reliance rather than reassure the timid.

Doing climbs myself not only increased the accuracy of my subsequent prose; it enabled me to decide how much detail a route description should include. Two anecdotes illustrate the considerations that went into these decisions.

Claude Suhl and I started up the right edge of the southwest face of Shark's Nose, as the wall's first-ascent party had described in the *AAJ*. We reached easy, right-sloping ramps leading to a notch near the top, looking too late for the traverse toward the center of the face that the first ascensionists described "eventually" making. We reached the summit but returned to the same face a few days later, diagonaling up left after two leads. Here we found half a dozen of the most exquisite pitches of crack climbing I have encountered anywhere. Crossing between parallel cracks kept the difficulty moderate but required routefinding vigilance. Angling left on the third pitch had lured us into adventure; I chose to specify this traverse precisely in the guidebook description. Paradoxically, this piece of information forces a climber to be creative in his subsequent routefinding.

The south ridge of Haystack, however, is a quick climb, a few trivial pitches and one that has long been rated 5.5. The obvious feature of the crux pitch is a crack, but it overhangs and is too wide to jam. While I doubtfully rattled my fist in the crack, wondering if I was stupid, wondering if the 5.5 was a mistake, Muffy Moore, my belayer, kept suggesting an alternative, which I kept ignoring. Eventually I listened; her way involved unlikely—but only 5.5—face moves. Puzzled friends have since turned back, angry at my brusque mention of a "routefinding dilemma," but the ridge is more memorable, less violated, and the satisfaction of success greater when a climber—or his belayer—must study the rock.

I also had to choose a style of language. Guidebook prose is typically laced with imperatives—"traverse left" and "ascend the corner." These cookbook directions, terse and unyielding, may be one reason some climbers feel that guidebooks "ruin" climbing. Descriptions take the form of commands because imperatives make short sentences, and brevity saves trees and reduces the weight in the pack. I used this traditional style, but I hope that climbers take such commands as free spirits should, studying the route from below, making up their own minds about where it goes. Steve Roper, author of a guidebook to Pinnacles National Monument, once saw a neophyte climber staring, book in hand, eyes agog, at an overhanging wall. "But it says start fifty feet left of the tree," he told his partner. Roper wanted to shout, "Don't believe everything that cretin says in that book!" When a climber gets so far off route that he can see the back of his head, he should be able to blame himself for using poor judgment, not castigate a guidebook writer.

A climb of Musembeah Peak and my subsequent quandary about how to describe it illustrates a few of the nuances of guidebook writing. At 4:00 A.M.

clouds were billowing over the nearby mountains. Going back to sleep was nearly irresistible, but Richard Goldstone and I had hiked sixteen miles—too far for us to give up quickly. Our objective was Musembeah's 1,500-foot-high west buttress. We knew little about this obscure, remote route: we had seen it from other summits and read Fred Beckey's sketchy account of his ascent with Layton Kor—an account that told more about a violent storm that caught the pair well below the summit than it did about routefinding details. Still, Richard and I owed it to ourselves to climb until the expected storm arrived, then retreat with honor.

When I feel right, I can make a dawn approach in a blissful trance. Knowing, though, that we were merely going through the motions until hail or snow allowed honorable retreat, I stumbled through the talus hesitant and irritable. I tied on the rope without enthusiasm and indecisively started climbing a corner. When it became harder, I decided it was the wrong corner and retreated to let Richard try a different one. But he sprinted up my corner without hesitation, and, unburdened of uncertainty, I followed with embarrassing ease. Although the time I had wasted further diminished our hopes, we continued.

The fourth pitch was my lead. Above rose a steep face that appeared to have sufficient holds, but the route was not obvious. I saw no cracks in the next forty feet; I would have to make moves that I could reverse if I reached an impasse. Probing, pondering, retreating, and meandering, I climbed the forty feet to a flake I expected to slot a nut behind. The flake, however, was loose, useless. We were alone, far from a road, several days from being missed. An eighty-foot fall being unthinkable, I had to concentrate and be realistic, decide whether to go up or down. The next section *looked* easy. I continued and after a few moves found an unexpected crack that was perfect for nuts. This outcome was anticlimactic, but we were now involved with the rock. We stopped looking over our shoulders at the sky and began scanning the wall above to locate the route.

The upper 500-foot headwall proved equally intricate, but, alert and confident, we threaded our way up a labyrinth of cracks, corners, and overhangs without misadventure. As I led onto Musembeah's flat summit, snowflakes floated from the long-forgotten sky.

An adventure that calls for concentration and commitment to a lonely, complex wall forms the essence of climbing. We had needed wits—and

luck—to overcome obstacles both without and within; we succeeded in our quixotic venture by persevering.

Soon it was winter, and I typed "Musembeah Peak—West Buttress" onto a blank sheet of paper. What information should I provide? Should I identify the initial corner, depict the steep, unprotected face in enough detail to spare climbers anxiety and make the pitch safer? Should I specify the exact route on the upper headwall to facilitate quick ascents? Should I depict our adventure or the first-ascent team's?

I recalled my elation—and relief—while belaying above the unprotected face. With a detailed recipe I could have climbed it quickly, but my satisfaction came from figuring out the route for myself. So, in the finished route description, I mentioned that the first pitch involved a "tricky corner," without identifying the corner; that the unprotected face was "intricate but not difficult." Having gotten climbers to the upper headwall, I left them on their own. (Here I didn't "creatively withhold information"—a phrase contained in advice from Doug Robinson. During our ascent I was too preoccupied to make mental notes.)

The noncommittal phrases of the description would be unlikely to tempt anyone to walk sixteen miles; I also needed to evoke the ambiance of the west buttress. The obvious method would have been to recount my adventures and feelings—my mental anguish and eventual satisfaction—but I then risked crossing that indistinct line between characterizing the route and dictating how future climbers should feel about it. "You vill ascent dis vall, und you vill enjoy it."

I once came upon a warning given by John Fowles in an essay concerning the art of seeing nature:

Telling people why, how, and when they ought to feel this or that—whether it be with regard to the enjoyment of nature, of food, of sex, or anything else—may, undoubtedly sometimes does, have a useful function. . . . But what this instruction cannot give is the deepest benefit of any art, be it of making or of knowing or of experiencing: which is self-expression and self-discovery. The last thing a sex manual can be is an Ars amoris—*a science of coupling, perhaps, but never an art of love. Exactly the same is true of so many nature manuals.*

And, needless to say, of climbing guidebooks. Guidebook writers must be on guard against self-fulfilling prophecies. Call a route "obligatory for hard men" and hard men feel obligated to climb it.

Nevertheless, climbers planning a trip at home or in a base-camp tent want to know if they are likely to enjoy Musembeah, not that the first pitch involves a tricky corner. They want to know if a

This striking, unnamed buttress, located only a few miles from the Cirque of the Towers, awaits its first ascenders.
JOE KELSEY.

particular route is friendly or hostile, exhilarating or intimidating, elegant or illogical. So my science of coupling climbers and climbs characterizes the west buttress as "long, exposed, committing, and isolated." And, these adjectives being not quite sufficient, I presumed to declare the route a "classic."

"Classic" is not quite synonymous with "enjoyable" and is slippery to define. Yet certain routes make memorable experiences—ascents that seem important personally—to a striking proportion of those who climb them. I was struck by the number of Roper and Steck's "Fifty Classics" that had been important climbs for me. A route's history is one of the ingredients that create a classic, and a guidebook is a medium for passing on history. But we must be careful about creating classics by our own fiat: I know of a route that, after a single ascent, was "destined to become a classic," according to a guidebook. Innumerable climbers have since judged the route mediocre; yet it remains well traveled by guidebook readers.

If decreeing classics is presumptuous, then describing a route as "pleasant" may be even more so. Not long ago, three climbers—habitués of Yosemite, where difficulty is mistaken for pleasure—visited the Wind Rivers and went straight to the range's best-loved route—and one of the "Fifty"—the exposed, picturesque, improbable east ridge of Wolf's Head. They discovered that five-foot-wide, low-angled slabs bordered by thousand-foot drops and towers traversed via two-inch-wide ledges were not commensurate with their dignities. The trio left the Wind Rivers after this one climb, complaining.

We find in the writings of our heroes reasons why climbers "have risen above themselves, and . . . labored unceasingly to create the higher standards"—to borrow from the dedication in Art Gran's Shawangunk guide—but who has explained the pleasures of a route of only moderate difficulty? Until some pundit tells us, perhaps we should restrict ourselves to objective characterizations as "solid" or "exposed" or "steep." Yet a shared sense of hedonism, whimsy even, unites the mountaineering fraternity and, incidentally, makes guidebook writing almost enjoyable. Let the would-be hotshot learn to look beyond the words "classic" and "enjoyable": even the Wind River Range offers flaring off-widths and overhanging fingertip liebacks.

Several climbers told me that a guidebook should include only the best routes, to keep the book compact. Fred Beckey, on the other hand, who has devoted his life to first ascents, believes a guide should be complete—not to keep him on route, but to keep him off existing routes! I easily resolved these contradictory requests, describing good routes in some detail and inferior ones but briefly. I can only hope that certain routes do not become popular *because* they are well described, or others ignored *because* of a sketchy description.

Writing guidebooks is not just a matter of researching various sources and then setting down thoughtful descriptions. One must be concerned with numerous details that, if perhaps hovering on the pedantic, can prove fascinating. Take nomenclature, for instance. When possible, I took names from the maps published by the U. S. Geological Survey. But many prominent Wind River peaks, unnamed on the map, have been named by climbers; convention dictates that such names be enclosed by quotation marks. Since I felt that such a household word as Pingora looked silly as "Pingora," I wrote to the U. S. Board on Geographic Names, the agency that gives legitimacy to place names. My questions were aimed not only at extricating Pingora from quotes but also at resolving more monumental concerns, such as the difference between a mountain and a peak.

It turned out to be a mistake to mix the general with the particular, but it was comforting to learn that the USBGN thinks bureaucratically. A mountain, I found out, rises 1,000 feet above the "surrounding territory." A peak is a "sharp point on a mountain ridge." What I didn't learn is why Wyoming's highest point is Gannett Peak, while Mount Koven rises less than 500 feet from Gannett's north ridge. The word *however* figured in many of the USBGN's transitions from the general to the specific. My astonishment that a single quadrangle portrayed three Indian Passes elicited this answer: "We agree that it is not a good naming practice to apply the same name to several nearby features. However, the three Indian Passes were probably found to be in use when the area was being surveyed." In reply to another query: "The Board has a policy of not approving new name proposals for living individuals. However, . . . "

My correspondence with the USBGN emboldened me to use what names I pleased. Not only did Pingora lose its quotation marks; so did Little El Capitan and Peak Lake Peak. I even disregarded map names on occasion. For decades climbers have called a certain summit Ellingwood Peak after the pioneer who, in the mid-1920s, made the first ascent of it and several other of the range's highest points. Yet on the 1968 topographic map it had become Harrower Peak, commemorating a late mayor of nearby Pinedale. According to the USBGN, the local historical society, which proposed the new name, could find no existing name, even though the peak had long been Ellingwood in the Bonneys' guidebook.

More than one climber has gotten off route on the complex north and east sides of Pingora. JEB SCHENCK.

Climbers have not been quick to adopt the name change, nor was I; so the peak now bears two names, one for those ascending it and one for those admiring its profile from Pinedale's main street.

My editor and I had an especially animated discourse about apostrophes in possessives. The USGS omits apostrophes on its maps for arcane cartographic reasons. Should a guidebook writer reinsert them? Years ago David Brower appended to a *Sierra Club Bulletin* article on Devil's Tower a witty note in which he pointed out that while "Devils tower" is a complete, though short, sentence, it fails to convey the intended meaning. Apostrophes in place names are "house style" at the Sierra Club; so I was sent scurrying to learn for whom Roberts Mountain was named and how many fiddlers fiddled at Fiddlers Lake. The man was John Roberts, not Robert somebody; so the peak is Roberts'. One fiddler in the mountains being unlikely, but two fiddlers even more unlikely, we chose Fiddler's Lake. We arbitrarily chose Dad's Lake, but when we got to Adams Pass, the wine that characterizes editorial luncheons had worked its magic, and in a moment of inattention we let the pass escape without an apostrophe.

In the autumn, when typesetting had put the text mercifully out of reach, I hiked in to Island Lake, not with pencil and notebook, nor with thoughts of apostrophes cluttering my mind, but with ice axe and crampons. Jack Clinton and I crossed one of the three Indian Passes and studied two wide couloirs—both characterized in the guide as pleasant, seven-pitch ice routes—on the north side of Jackson Peak. The bergschrunds looked too wide to cross, though; so we headed for a less-conspicuous gully between the two, unmentioned in the guide but offering a negotiable bergschrund. Jack led over the lip of the 'schrund, and we were in the gully. The ice was perfect—hard without being brittle—and I rediscovered the joy of moving on ice. Snow fell as we climbed the final pitch, giving us the sine qua non of ice climbing, a spindrift avalanche.

Having started late, we reached the top at sunset. The storm had passed Jackson Peak, but ragged clouds lingered across the way on Ellingwood Peak. Mountains and sky were shades of red, yellow, and orange. The descent would be down snow to a shoulder of the peak, then down a chute to the basin below. I had been in the chute years ago but could remember only that it was hard to locate from above. Soon it would be dark. If we found the chute quickly, we could stumble three miles through the dark to camp. If we searched too long, we would spend an interminable October night on the 12,000-foot shoulder.

Reluctant to leave, we looked again at the peaks, now lit a fierce gold, the clouds darkening from pink to purple, the valleys in shadow. Then we began running down the snow as fast as we could.

Olaf Sööt

Portraits of Patagonia

Above: Lenticular clouds dominate the sky above the
Cordillera Paine.

Facing page: Patagonia's most spectacular spire, Cerro Torre,
dominates its neighbors, Torre Egger and Cerro Stanhardt.

Opening page: The massive bulk of Fitzroy, as seen across
the Río La Leona; Cerro Torre and its satellites lie to the
left.

Overleaf: The eastern faces of the South, Central, and North
towers of Paine, as seen from the Paine Chico. The route
described in Bobby Knight's article ascends the left edge of
the Central Tower.

Above: Rock island, Marinelli Glacier, Cordillera Darwin.

Facing page: Los Cuernos del Paine from Lago Pehoe.

Overleaf: The Central and South towers of Paine, viewed from the southwest.

Bobby Knight

Dreams and Doubts

Six Weeks in the Paine Cordillera

M Y FINGERS THROB WITH PAIN. My eyes—mere slits abused by the wind—feel as if they have just been through a Sahara sandstorm. Every joint aches. The rest of my body lacks any sensation. It is still too numb from the past twenty-four hours of torture. Exhaustion overpowers me, and I find it difficult to stomach food. I crave sleep. Sleep! All I wish for is a few uninterrupted hours of rest.

The stillness and warmth of the snow cave provide a blessed sanctuary from the fierce Patagonian elements. From our cave, twenty feet deep in the glacier at the base of the Towers of Paine, we hear the storm outside continue to rage. One look at Alan Kearney tells me he is as content as I to remain in this womb for now. Sleep doesn't come easily, though. My mind is still fixed on the ghastly experience of the past twenty-four hours.

Psychologically, we have taken a severe beating as well. This morning at dawn we were forced to crawl off our bivouac ledge high on the Central Tower. We were spent and humbled, ready to admit that the weather was far too brutal to remain. To continue climbing was unthinkable. Our consuming fear was that we might not have been able to escape to the glacier, 1,200 feet below.

How did we allow ourselves to believe we could camp perched on the side of a rock spire completely exposed to the Patagonian storms? We were forewarned. The climate's lethal character had been described vividly by a friend back in the States: "We were pinned down in our approach to the climb for forty-five minutes. Lying prone on the flat glacier, we had to use our ice axes to avoid being swept away. The wind drove the rain through our cagoules, and in a few minutes we both were soaked. If the tempest hadn't let up, our lives could have been endangered." His warning was made even more dramatic when he pointed out that my small stature would make me susceptible to being easily toppled by the ferocious gusts that plague the place. The conversation closed with, "I know you'll go anyway, but you're crazy for wanting to go to that Godforsaken place."

The admonition was well put. The dozen climbing accounts we had reviewed before the start of this adventure also prepared us for severe and unrelenting climatic conditions. By the time we stepped onto the plane for South America, we were thoroughly versed on the Patagonian elements.

The events of the past day come back to me vividly; our first attempt on the Central Tower had been a true nightmare.

A small, snow-drifted ice ledge had seemed an

Bobby Knight leads a pitch on the Central Tower.
ALAN KEARNEY.

ideal place to pass the night. Besides, we weren't able to find any other suitable places to pitch our small bivouac tent. We reasoned that if we still had extra time after setting up camp, we could continue climbing until dark and fix a rope or two above the ledge.

So we dug into the bank of snow, making a well-protected niche for our uniquely designed nylon shelter. Its vertical backside nestled securely against the rock wall, and the excavated hollow acted as an excellent windbreak for the tent's narrow profile. By the time we finished the construction it was twilight, and the westerly winds were picking up. We abandoned thoughts of climbing further that day.

From our exposed perch we detected a sound so faint that my heartbeat almost obscured it. In a few seconds the sound became perceptibly louder, and a light breeze stirred. Then an unbelievable rush of air smashed against the rock, deafening me and permeating my very soul. The power of the wind intensified as it slammed against the sheer granite walls of the Paine Cordillera. The gale had no place to escape except through the narrow gaps that separated the towering rock spires, and the funneling air created a myriad of eerie, frightening sounds. Savage blasts boomed like cannons between the calmer moments of muted howling. The most terrifying sensation, however, was the slowly building roar from miles away that grew in intensity until it sounded like a freight train about to pass by.

Unbelievably, the storm grew stronger. During the next anxious hour we witnessed the gradual destruction of our humble abode. As the seams on two walls began to disintegrate, I hurriedly laced my double boots, stuffed my sleeping bag, and crammed every loose item I could find into my pack. My wariness prompted Alan to follow suit. Neither of us wanted to watch our fabric and gear explode into oblivion. We had to decide to either retreat to the cave on the glacier or find some type of natural shelter. Imminent darkness decided for us—stay put and dig in for the night.

Hours of digging by both of us produced only one narrow passage sandwiched between a large, detached flake and the ice. The slot tilted at thirty degrees and its width would not even allow a small person to turn over. Even if there had been room for two, the thought of staring at a granite block three inches from my nose wasn't at all appealing to me. Alan took the slot, and I settled onto a nearby snow shelf.

My granite backrest provided some protection from the wind, but I couldn't shut out the feeling of doom that swelled with each blast. The pattern became consistent in the next few hours: each new wave grew in force. With each passing minute I fought the obvious fact: the storm had not yet reached its full potential. The shallow hole I had scratched with my hammer barely accommodated my lower torso, which was squeezed into my sleeping bag. My exposed upper body was pounded by the loose snow that whipped about with tremendous velocity. Physically, I knew I'd survive, but the wind and the isolation were robbing me of my sanity. The next blast was so fearsome that I dragged the haul-bag sheath out from under my body; I desperately needed to cover my head. The frantic struggle to wriggle into the tiny tube seemed to take hours, but finally the dreadful noise, muffled by the sheath, ceased to intimidate me.

Alan may have been faring better from the elements, but I was not envious of his claustrophobic chamber. Although we were only ten feet apart and awake all night, we spoke not a word. The sound of the wind formed a wall between us. Since I couldn't share my doubts with Alan, I settled down to a long night of restless contemplation. First light was a glorious blessing, even though the wind continued to howl. We began to descend; our first attempt had failed.

From our snow cave we watch swirling clouds caress the upper reaches of the three Paine Towers as the storm passes toward the arid lands to the east. The Towers change appearance frequently as the tempests engulf them. On the rare clear days the smooth granite monoliths stand tall and straight, reaching 4,000 feet or more out of the snow and ice that even now continues to carve them. Their shapes are exceptionally striking in the morning, when cold hues of gray turn to warm ambers, and again in the evening, when they burn with fiery reds. The Central Tower, though just shy of being the tallest of the three tightly grouped spires, dominates the landscape from the east. Its sweeping vertical lines and enormous east face have no equal from this perspective. Its more massive neighbor, Paine Chico, composed of strange, darkish rubble, rises to the south. To the north soars a granite wall capped with unusual flutings of black slate. The small eastern cirque that is surrounded by these massifs drops 2,500 feet to the Río Ascencio Valley and our base camp.

Two days later the storm has diminished in vio-

lence. Since food is running quite low, we decide to return to base, not only to replenish supplies but to bolster our psyches as well. A change of scenery will be therapeutic for our near-catatonic state. Hiking down the cirque is refreshing and not excessively strenuous. It is one of the few moments I can enjoy my environment. The upper end of this tiny glacier system still abounds with snow, but its lower reaches are already bare. Immense rock benches, polished and scarred by the ice, drop off hundreds of feet into a minuscule tarn that is dammed by large piles of morainal debris. It is testimony to the larger mass of this glacier in an earlier time.

Once off the glacier, we weave along the snake-like lateral moraine and emerge into the world of living things. The transition from that barren land of rock, ice, and snow to this one of lush greenery is sudden and extremely welcome. The smells of growing vegetation are everywhere. Each time I have made this hike I have marveled at how my senses respond to the reentry into the beech forest. Colorful wildflowers are beginning to bloom on the hillsides, and birds chatter ceaselessly. Springtime has arrived in this land south of the equator—a November springtime.

A small stand of beeches borders the glacial debris and houses our modest base camp. Though the treetops sway violently, at times arching their backs toward the ground, the winds fail to penetrate the thick canopy. Branches groan audibly at each powerful blast; yet my candle hardly flickers at the entrance of the tent. An air of security prevails within this jungle of twisted, low-growing trees.

This particular spot has been used and misused by previous expeditions: a large pile of trash blots a hillside above the stream that flows through our camp. An elaborate cooking and dining area are the products of someone's idle hours. The British and Italians passed through this area in 1963, when they dueled for the first ascent of the prized Central Tower. I am certain that this place served as one of their intermediate camps on the way up the Río Ascencio. The South Africans who climbed the east face of the Central Tower in 1974 also used this site as their base. A flattened tin can, scrawled with names and nailed to a tree, attests to the former presence of an Irish expedition. Over the years numerous wanderers must have paused at this spot, resting their weary bodies before ascending to gaze at close range upon the pride of the Chilean Andes, Las Torres del Paine.

The storms continue. For a full week we have had to contain our restlessness amid diminishing hopes for better weather. Rain has turned to snow at times, and, on one occasion, we awoke to find six

Knight follows a steep pitch near the top. ALAN KEARNEY.

inches on the valley floor. The winds are still releasing their venom. Alan swears that some of the moisture we are receiving is wind-blown water from the river, seventy-five yards away. After my last bout with the wind, I do not doubt this phenomenon. Lethargy has replaced relief, and our initial mood of optimism has slowly been eroded by our confinement. Now the darkness and dampness of the forest filters into our hearts. The days of inactivity wear at my patience. Nights have become hideous ordeals of tossing and turning, listening, and longing for silence. The endless rolling drumbeats of the Patagonian giants fill my ears.

Our barometer is creating additional problems. Its forecasts are unreliable and don't give us any advantage; the storm systems move so fast that they arrive about the same time a change is indicated. Yet every time I detect a lull in the rustling of trees, I rise in anticipation and check the damned instrument. One of these nights I will dash it against the rocks in sheer frustration.

The social veneer is wearing extremely thin already. With thoughts of our failure fresh in our minds, as well as the knowledge that we must return to the climbing arena once the weather finally clears, we are anxious and tense. Communications between Alan and me are minimal. I'm afraid any words that come out of my mouth will create antagonism. Living in such close quarters, it is easy to release our pent-up frustrations on each other. Different personalities, annoying habits, and idiosyncrasies are all causes for verbal clashes. Base-camp food is becoming the biggest issue. I feel bad because Alan took on the burden of planning the menu alone, while I was running around Portland collecting personal equipment. Just mentioning the subject makes him bristle.

When tempers flare, the claustrophobic tent makes life unbearable, and one of us is forced to seek another place to pass the time. Within a day or two a truce is reached, and we reconcile, knowing many days of confinement are yet to come. Besides, it's lonely not having anyone to talk to. I'm grateful we don't have even more explosive differences, for this trip could come to an abrupt halt if we did.

Our forested prison offers more room than the snow cave, yet is just as confining in its own way. We have escaped from our cell high on the glacier only to be walled in here by our commitment to remain in position to climb the Central Tower. To stray for a day or two and miss a spell of good weather could cost us our goal.

We have indeed picked a worthy adversary. The sweeping lines of the exposed south face should offer 3,000 feet of difficult climbing—it would be a coveted climb anywhere in the world. During the planning stages it seemed feasible to abandon the siege tactics used by many past expeditions. A lightweight, two-man effort relying on speed and advanced climbing techniques seemed to be the answer. But the handicaps of alpine-style climbing are now apparent: we will be unable to continue upward or maintain a hold on the spire during adverse weather. Even if we climb at our best and don't run headlong into off-width cracks choked with ice or immense blank sections that require bolting, we have invested our meager savings in a risky and uncertain adventure.

What really makes me toss and turn in my sleep, though, is the vision of regaining a significant elevation only to be subjected yet again to an outrageous storm. Our strategy depends on traveling with a minimum of protection from the elements. Can we still believe survival is possible under the conditions we've witnessed? Retreat in the face of the Patagonian powers is possible—as we've already proven—yet the British barely escaped alive from the Cathedral a number of years ago when snagged rappel ropes forced them to downclimb through an unbelievable tempest. Dave Nichol's recollections from that nightmare are graphic: "Looking back, there would seem to be little doubt that had we not left ropes in place during the ascent we would be there somewhere on the mountain hanging from the unprotected ridge like sides of frozen mutton."

Finally the weather has cleared and we have left the beech forest to begin climbing up the bleak granite wall. Cleaning the last piton from an awkward aid crack, I pause to scan the horizon to the west. Damn! A thin line of luminous clouds is developing over the Southern Ice Cap. What have we done to deserve another flogging from this hostile environment? The terrifying bivouac a week ago was enough punishment for one trip. Four hundred feet below us, the ten-foot terrace on which we suffered that night looks like a haven compared to our present precarious stance.

The slight breeze that had arrived at midday begins to pick up momentum as I reach Alan's hanging belay. The last two pitches, requiring eight hours, have nearly depleted our energy. The angle eases off for a rope length or two ahead; most of this section should go free and help us make up some time. Before I take off on my lead I ask Alan what he thinks of the ominous streak of developing clouds. The question beggars comment, for it has preoccupied our thoughts for hours: the front is heading this way.

The next section is a delight, for the crack system provides a variety of holds and protection points. I become totally absorbed in the rhythmic climbing routine. Daylight is fading as I place several anchors on a small ledge.

Is it really possible that we can pull off this bizarre caper? Illusions of fame infiltrate my mind, and

I envision the headline: "Central Tower of Paine Falls to Lightweight Expedition by New Route!" The notoriety may even open doors for an invitation to the Himalaya. Suddenly the reality of the situation hits me: I'm standing on a six-inch ledge, 2,100 vertical feet into the ascent, with a storm approaching. There is no promise of glory and glamor in this hellhole. A sharp wind bites into me, and my mood spirals downward. Alan rounds a corner and hastily ascends to my narrow stance. Not a moment is wasted as we exchange hardware and worried looks. As darkness arrives, Alan affixes his headlamp and scurries upward into the void.

The wind is picking up to an alarming velocity. Night is swallowing us, and from my stance I can see no hint of shelter nearby. Another epic is unfolding, for on this attempt we had decided to go extra-light and leave our sleeping bags behind.

The penetrating cold pulls me from my rambling thoughts. As I rummage through the pack for additional clothing, I peer into the darkness for Alan. The surreal silhouette of my friend inches its way up the unforgiving rock, the beam of his headlamp creating dragon-shaped shadows as it moves left, then right, searching for holds. Clouds swirl overhead; kaleidoscopic movement transforms the sky. Hideous creatures materialize, then dissolve

Knight takes a well-deserved break. ALAN KEARNEY.

into nothingness. Sinister towers throw jagged outlines against the alpenglow. I am transported by the timelessness of these images.

Alan's muffled shouts bring me back from the spectral world. He is nearly out of rope, and his yell can only mean he has reached some sort of belay stance. A few sharp tugs on the rope confirm that he is off belay. I hope that he has found a better place to bivouac than what we've seen so far. It is unlikely we can proceed safely without more light.

I begin making final adjustments in my foot stirrups and waist ties. Everything is flapping in the wind, making preparation for ascending annoyingly difficult. My fingers are cold and clumsy in my mittens. Just when I think I have everything ready, my headlamp flickers. Damn! I would give anything to be nestled in my sleeping bag among the beeches. It is disheartening to be headed in the opposite direction.

As I make the basic mechanical motions of ascending, my chilled limbs receive a shot of warmth from the exertion. Within minutes the angle steepens, and my overstuffed pack pulls me backward, straining my shoulders and reigniting the pain that plagues the tendons in my tired arms. I overheat quickly, and the sweat pours off me. I can't believe I was freezing five minutes ago. My stirrup repeatedly falls off my foot and writhes wildly in the wind. After twenty minutes of swearing at my plight, I stop to adjust my clothing and equipment. I've covered only half the distance to Alan.

A piercing yell shatters my troubled world. Alan complains that he's extremely cold and can't endure much longer. His voice contains a tone of desperation. No wonder: he's wearing nothing but light clothes and a windbreaker. I've got all his warm clothes stuffed in my pack. I apologize for being slow and ask if there's any place we can pass the night. A few words—"Not really"—reach me before they are caught up in the roar. Just what I want to hear! The situation demands that I act quickly; so I choose a badly sloping ledge and start toward it. By the time I dump the pack and place a couple of anchor pitons, Alan has descended to my level. He is shivering uncontrollably and immediately tears into the pack for his extra clothing. A lot of good all that warm clothing is going to do us if this front brings rain instead of snow. We are going to look like frozen Popsicles once our saturated gear succumbs to the night's cold. I switch off my pessimism and get down to matters at hand.

The hardware has been retrieved from the unfinished pitch and is added to the rack for a possible hasty retreat. Every last bit of clothing is dragged out, and we climb into our packs. We light the stove and screen it against the wind with a small scrap of tinfoil and our bodies. Impatiently, we anticipate something hot to drink. The discussion turns to our precarious position. The prospects of continuing upward appear hopeless, unless there is a major reversal in the development of the storm. Retreat, difficult enough in the dark, will be even harder tomorrow if conditions worsen. What shall we do?

Neither of us has the answers to our plight, and we are too exhausted to initiate any action. We wait in silence and pass the hours deep within our own thoughts. The full moon creeps out from behind the summit of the Central Tower.

Sitting with my back to the wind affords me some comfort in this bleak situation. I can feel each new wave of wind attempt to uproot me from my moorings. It is only a matter of time before we must retreat.

Just how difficult will this route be to reverse? My mind has been working out the solution pitch by pitch. The first section will be straightforward, but once we turn a corner numerous problems abound. Loose flakes clutching at our ropes will prove a constant nuisance, and the overhanging pitches will be frightening and difficult. We may have to employ downnailing on occasion, a slow procedure indeed.

The hours pass with agonizing slowness. It would be better to be moving, one way or the other, instead of just sitting here immobilized, letting my fears eat at me. I wonder what makes some people perform admirably, with self control, in the face of near-hopeless odds, while others go off the deep end. I find this thought intriguing, since the seriousness of our situation could easily explode into overwhelming emotion. I struggle to keep my emotions at bay by rationally sorting out the situation. The next twelve hours could prove to be an enlightening experiment in human behavior under stress, though I do not relish being one of the guinea pigs.

Retreat is mercifully forced upon us. The convulsions of the wind are reaching beyond what we can physically endure; we are being purged by the guardian of the Central Tower. It is time to start down while the opportunity still exists.

A voice within me keeps repeating, "Hurry up. Faster. Let's get the hell out of here!" The rapidity of my thoughts contrasts sharply with the sluggishness of my movements. To rush the descent in our condition would be foolhardy. We reduce the rappels to sixty feet in the hope of avoiding costly rope hang-ups. Yet at any time the wind might sweep a loose end across the face and deposit it behind a rope-eating flake. My stomach sinks to my knees each time the rope jams; I cannot help thinking of Dave Nichol's epic years ago. We too have no back-up ropes.

One badly inclined section threatens to pendulum Alan out into a blank world of overhanging granite. Using his feet by pushing against a crack helps, but a tricky section below requires heroic efforts. Backing off onto the same rappel, I ponder the sensation of swinging out into the void. One last inspection of the rappel system stops me in my tracks: I stare in horror at the open gate on my harness carabiner. As I screw the safety catch tight, I realize that this rappel could have given me my final adrenalin rush.

Several more rappels and we will be on a bench; below it we can descend lower-angled slabs to safety. Feelings of gratitude begin to sweep into my being. The knowledge that the worst is over relaxes me, and once tied off to Alan's anchor system, I breathe a sigh of relief. But the meeting of our eyes shocks me. The deep creases in Alan's face and the abnormal redness of his eyes reveal the strain of the past thirty hours. The expended energy, anxiety, and frustration of this second failure have taken years off his life. And I, have I fared any better? I'm glad I don't have a mirror.

Writing in my journal, I am easily distracted by the continual gusts of wind that penetrate the makeshift rock wall we've constructed under a gigantic boulder at the foot of the glacier. The grit covering our floor whips about in a frenzy, making life miserable in the cramped quarters. I guess it's better lying in this semiprotected gopher hole than being lashed by flying morainal debris outside. Our new home serves as advance camp; our unoccupied snow cave at the foot of the spires was demolished by an avalanche three weeks ago.

I find it hard to believe that this is our fortieth day in the Paine Cordillera. The end is near for this adventure. Brutal weather caused us to halt our third attempt far short of our previous high point. Our food supply is vanishing; enough snack food remains for one final attempt.

We are waiting, ever waiting, to capitalize on the briefest of calm spells. We can't tolerate waiting much longer, yet neither can we summon up any enthusiasm to expose our battle-scarred nerves to the elements for the fourth time. General conversation and personal thoughts tend only to deepen the pervading pessimism. And yet we are still in the Cordillera and have not called it quits after enduring so much abuse. Something inside both of us will not permit us to abandon our endeavor. Why do we persist in the face of such staggering odds?

The question churns around in my head. Under the present circumstances the importance of attaining the summit has lost all significance. My desire to dance atop the granite spire is overshadowed by fear of disaster and the boredom of repeating pitch after pitch. The thrill is gone, replaced with distaste. The entire atmosphere has shifted from one of healthy anticipation to outright contempt for this

land and its relentless weather. I no longer care to test my skill and knowledge against these merciless hunks of rock.

I would have given up this ordeal weeks ago except for my commitment to Alan. A surprisingly strong bond exists between us after all the hardships we have endured together. My pride refuses to leave him stranded in this place, abandoned without a partner. Though I dread every waking minute, I exist for climbing here; I shall not give up until I am forced to go home.

The seemingly endless hours of inactivity force me to struggle with my personal misgivings. Is climbing the Central Tower worth the anguish? As always, my stubbornness makes it difficult to give up something I've started. But I wonder if this painful experience will have a lasting effect on my attitude toward climbing. The meaning of this trip eludes me even while I struggle in the midst of the fight.

Sometime later a break in the storm pattern allowed us to reach the summit after forty hours of continuous climbing. The rock eased after 2,400 feet, and we struggled up broken slopes through the darkness to within several hundred feet of the top. The morning of January 2 dawned clear. A few last pitches of rock and ice fulfilled our dream, our obsession.

Yet I still have uneasy feelings. The intensity of the final struggle has magnified the pointlessness of this endeavor and stolen some of the glory from the achievement.

Rick Slone

Mrs. Robertson
Is Climbing Again

SAM SHENNAN IS DRESSED FOR DINNER. Hair pasted down, tie tied, neck jutting out of his collar like a broomstick in a barrel—this is what you see of him across the table. "I had some rough weather at sea last night," says Sam, who's been retired from the merchant marine for fifteen years.

"Rough weather, yes," says Sam's wife, Isa, whose habit it is to echo Sam's words. By coincidence we've met them here, although Norah has known them for years. Near where we are in Glencoe, and all over these Scottish highlands, Norah once climbed with the Shennans' sons, men themselves in their fifties now, the mountains no longer a part of their lives. "They've lost their keenness for the hills," is how Isa puts it, and it is something she could also say of the other climbing partners Norah has seen come and go. John Bethel, for instance, who as a boy was a constant and eager companion, simply grew up. Peter Connelly married a jealous girl. Crawford and Bert Shennan eased into sedate middle age. Now there's me, and Norah tells the Shennans that tomorrow we plan to climb the

Buachaille Etive Mor. "Oh, that will be lovely," says Isa. "Sam, dear, Mrs. Robertson and her friend are going to see the Buachaille tomorrow." Corrected, Isa flings a hand to her cheek. "Oh! Climbing! My word! Sam, Mrs. Robertson is climbing again!"

Isa's words hit Sam, who is staring at Norah, like darts on a metal bulkhead. After a moment's thought he tilts stiffly back in his chair and looks at the ceiling. "The highest waterfall in Britain is up at Eas Coularin. . . ." he says, and somewhere near the fluorescent light he contemplates a possible line up the slippery face. "But it's a very dangerous route. I wouldn't want to climb up there."

"Dangerous, aye, yes," says Isa. "Don't you feel cold, Mrs. Robertson?" Isa's brown cardigan is buttoned over breasts drooping to her stomach. Her pockets are stuffed with tissue. She puts on her coat while Sam continues to reconnoiter the ceiling.

The meal, served family style, is mashed potatoes, roast pork and gravy, applesauce, and vegetables. Norah piles her plate high. The food on Sam's plate and Isa's makes small islands on a white china sea. The way Isa works her fork, she could be dissecting a newt. "I won't be having the pudding tonight," she says, and orders the safer cheese and crackers. Sam orders ice cream, then changes his mind. "Too cold for ice cream." Isa agrees. Norah and I get Black Forest cake with cream. She wolfs

The east side of Buachaille Etive Mor—"the Great Shepherd of Etive"—as seen from the fringes of the Rannoch Moor. JOHN CLEARE.

hers down and, finished, oversees me. "You left some cream," she says, pointing at my plate with her spoon.

Tea will be served in the sitting room, and Norah is first up the stairs, taking them by twos. "I've always done them two at a time, all my life," she says. She's wearing lime-colored slacks, a white blouse, a scarf around her neck, lipstick, and eye shadow. Next goes Sam, hand-over-hand up the bannister, grunting at each step. Handicapped by swollen ankles and a big handbag, Isa finishes a landing behind.

Norah—there's something about her. You sense it right away, like Sam did at dinner, like I did when I first met her five years ago. Slim, erect, bright-eyed, she's a nice-looking woman, all right, and there's no need to add "for seventy-five" to make it true. But it's not wholly her looks; she has something else, and it shines as clearly and steadily as the flame from a welder's torch.

Tea comes on a silver service. There are lace antimacassars, dark oil paintings in heavy gold frames, a shelf of paperbacks—all Louis L'Amour—and an eagle in a glass case. Isa warms up in front of the fire. Another guest puffs his pipe and reads. Sam sits listening to Norah, as still as the eagle in its case.

Norah Robertson pauses during the ascent of Buachaille Etive Mor. RICK SLONE.

I got married when I was twenty-three, and a year later I began to get stomach pains pretty regularly, a terribly full feeling. I didn't tell anybody, and I didn't do anything about it. I always found an explanation for it. Some circumstance or other made my stomach churn; it seemed more to be the seat of my emotions than the heart.

I had a very happy childhood in England and a very successful career, and I married intending to go on freelancing as a commercial artist. But after the wedding I got put into a Glasgow tenement surrounded by five sisters-in-law. My husband's sisters disapproved of their brother marrying an Englishwoman, a foreigner. They were very narrow-minded, and they said it was quite out of the question for the wife to work when the husband had a good job. There was continual criticism. They attempted to mold me into a Robertson. They were The Robertsons, and I had to conform to their way of life.

At the time we got engaged Willie worked both day and night. He was a teacher of science at Clydebank Technical College and four nights a week was headmaster at the evening school. Friday night he was too tired to be interested in anything, and Saturday and Sunday he spent entirely on the golf course. Willie enrolled me at the golf course, and I took one or two lessons. I was quite promising, but I had to play with Willie's sisters. Women weren't allowed to play with the men—it was segregated then—and I hated his sisters.

We had no room for fun. When I saw his ambition, I told Willie, and he seemed to see my point. He asked, "If I gave up the night school, would that be all right?" Oh, yes, I thought, he understands; he's willing to meet me part way. The day after we were married he told me he'd lied—he had no intention of giving up night school. I felt betrayed, and I couldn't ever trust him again.

I got wrapped up in the hate, fear, and anger that my life had turned into. My lovely life was spoiled. What got me the most was the way they were going to mold me, turn me into one of themselves. Willie's sisters would say, "We never expected Willie to marry an English doll." Doll wasn't a flattering word then. I was tall and thin and never had to do anything about my figure, and they were short and squat, like bolsters tied in the middle. They were always at me about how I did it. "What is the name of those pills you're taking, Norah?" They were always on a diet, taking pills, starving themselves, and so on. Of course, I wasn't taking any, but I was getting thin, gaunt really.

After five years I finally did go to a doctor. It was obvious I was ill. The doctor took me to a specialist, who took X-rays, and I was found to have cancer. It was in my womb. They didn't tell me at the time. Nobody knew but Willie and the doctors. As this thing progressed I got weaker and weaker, and the sisters continued their third degree. One after the other they would come to see me in the hospital and ask, "Now, Norah, no one will be angry; just confess, what were those slimming pills you were taking?" The eldest sister was in the room questioning me when I got hysterical. After that they were forbidden to come back.

At first the doctors thought they could operate. Later they said it was useless—the thing had too great a hold. The best thing seemed to be to go home to England and be nursed by my mother, and I went. I stayed in bed and took massive doses of morphia; that's all they could do in those days. Willie very rarely came to see me.

I had lost sixty pounds, my hair was falling out, and my teeth were decaying; I was a mess. My mother was retired and she took care of me. I could be out of bed a little bit each day, but I would have terrible attacks of pain. The family doctor came regularly. Eventually I took the morphia to no effect. I could do less and less until finally I lay in bed just longing to die. I was twenty-eight years old.

I knew I had cancer, but they were trying to keep its seriousness from me. They wouldn't tell me outright. I asked, but they always turned my questions aside. I was fourteen when my father died of cancer in horrible circumstances, and I had this fearful conviction that I too wouldn't escape. Not only my father, but my grandparents on both sides had died of the same disease. And while it wasn't apparent at the time, my mother was dying of cancer too. I was so obsessed with the cancer that I could think of little else.

My religion was no help to me. I had been brought up in the orthodox church, the Church of England, but I had given it up in my midteens. I couldn't accept a God of love from the evidence I saw around me. I thought people were hypocritical in their professions of faith; they couldn't live up to their beliefs. The Bible was a closed book, full of contradictions.

I weighed less than ninety pounds, my skin was yellowish, and I had this perpetual pain. They knew I knew. It wasn't concealed from me anymore. This would be February 1935. The doctor told me I'd last a year, maybe two. They could do no more for me. If I could have gotten up, I would have ended it—committed suicide. I didn't care. I wanted people to leave me alone and let me die. I was always asking the doctor for something to end it quicker. I didn't care about anything.

In the midst of all this a thought came to me, just as if someone had said it: "Try Christian Science."

That startled me because I'd only heard it ridiculed. But still this thought persisted: "Try Christian Science." It went on and on in my mind.

While lying there, I recalled a girl I knew from childhood who was now a Christian Scientist. She came over, and I asked if her religion could cure cancer. She said yes, it cures everything. Instead of being hopeful and pleased, I was angry. She was doubting my cancer. I told her to clear off, and she did, but not before leaving her Christian Science textbook on my bed.

I remember that when she left, a great wave of indignation came over me. I was determined to uphold my misery. But I opened the book anyway, and the first sentence I saw was: "There is no pain in truth and no truth in pain." I hurled the book across the room.

Later, I started again, this time at the beginning. I thought it was a big con at first. Then I began to read the chapter on prayer, and after several pages something seemed to snap. In that moment I saw that everything is as God made it to be. I cried when I saw how wrong I was in my whole attitude of being a helpless victim, a victim of the cancer and of Willie and his sisters. I had only myself to blame. I knew I didn't have to submit; I had it in me to respond to something else. It wasn't clear then what it was, but I had a glimmer that I wasn't condemned to suffering and death; something was bigger than myself. It was a change of consciousness.

I studied the book. I stopped taking the morphia. The book said I had to go one way or the other: I had to rely on the spirit or the medicine. The pain persisted; but the intervals between attacks seemed longer, and I stopped wanting to die.

A week or two later I was up and trying to do things for myself. I began to put on a little weight. I went to the dentist and had all my teeth removed and a denture made. My hair grew back. In three months I went home to Willie. We had our two boys, Michael and Colin. I stayed with Christian Science, and for forty years I had no need to visit a doctor or take a pill, not even so much as an aspirin.

This is the story I heard five years earlier, and I don't know now any better than I did then what to make of it. If we hadn't climbed Aonach Eagach yesterday and the Cobbler two days before that, if I hadn't watched Norah step unroped onto a narrow ledge 300 feet up, or seen her skin her knees in a Mummery crack, or seen her fall, pendulum on the end of the rope, then get back on the rock and finish the climb—if I hadn't seen all these things myself, had only heard about them, I could more easily dismiss her as an old woman, a screwball harping on God.

Sam and Isa go to bed, but not the other man, who, engrossed in his book, seems oblivious to us. He's wearing a tweed suit with leather patches on the elbows, a vest, a tartan tie, and hiking boots. Missing is a deerstalker hat. "Aren't you Jeffrey Bogsley?" Norah asks. Brought back abruptly to the sitting room, the fire, the stuffed eagle, the man hesitates in order to get his bearings. "Aren't you?" Norah demands impatiently.

"Pugsley," he says. "Jeffrey Pugsley." Norah tells him that they met twenty years ago, but Mr. Pugsley doesn't remember. We see him again at breakfast, where Norah says, "Good morning, Mr. Bugler, good morning." Sam reports another night of heavy seas. The day is cloudy and threatens rain. He and Isa aren't going out.

As with all mountains, the Great Herdsman—the Buachaille Etive Mor—has tougher and easier ways to the top. Ours is an easier one, mostly class 4 with some class 5. There are places where beneath you the mountain drops clean away, where if what you want is to scare yourself, you'll have the chance. The trail passes first through the moor. "I'm an experienced climber, and even I wouldn't go there," Norah says, turning to face me. I don't know what she's talking about. "That's what Mr. Piggley said to me twenty years ago. I remember distinctly. He asked me where I was going, and I said the Saddle in Glen Shiel. 'The Saddle! You can't go there,' he said. '*I'm* an experienced climber and even *I* wouldn't go there.' That's exactly what he said. 'That's a rock climb. That's done only with ropes. Where are you really going today?' he asked me, the self-important little man. I told him again, and I told him I'd already done it several times, but he didn't seem to believe me. He argued that it was quite impossible for me to climb the Saddle, and he brought out his map to prove it.

"I don't want you to think I was a big cheese or critical of Mr. Pugsley. It wasn't a very difficult route as rock climbs go. If if were, it would have been listed in the guidebook, and it wasn't. But that was the kind of opposition I ran into. He demanded that I point out the Saddle for him on the map, and, of course, I couldn't find it. He was triumphant and quite rude. I just left the hotel and went and did it. When I got back, I told him where I'd been. 'What you have described to me is the Forcam Ridge on the Saddle. Everyone avoids that,' he said. He said he didn't believe I was on the mountain at all. I was furious. 'Are you calling me a liar?' I asked. He sort of shrugged his shoulders and walked off. I ran into opposition like that a lot."

Where a stream crosses the path, I find a narrow place and step to the other bank, but Norah climbs a waist-high boulder and leaps to the opposite side. I ask her if she wouldn't mind doing that again, that leap, so that I can take a picture. She recrosses the stream and climbs back on the boulder. I set the meter, focus, and give her the go-ahead, but I haven't cocked the shutter. She volunteers to do it one more time.

Norah climbs slowly up the steep path, stopping to rest every few hundred feet. Despite the cold, she's sweating, and she's tied her jacket around her waist. She hates the uphill walking, but once we get onto the rock, she's renewed. She leads. She's been up here who knows how many times? The climbing's not difficult—good holds, wide ledges—but she doesn't go the easiest way either, instead choosing vertical sections we could scramble around. There are places I wish we had a rope.

We stop to talk about how to do a crack in a smooth slab; there's nothing for the feet, and it looks like a lieback to me. The move demands more muscle than Norah thinks she has. Having come this far with her, I wouldn't be surprised to see her spring to the next higher ledge. At the same time, I think she can't do it; no way can she make that move. Worse, I think she may fall.

Three men move onto our stance from below; one, Bill Sutherland, Norah met years ago in the Black Cuillin of Skye. Pleased to see her as he is, he is also surprised she is still climbing mountains. With five of us on the ledge it is crowded, and someone must move. Norah climbs the crack. When I reach her, she is out of breath, flush, and exhilarated. "I didn't think I could do it," she says, "but I didn't want to embarrass myself in front of the others."

Higher up is a narrow ridge, two feet wide. The drop is ten feet to a shelf on the one side and twenty feet on the other. I'm first and put up one foot, but I don't step up with the other. It's a move that would be easy if we weren't so high, or if there were a place for my hands, a hold to steady myself—something, anything. I don't trust the foothold and won't commit my weight to it, not until Norah puts her hands on my rear and boosts me up. It takes some nerve to stand up straight, and I want to crawl the ridge on all fours. The road in the valley looks as wide as a wire. Norah is right behind me. "You've got to be pushed off here to fall," she says. I don't think so. I think a breeze would do it. I think about Isa, for whom pudding was a risk. "Yes," she says, "someone's got to push you off." Two cautious steps further along she adds, "At least that's what I tell myself."

On the summit we share a can of grapefruit. Beyond the gray of the rock is the red-brown moor. A lake gleams like dull metal in the distance. There are clouds and mist and wind.

Ben Nevis, the highest summit in the British Isles.
JOHN CLEARE.

I remember when I first told Willie I intended to climb. "What! With your weak heart and chilblains?" he said. And I thought, chilblains or no, I'm going to climb. I was forty-five years old. Willie was a dour man. He thought pleasure and joy were things to feel guilty about. I'd come in from a wonderful day on the hills all grinning and say, "What do you think I've just done?" And Willie would look stern and say nothing. His reaction made me even more determined. My breaking the conventions bothered him. "Why can't you be like Mrs. Miller?" he'd say. She was a stodgy neighbor two doors up. "Learn to play bridge and go to the cinema." I'd go into a terrible rage or rush into my room crying, although I never let Willie see me cry.

As time went on, the situation got nastier. I was climbing with these young boys and they treated me like one of them. It was the only way I could have done it. If they had treated me like an old lady, I would have acted like an old lady. Every time I went out I seemed to carry this great load of disapproval, of being headstrong and willful and selfish. I put myself in the ridiculous position of trying to keep up with young men when I was a silly old woman.

Willie thought that climbing was just an excuse to get away with other men. It sickened me. He tried to break up every relationship I made. He called up Peter's wife and fixed it so we couldn't go out together. I must have been seventeen or eighteen years older than Peter. I tried to find other women to climb with. I even tried to teach some. None of them would have any of it.

Later there were Crawford and Bert Shennan. We had twenty-five years difference between us, but Willie phoned Sam and warned him about me. Crawford and Bertie were at our house, and Willie said to them, "How would you like to have a wife like mine who does nothing but chase after men?" And another time Willie asked Bertie, "Why don't you get a young girl to go out with you instead of my wife? She's an old woman compared to you."

And Bertie smiled broadly and said, "Old woman or not, we can't keep up with her." That's a bit of an exaggeration, but I could keep up with *them*. I was very lively at that time, twenty years ago. I could go some rate.

The wonderful thing was that although all this trouble was stirred up with the families, none of the boys accepted it. Things came together again. They began to see it was Willie who was so obsessed.

Later Willie would apologize and tell me how much he loved me. He would tell me there had never been another woman for him and say it was only his jealousy that made him act so. But don't think I always won and Willie was the little maggot who couldn't. I used to bluff in defiance: "You can't win; I'm always one step ahead." I see now it must have been very trying for him, living with such a woman.

The whole world's disbelief came with me when I went climbing. I would go laden with guilt. Sometimes I would be sick and vomiting, but when I got on the hills I would forget it all. The week after Rodger and I had fallen on Aonach Beag I came to church with a bruise on my face. A lady said to me, "Well, now you've learned your lesson." She seemed delighted.

I knew what she meant, but I said, "What lesson?"

"You've been headstrong and foolish. We must all learn our lesson. Now you know not to do these things. It's very unwise. It upsets other people."

I heard that a lot in church: "But is it wise?" In other words, I had a responsibility not to upset other people, to behave as I was expected to behave. The only lesson I knew was how wonderful the mountains are and how excited I was to be going off to Skye the following week.

You see, it wasn't only Willie—the whole world's belief was against me. It wasn't enough for me simply to climb. I wanted to do it for the right motives. If I did it to break down the limitations imposed on me by world belief, it wouldn't have worked. I did it for the joy of it and at the same time found joy in breaking those beliefs. Lots of people who condemned me before now boost me to the skies.

We don't stay long on the summit. There's nothing there to keep us, not even much of a view. It's cloudy and cold and miles back to the car. We finish the grapefruit and pack the can away. As we start down, a stone catches my eye; with lichen on one side and colorful streaks on the other, it is beautiful, and I pack it away, a memento. We take another route back, down 500 feet of scree. Each step trips a small slide of dirt, loose rock, and small stones. I fall several times, and so does Norah. In an hour we are down—four hours up and one hour down.

Norah's face is red with exertion, her eye shadow matches the fine blue network of veins at her temples, and the L-shaped scar on her cheek is faint, like lipstick left from a kiss. She looks back toward the mountain and then to me. "Is mar-i-ju-ana better than that?" she asks.

Inside the car she fixes her hair in the rearview mirror. "If you've got a body, you might as well make the best of it," she says. There is dried blood on her palm from a fall on the scree. She wets her handkerchief from the water bottle and wipes it clean. She could be wiping a dirty dish. "Blood? What's blood? It's just sticky, red fluid. People talk about lifeblood, but there's no life in blood. People are spirit, I'm spirit, and spirit is bloodless."

On the return to Glasgow the following day we detour to Glen Nevis, the valley beneath Ben Nevis, Great Britain's highest mountain. The trail leads through the trees and traverses a hill with a gorge on one side and a stream at the bottom. The stream is out of sight, but we can hear it down below. The path enters a wide meadow, the glen, and here the stream is wide, quiet, and shallow. There is a bridge of sorts, three cables strung across the stream, one to walk on and two to hold on to. Eight feet off the water and twenty feet long, the bridge is a tightrope with handrails. There's no need to go across since the glen is what we've come to see, but I want to do it anyway. I'm careful to put my feet squarely on the cable, which swings in short, rapid arcs. This small risk makes the afternoon. When I turn around on the far side, Norah is right behind me. She loses her balance, recovers, loses and recovers again. She laughs and the cable swings. I feel like a parent seeing his kid way up a tree. Is she plucky or rash? "I wasn't going to sit on the bank and watch you have all the fun," she says. "You didn't think that, did you?"

She has come here often to the glen and to Ben Nevis itself, snow-topped over the green meadow, and it was near here, she tells me, amid this peace and beauty, that she had her worst climbing accident.

Aonach Beag, just to the east, is rarely climbed because it's remote and because most people go to Ben Nevis if they're up this way. Aonach Beag is 4,000 feet high, and at about 3,000 feet this ridge becomes a narrow arête for about 500 feet. The guidebook says there are no great difficulties except under winter conditions. This was in the winter of 1965, and it was stupid to go in winter for the first time.

The last section was a chimney full of black ice. The face is about 200 or 300 feet, and it gets progressively harder. There was a traverse over a 100-foot drop that leads into the chimney, and the traverse was icy. Rodger led the traverse and started up the

The northwest side of Ben Nevis, with the Great Glen in the foreground. JOHN CLEARE.

chimney, and I was horrified at the thought. A few feet up Rodger said in a small voice that he couldn't do it, he couldn't go on because of the black ice, and he couldn't reverse the move—he'd have to jump off. "Be ready," he said. "You'll have to hold me."

I couldn't have held him. He was twice my weight and had a sack full of ironmongery. There were about fifteen feet of rope out between us. It ran through a piton near my head, and the end was tied around my waist. A second rope tied me close to the wall.

We were where we didn't belong. The funny thing was that Rodger thought he was with a Christian Scientist practitioner and nothing could happen to him. And I thought nothing could happen to me; I was with a big, strong boy.

I had never had to hold anyone. I was horrified and nothing registered. When he dropped off, I wasn't ready. The rope pulled away and all of it, 120 feet, ran out. Because the rope ran through a piton and around my waist, I was jerked up and against the rock. That's all I remember. I was knocked unconscious.

The piton held, and both of us were hanging from it. Rodger yelled from below to give him some slack so he could climb up. He told me about it later because I never heard him at the time. The next thing I remember was this bloody head moving up

to my stance. I was just dangling from the piton. The left side of my face had struck the rock, and my crampons, which were tied to my rucksack, clawed at my ear.

Rodger pulled me back onto the ledge. He said I was a gory mess. I was so badly concussed I didn't know what I was doing. Rodger just lowered me down off the face. It was freezing cold and dark, and I fell again moving around a bulge. Rodger held me, but the rope severed the tendons in two of his fingers. We still had miles to go to the car. I would collapse and he would bring me around, and then he would collapse and I would bring him around. But I was determined to get home without troubling anyone; I didn't fancy being found by the mountain rescue and all the fuss in the papers.

It was pitch black when we got to the car. We tried to clean each other up. We both were covered with blood, our heads and our hands. We drove to the police station at Fort William. It was the small hours of the morning. I had to concentrate to get up the steps of the station. We thought our families may have called looking for us, and we wanted to call home. Rodger asked me to make the call. We agreed to say that we had just lost the route and taken the long way back and to say that we were on our way.

My son answered the phone, and I told him the story. He didn't seem too anxious. Willie was asleep. All the way home I held onto the thought that there was no suffering and we could not cause suffering. I prayed to see this as a good experience. We got home at six o'clock in the morning; I remember the milk was being delivered. When I walked in, Willie was blocking the way. For many years we had had separate bedrooms, and I just pushed him aside and said I didn't have time to argue.

I spent half the day in bed. The side of my face was all black and blue and my ear was mauled. Roger was in bed two or three days and off work the whole week. He worked in a foundry and couldn't use his hand. He came to me for treatment. I assured him it would heal if we got the right idea. We must have, because by the end of the week his fingers healed. The tendons grew back together, although he couldn't straighten the fingers completely.

But by the following week, when we went off to Skye together for holiday, the fingers straightened out. We were like wounded soldiers, but we refused to give way to the material law.

She names each peak we pass and points out routes, gullies, and ridges on the drive out of the Highlands. We pull to the side of the road for another look at the Buachaille Etive Mor. Yesterday we stood on top. We climbed 3,000 feet yesterday and 3,000 feet the day before that. She's seventy-five years old. For others her age, a flight of stairs is reason not to visit a neighbor; a patch of icy sidewalk means a broken hip.

She says she can't explain, not really.

"Look at me. I'm an old woman. I'm weak. You know my muscles are weak. Feel my arm." The muscle around the bone is soft, the bone a bone of a bird. "I don't have an explanation. I can only say that I live in the spirit and the spirit is weightless. I throw off all the arguments and all the reasons why I can't, and I move up freely and naturally, quite easily. I've learned this through mountaineering, and what is true for me is true for everyone. The mountains were where I had to prove that I accepted these ideas. Of course, it is easy to think these thoughts when all is physically well, but they're hard to hold in the face of the opposite sensation. I don't have an explanation, but I do know that if you argue for your limitations they are yours for sure. That I do know. God, I couldn't say this stuff if I hadn't proved it in some measure for myself."

Norah's house is one in a row on the very edge of Glasgow. Across the street, the city ends and the pastures begin. Her living room is small and clean and cluttered. There are plants, glass and ceramic animals on the tables and mantelpiece, stuffed animals on the couch, and a big stuffed penguin by the door. Pictures line the wall: Nanga Parbat's Diamir Flank, Mount Foraker, the Col de la Grand Vacheuse, the Aiguille Verte. Two ice axes stand in the corner, their wooden shafts nicked and gouged, the lacquer worn away. There is a picture of Colin and her other son, Michael, dead twenty-five years. There is no picture of Willie. Books fill the bookcase and books are stacked by her favorite chair. Beneath the Bible is *The Challenge,* by Reinhold Messner, part of a mountaineering library that includes W. H. Murray, Haston, Habeler, Bonington, Joe Brown, Rébuffat, and others. The stone with the lichen and the colored streaks, the one from the top of the Buachaille, lies on the coffee table. On the mountain, wet and shiny, in light filtered through mist, it seemed beautiful, singular, but down here, although pretty enough, it is just another stone.

The telephone rings, and Norah, watching a Sunday afternoon soccer game on the television, answers. Five minutes pass before she says a word. When she speaks, her voice is without pity or sympathy, but not without compassion. She is a Christian Science practitioner, a healer, and has been one for twenty-five years. It is how she earns her living, and it is a patient on the phone now. Norah tells her that no matter how things look, it is only the appearance of things, a spell that can be broken. "Like the air we breathe, thoughts of age and sickness enter in. Sickness is an argument. Let the argument pass away." She hangs up and turns her attention back to the game. "If you can't get through life happily, there is something wrong with your ideas," she says. "There is nothing wrong with life."

"I did this one, and this one, and that one, and this one . . . ," Norah says later, as she runs a finger down the index to *The Guide to the Central and Southern Highlands.* The names of the mountains rush out in a Gaelic blur. She estimates she's climbed the Cobbler a hundred times since she started climbing in 1950, the Buachaille forty times, Bidean thirty times, Aonach Eagach fifteen. There are 543 mountains in Scotland that rise higher than 3,000 feet; the Munros, they are called, and climbers often count them—keep track of the Munros they've climbed. Norah doesn't but guesses she's done 400. She does keep climbing journals, now running several volumes, written in ballpoint in a small, neat hand. The journals have notes on where she was, whom she was with, and a bit about the climb: Good route, good day. Saw eagle. Fiasco. Snow, mist, rain—good glissades. Soaking wet. Treacherous and icy. A few falls but no damage.

The following day I will be leaving, and Norah,

with another friend, is going to climb Ben Lui, her fourth mountain in seven days. The soccer game is in its final minutes. The flickering light from the television plays on her face. She sits in her favorite chair, wearing plum-colored slacks, a suede vest, and a striped blouse—the clothes she wore to church that morning. It takes some effort to recollect where we've been this past week, to place her back up on the Buachaille, her toes inching along a ledge, her heels hanging over empty space. She's a nice-looking woman, all right—and, like the stone on the table, pretty enough—but here in this room and in this light, she looks like just another granny.

Charles Hood

Twelve Scenes from the Life of Crow

1. Clever Crow

ALL DRESSED UP, AS THEY SAY, and no place to go. Crow shuffles in his double boots, trying to find a comfortable stance on the ice ramp. He cranes his neck to stare up into a world of black mists, plum-dark rock, stiff moss, and patchy ice runnels. Crow toys with the tip of his axe but makes no attempt to move out onto anything. Down a dozen depressions trickle small braids of water, some frozen, some not, none climbable.

2. Crow on Errands

Step, stamp, snap. The racing bindings click, and Crow poles off with a lunge, gliding swiftly out of the snow cave, down a steep bank, and out into the winter forest. He skis steadily along the blank path, chanting Eskimo words to keep his measure. *I-kag-nak.* Pause. *Ko-guk'-pûk.*

A gray day, and the porridge pot finally boils over, sending down large, fuzzy flakes. These settle thickly on skis as he takes off his pack, coaxes out a wool robe, and drapes it around himself. His spindly wrists poke out like two weeds. He grabs his poles and goes on, snow's ghost. Gaunt aspen striplings flicker by like framed rows of headstones, but Crow does not notice.

3. Crow Goes to Antarctica

Inside the shuddering tent, Crow is hunched over his sleeping bag. "Penguin," he mutters, stalking forward on all fours. "Penguin." He crouches very still, tensing for the spring. Quietly he says,

"The polar bear is in no way indigenous to Antarctica." "How do you know? Have you ever been there?" he replies to himself. Crow wrinkles his snout and crawls forward. "Penguin," he says. He leaps across the tent and lands clumsily, a dirty canteen squirting away with a pop. In an instant he is on it, wrestling it and gnawing at the lid with his teeth. "Got the sucker," he says with glee.

Outside the thin nylon dome and the stacked bricks of snow wall, the wind tears across the polar ice, as it has for eight days. All of Crow's skiing and climbing equipment is out there, staking the rimed tent. He endeavors to hold the penguin down with both paws and twist the cap with his jaw. No luck. Pushing it with his nose, he tries to wedge it against a creaking tent pole; refusing to cam, it slides free. Finally, he sits on the canteen. "Polar bears are not indigenous to nylon tents," he says. "Only penguins are."

He bats the canteen and pounces on it again. "Polar bears are on the verge of extinction due to excessive boredom."

He finds the other canteen, the one being used as a pee bottle, and fills it.

Crow is not enjoying his trip to Antarctica.

4. Naturalist Crow

Crow lies naked and belly-down on the hot sandstone. *Uta stansburiana*, the side-blotched lizard, faces him, doing short pushups. Crow, too, does pushups. He and the lizard take turns doing pushups for half an hour. The lizard stretches its tongue. Crow's pink tongue almost touches his nose. The lizard skitters across the dome of rock, pausing near the brink. On fingertips and toes, Crow follows.

The gorge below is a brindled mass of sienna-, rust-, oxblood-, and ochre-colored stone, peppered with desert willow and stitched to the sky by the darting needles of cliff swallows. Crow does more pushups.

He has painted gray and brown rosettes down his arms, legs, cheeks. A solid azure circle stretches out under each armpit. As he sweats, the colors loosen and run. Crow lies on the rock, a tired side-blotched lizard. The real lizard sprints over the lip of the escarpment.

Crow crawls slowly to the edge and stares down. The lizard, tail high, scurries away and disappears into a crack. Crow sits up and puts on a pair of EBs. He stands, stretches, flexes his arms and fingers, and starts scouting a way down.

5. Crow in the Himalaya

He has never been this high before. Dimly he knows why: it has always before been too much work. His lungs, feet, heart, legs, throat, and eyes agree that even now it is too much work. His brain agrees as well. It spends minutes not doing anything, then bursts awake to tell Crow about the hard work. It also tells him about the scenery, about the Kodachrome film in the Italian camera in the French rucksack. It tells him about the fingers pushing metal raisins, clicking sounds, certain credits in magazines and books, certain sums of necessary money. "Raisins?" he wonders. His arms and legs try to remind him of the earlier message. "Oh, why is Crow so stupid?"

"This is too much work," agrees the brain, "but why won't he take pictures at least?" Stupid Crow.

6. Crow Entertains Himself

The government station wagon glides around the campground's dirt road, stopping only once to let the ranger emit a vague warning to a group of hacky-sack players who, it seems, have once again overstayed the park's fourteen-day stay limit. Crow, industrious in the chilly twilight, tears up orange crates for kindling. The station wagon's headlights X-ray each tent and Winnebago in succession, and Crow stiffens as the beams reach his tent. Eventually, the taillights turn toward the highway and fade like sleepy embers.

Crow builds a fire. It flickers at first, then flares up brightly, turning the monzonite boulders crowding the site orange as pumpkins. In the firelight the rocks dance and melt. Nearby Joshua trees stand as hard and rigid as medieval weapons.

Out of a dirty haul sack Crow takes three small jars and several foil packages. These he carries behind one of the boulders and sets before a shallow overhang, along with a candle, a page torn from a book, and a hollow tube. He mixes the contents of two of the jars and pours the resulting scab-red powder into the tube. Crow clenches the tube in his teeth, blowing steadily. The pigment fogs over his hand and clings to the granite like chalk, neatly outlining Crow's palm and fingers. Above this cavort two horses and a stylized bighorn sheep, already finished.

This is Crow's new project, a series of murals on crags and boulders across the country. "Crow's Neolithic landscape," he calls it.

He goes back and piles more wood on the fire.

7. Tarot Crow

He hangs by his heel. One EB is tangled in an étrier, the other waves free, kicking impotently. Crow, the Hanged Man. Slings and 'biners dangle out of the split roof like inverted clumps of grass. The gear sling, terribly anxious to hammer into the talus, continually pushes Crow's nose into his forehead. Crow claws at the rope peeling off his seat harness, his hands too watery to maintain a grip. He twists and tries to do a situp, at the same time fighting a great duel with the gear sling. The second EB pops out of the étrier step, dropping Crow five feet and completely clear of the overhang. Head down, arched like a banana, he revolves in slow gyrations. "Up rope," he calls hoarsely, "up rope." A minute later there is an indistinct call and the rope eases down another five feet.

8. Crow Briefly Works Retail

"I need some brown one-inch webbing." "We have green or white." "No, you don't understand. A sort of medium brown, to go with these pants." "Too fucking bad."

9. Social Crow

As usual, Crow has to take a leak. He worms reluctantly out of his sleeping bag, switching on a headlamp as he stands. The talus cave is cramped, and he picks his way carefully.

"Excuse me," he says. "Would you mind turning your back? I must make water."

Finished, Crow stumbles back to his bag, the beam from his light playing quickly over the Inca mummy at the end of the cave.

"And after water, we make *chai*. See? Success in mountaineering is all in the ritual." He primes the pot of snow with water from a canteen and lights his MSR. The cave fills with the stove's steady cobra hiss. Crow turns off the headlamp, trading its white insistence for the stove's eerie blue glow.

The mummy lies on a shelf of rock diagonal from Crow's bivouac site. Withered, sepia-dark skin puckers tight across its skull. A rotted basket rests beside it, and fistfuls of blue beads lie scattered amid the scree.

"And after tea, we eat biscuits." He slides a Ziploc baggie of granola out of his pack, along with two tea bags. "And, having bathed and dined, we proceed with the remainder of the descent, and then have left only the inevitable short yet epic hike back to base camp." As the water heats, he drops tea into the pot.

"Aren't you excited? Isn't climbing"—Crow turns on the headlamp a moment and stares at the corpse—"fun?"

10. Crow Waits for a Train

Rain sings down endlessly, beating out of the cement an unpleasant, sick smell. On the cold porch Crow shivers in a thin sweater. The station lobby will not be opened until 7:00 A.M., four more hours. He wishes he were in a sunny place. Sighing, he drags his rucksack from the one dry corner of the porch. He pulls out a wad of soiled slings, a nine-millimeter rope, and a heavy aid rack, which clinks hollowly in the chill air. Using bat-hooks and copperheads, he eases up the masonry of the building's façade.

From a high point under the eaves he tries to lasso a nearby transom window latch with his sling. The runner catches on the fourth try. Crow jumps, leaving the sling dangling from the transom. He then walks to the edge of the porch and stands under the lip of the roof, rain pouring onto his head. He leaps up, grabs the roof's edge, pulls, and holds, shifting into a one-armed mantle. With his free hand he slides a piton into a gap between a rafter and the roof. He clips two carabiners to this and feeds through the free end of his rope. Dropping back to the porch, he pulls several loops of rope through the bottom carabiner and ties a heavy hex onto the end. This he tosses through the transom runner. Crow unties the hex, ties the rope directly to the transom sling, and then walks back to the edge of the porch. Pulling on the rope, he hauls in the slack perlon so that the transom sling is pulled tight to the roof. The rope runs along the roof to the carabiner and down to Crow's cold hands. "Let there be leverage," Crow announces, pulling steadily on the rope. The transom window unlatches and swings open.

He cleans the pitch and puts the gear sling back in his pack, leaving out only his Edelrid. He ties a loose slip knot in this and tosses it through the lobby window. It snakes down the glass door to the lobby until it halts at the door latch. A dozen tries and Crow has the rope around the handle, which opens easily.

He sits before the electric heater in the manager's office, coiling his rope. "You know, Crow," he says quietly, "it would have been simpler just to have bought a new cagoule."

11. Crow's New Attitude

Mara sits alone in the busy café patio, sipping her *cerveza* and wondering about unemployment and alienation and the existentialism of solo life abroad. A gust of wind catches her bare arms unexpectedly, making her shiver as her mind flashes back on Alaska eleven months earlier. She sees again the snow and rock of the Cathedrals, remembering every detail of that horrible expedition. She shakes her head in an effort to dislodge the ice-gripped imagery, taking another long drink. "Long ago and far away. . . ."

She is still there an hour later, trying to decide to leave. "What?" she says, turning with a start. Her sudden question meets only the usual babble of Spanish and a panorama of people at tables, eating.

A waiter comes over. In clumsy Spanish she must explain that she thought she had heard someone say "wolf" in English and that she wanted to speak with him if he was American or British. "*Sí, sí, un lobo,*" the waiter says with a patronizing expression, walking away muttering about the stupidity of drunken Americans.

"Fuck him," Mara says, following herself with "*tan loca como una mujer*" and a funny laugh. Then she freezes in midsmile as she focuses on a figure walking through the patio. Tall, bearded, his head is half black bandana, half an eruption of wet, straw-colored hair. A rucksack bulges behind him, and expedition boots keep his stick legs from driving into the ground. The boots stand out all the more because, instead of pants, he wears faded Chouinard shorts. Seeing her, he strides toward her table.

Mara starts to rise, but he stares her down. He neither smiles, nods, nor extends his hand.

"I am Crow," he proclaims.

12. They Live Together

The predawn trucks roll east with the soothing clatter of a rain squall. She sits awake, the covers a tower over her knees.

"Crow, have you ever been in a motel before?"

"No."

"No?"

He reflects. "Jail, gutter, lifeboat, cave, yurt, tent, trailer, hut, cabin, crevasse, igloo, hostel, pension, cheap hotel, yes. Motel, no."

"Lifeboat?"

"I was on a boat. It sunk."

"Have you ever been in New Mexico before?"

Crow shrugs. "We have many lives."

Tom Higgins

Tricksters and Traditionalists

A Look at Conflicting Climbing Styles

C OLORADO CLIMBER PAT AMENT recently watched people dragging a thirty-foot ladder up scree slopes in Boulder Canyon. Were they on their way to a high-wire act, he inquired? No, no act; they just needed to preprotect a new route with a bolt twenty feet off the ground.

In Yosemite Valley, holds are chopped ("sculpted," say the defenders of the action) into the rock to allow tries at free climbing El Capitan. At the other end of the Valley, on Glacier Point Apron, a string of aid bolts is placed to protect free climbing on Hall of Mirrors. Reportedly, protection without aid was possible, but on a less direct line. The route is then touted as one of the greatest new free climbs in Yosemite.

In Tuolumne Meadows—in the high country of Yosemite National Park—routes on every major dome are done by placing bolts and pitons while on rappel, by standing on bolts to place others, and by

The ultimate refinement of "traditional" climbing: John Bachar free soloing a classic jamcrack on the second pitch of Outer Limits. Since a fall during unroped climbing high above the ground proves uniformly fatal, few climbers practice the pure but risky style portrayed in this and the following two photographs, all taken in Yosemite Valley. LANNY JOHNSON.

creating bolt ladders to protect free climbing. In the latest Tuolumne innovation, leaders place protection bolts while hanging from hooks attached to flakes and knobs. In the same area even the long-standing agreement to respect the protection style of the first-ascent party is weakening: a bolt was recently added to an established route on Daff Dome.

In every major climbing area in the country, it is possible to see climbers rappelling cliffs in order to preview crux sections of proposed new routes, to rehearse moves, and to place protection. When these climbers finally decide to do their routes, they often fall repeatedly and rest on their protection. The new protection devices, Friends, encourage this behavior; since the protection is more easily assured, climbers can push closer to the point of falling.

Clearly, rockclimbing styles are changing. "Tricksters" are bending and altering the traditional rules of the climbing game. In the traditional style, climbers do not alter the rock in order to free climb it. Nor do they preview routes on rappel, or fix protection on aid or on rappel with the intention of immediately trying to free climb. Aid climbing is done to get to the top, not to set up a route for free-climb attempts. Likewise, in traditional style the climber might fall a few times trying a free climb, but he or she doesn't rest on the protection between attempts. The traditionalist knows there is a time and place to give up.

The conflict between tricksters and traditionalists is no small issue. Before 1970 there were few, if any, tricksters; nearly all the routes were done in traditional style. Now, tricksters are continually creating new routes with their controversial methods. Also, capable and respected climbers subscribe to the methods. Vern Clevenger tells of times and places he stood on protection bolts to place others and previewed or rehearsed while on rappel. Jim Bridwell has doctored rock selectively and has placed bolt ladders to protect free climbing. John Bachar rests on hooks while placing protection bolts. Reportedly, Ray Jardine "sculpts" holds on El Capitan. These expert climbers, of course, do not use the controversial styles everywhere or every time. They all have climbed ferocious routes in traditional style.

Nevertheless, respected climbers not only use the new styles, they defend them. In an article on face-climbing styles and standards in the 1982 *American Alpine Journal*, Bruce Morris reports that many climbers in Tuolumne now subscribe to "the construction of a line of technical difficulty at almost any price." He quotes "notorious local Claud Fiddler," who asks, "How can a route be worthwhile unless 'questionable methods' were employed on its first ascent?" Of Vern Clevenger, Morris writes: "He demonstrated a willingness to cheat selectively . . . as long as it extended the upper range of the free-climbing spectrum." The attitude seems to be, so what if protection bolts are placed on aid or rappel, as long as the resulting climb is a good one? So what if a flake or crack is slightly altered to make a great free climb? Why should climbers be bound by old rules—or any rules—when creating new routes or trying to free climb old routes?

The conflict between traditionalists and tricksters extends to methods of reporting new routes. Whereas climbers once agreed to report their first-ascent style openly, now information about style is not readily forthcoming. Some tricksters simply refuse to say how they did a climb, perhaps believing the style of ascent is no one's business. They may not lie about how they climbed, but often they remain silent about their style of ascent until asked directly. Their silence creates an awkward and misleading situation. For example, Morris remarks of a Tuolumne first ascent: "No one will ever know for sure whether [the leader] drilled all the bolts strictly on the lead." And referring to Pièce de Résistance, another Tuolumne climb, Morris states, "Only one bolt—but [the climbers] would never say which one—was supposedly drilled on aid." Other climbers acknowledge their aid ladders or rests on protection, but only to close companions. The information rarely gets into print. Journal articles relate heroics, not style, and modern guidebooks, short on history but long on route maps, contain few references to the style of ascent.

Climbers arguing for full disclosure of style perceive a glaring contradiction in the paucity of reporting. Why are tricksters so loud in defending what they are doing but so reluctant to reveal their style of ascent? It appears tricksters want a free ride on the backs of people climbing in traditional style. Because tricks are a relatively new phenomenon, climbers unaware of the inside story presume traditional styles were employed and give their respect accordingly.

It is time to reexamine the issue of climbing styles. The first question is obvious: why should there be *any* agreement about styles? The answer is equally clear: because these agreements safeguard the climbing enjoyment of others. Some agreements between climbers aim at facilitating the competitive side of the sport. Contrary to cherished belief, climbing *is* a competitive sport. Climbing a route all free, with limited protection, and on the first try means much more than climbing it after rehearsing moves or placing protection on rappel. Consequently, climbers should agree to reveal how new routes, particularly hard ones, were done. Only in this way can climbers test themselves by trying routes in the same or better style.

Climbers are not alone in making agreements about competition in their sport. Bagging game with a bow and arrow is much more impressive than with a rifle, and kayaking a rough river is a greater achievement than doing it in a tube raft. People participating in these sports agree to reveal what technique or style is used because the achievement and stature of those responsible are thereby defined. The achievements in any sport are remembered, written down, and discussed for many years. For that discussion to have any meaning, people agree not to imply they used a bow and arrow when they used a rifle, or used a kayak when they used a raft.

Other agreements guard against actions climbers find offensive. For example, when climbers agree not to paint their names on walls, blast out ledges, fix cables, or otherwise drastically alter the rockscape, they do so because most climbers are offended by the result. Similarly, many climbers are offended by an extra piton or bolt added to an established route. Upon finding such additional protection, they feel the same as they would coming across names spray-painted on the rock. A bolt and a pin added to a route at Lover's Leap, in California, once caused much debate. Several climbers still feel the protection should have been left as it was originally placed. The thirty-odd bolts placed on the regular

Bachar on Crack-A-Go-Go. LANNY JOHNSON.

route of New Mexico's Shiprock over the years so outraged climbers that one fanatic spent half a day removing them. On Yosemite's Lost Arrow Tip, six extra bolts were added in the 1950s to John Salathé's original ones. Some thought the bolts demeaned Salathé's efforts and should be removed. They were. In short, agreements between climbers about style are useful and important because they enhance or protect the climbing experience. Contrary to what tricksters say, climbing style is not a personal matter.

Of course, there is an exception to the agreement against altering protection on established routes: the first-ascent party may indicate better protection is needed. The Snake Dike on Half Dome provides a good example. Seasoned climbers, making the first ascent using marginal protection, realized only at the top that the moderate route was destined to become a popular climb. Therefore, they gave the next party permission to add numerous bolts, thus ensuring that beginners would have a safe and enjoyable time.

It is not only on established routes that climbing or protection styles are more than personal matters. The same is true for first ascents. There were once plenty of new routes for climbers to "hunt"; so it didn't matter that some people used "bows" and others used "guns" to do the coveted climbs. Plenty of "game" existed for each. But now that game is scarce, climbers employing different styles are in competition for new routes much more so than in the past. A first ascent accomplished by preplacing bolts or pitons on aid or rappel removes the opportunity for another party to make the first ascent without using these techniques. The same is true for first ascents done by rehearsing or resting on protection.

Tricksters defend their actions by means of two popular but fallacious arguments. The first is that no matter how a first ascent is done, traditionalists can always climb the route in their preferred style. They can bypass protection placed on rappel, and they can try a route without rehearsing or resting on protection. In so doing, they can experience their own "first ascent." The problem with this contention is that it discounts the importance of first ascents for others. Removed forever is the unique opportunity for a first ascent in traditional style. Obviously, a special satisfaction comes from doing a first ascent, naming it, telling others the story, being recognized, and adding one's name and accomplishments to the history of climbs in an area.

Tricksters raise a second argument: "Tough luck." They say the first-ascent party always has denied others the opportunity for a first ascent, no matter what the style. To be sure, people using traditional styles do deny first ascents to others, including climbers employing the new tricks. The rebuttal, however, is simple: bullets kill more easily than arrows. Where game is plentiful, it doesn't matter who uses what weapon. But when game is scarce, it certainly does matter. Guns remove more game for bows than vice versa. It is for this very reason that bow users are allowed to hunt before the regular season opens. It is also the reason that certain weapons are restricted in hunting and fishing. Consider the rightful ire of a flyfisherman observing someone building a trap or dynamiting the water!

Not only do tricks remove opportunities, they create certain dangers. Where a first ascent is rehearsed by top rope and preprotected, for example, traditionalists may be endangered in subsequent ascents. Traditionalists may not be able to place protection on the lead and, not having rehearsed the moves, may fall at a dangerous point.

Again, climbing style is not purely a personal matter. It affects other climbers in various ways. On established routes, adding protection offends climbers who wish to do the route in its original style, or as the first-ascent party intended the route to stand. Consequently, many climbers still agree to honor the protection style of the first ascent. On new routes, both climbing and protection style can affect others as first-ascent opportunities grow scarce. In this case, climbers employing preprotection, rehearsing, and resting on protection are more easily able to do first ascents than climbers choosing not to use these styles. For all these reasons a majority of climbers prior to 1970 agreed not to employ certain styles on first ascents. If a route could not be done in the traditional manner, the prevailing agreement was to leave it for better climbers—or future generations—to try.

Tricksters should reconsider what their climbing styles are doing to others and change their actions. First, where preprotecting, rehearsing, and aid ladders are employed, they should be widely reported. Guidebooks and climbing magazines should report the style of ascent. Without this information, other climbers cannot know what challenge has been set before them. Trusting climbers who presume traditional styles of ascent may even be endangered as they try to repeat certain routes. Second, tricksters should stop using their techniques on new routes in areas where first-ascent possibilities are scarce and where other climbers want to employ traditional styles. Third, and as a last resort, tricksters might confine themselves to places where the opportunities for new routes are plentiful. In such places they are less likely to happen upon established routes they feel need alteration in protection or in the rock itself. If they want to preprotect, rehearse, or create

Near the top of the spectacular climb known as Hardd, Bachar works up a wicked fist crack. LANNY JOHNSON.

bolt ladders for free climbing, their actions will not greatly inconvenience traditionalists.

The last two points are the most difficult for tricksters to accept. After all, they believe their style is applied only when traditional styles cannot be used. Perfectly capable of climbing in traditional style, tricksters feel they know its limits. They feel that few, if any, climbers will be deprived of first-ascent opportunities.

A recent case in point is the Bachar-Yerian Route on Medlicott Dome in Tuolumne Meadows. This spectacular route ascends a black water streak on a dead-vertical golden wall. The leader placed protection bolts while hanging from hooks affixed to knobs. The climb is superb, the line is direct, the protection is scanty; it is hard to imagine the route could be protected without resorting to a trick such as hanging from hooks. Surely, say the tricksters, no opportunity for traditionalists was removed in *this* case.

Perhaps the Bachar-Yerian Route could not be done any other way, except by rappelling to place the bolts. If all the routes done by tricksters were this impressive and difficult, there would be less to discuss. Within a few miles of the Bachar-Yerian Route, however, numerous examples abound of climbs where tricksters have removed very real possibilities for traditionalists. Handjive, on Lembert Dome, originally protected by placing bolts on rappel, lay well within the capabilities of climbers of the time to protect on the lead. Hoodwink, on Harlequin Dome, was first done with an aid ladder to protect free climbing. Traditionalists of the day could have done the first ascent without the ladder. Death Crack, once rehearsed by top roping, is now led occasionally on sight. Blues Riff, once protected on aid, is now done without this style. In the last two cases climbers of today were deprived of the opportunity for first ascents in traditional style. Other examples exist where climbers of the era, or those of the next generation, could have done—or would have wanted to try—trickster routes in traditional style.

The irony of the Bachar-Yerian Route is that John Bachar's usual climbing style suggests how the route might have been done to no one's objection. Since Bachar free solos routes of the highest standard, one gets the impression he put in his bolts for subsequent climbers. Suppose he had put in only those bolts that could have been placed without hooks and let climbers scratch their heads for years to come. Neither the traditionalists nor the tricksters could then object to losing the first-ascent opportunity to such a fine climber and so pure a style.

Whatever real or supposed opportunities were removed by the Bachar-Yerian Route, the style of ascent still disadvantages climbers preferring the traditional style. In the hands of lesser climbers, "hooking" is certain to remove ever more first-ascent possibilities for traditionalists of today and the near future. It is possible also that advances in protection technology will allow routes like the Bachar-Yerian to go without hooks, rappel placements, or aid ladders. Or perhaps more climbers will soon accept less protection, in line with Bachar's usual climbing style. The point is that tricksters should not presume to know the limits of traditional styles or styles less dependent on protection. Also, they should not presume to know how many climbers prefer traditional styles now or will in the future. Traditionalists may be a silent majority or weekenders who rarely have the time or contacts to make known their preferences. Considerable unthinking arrogance lies in the presumption that one knows the capabilities and preferences of everyone in the growing population of rockclimbers. Tricksters should also realize a first-ascent opportunity comes only once. Restocking can revive game populations for those fishing and hunting. But once the first ascent is bagged, it is gone forever. This fact alone should give pause to those who use weapons others in the sport refuse to employ.

Unfortunately, much of the discussion about climbing styles is so off base as to discourage serious debate. For example, tricksters say their style brings them closer to physical and psychic frontiers. Bruce Morris claims that to climb beyond "temporal ethics" is to take "mystical steps toward achieving a deathless super-consciousness." Does this Nietzschean rhetoric really clarify matters? Traditionalists say their style makes routes more challenging because there is less reliance on equipment and more emphasis on the act of climbing. Arguments go on endlessly about psychic rewards and purity of heart; it all sounds like a Sunday sermon. No wonder so many dismiss the whole matter.

The way to wake up the debate is to shift the focus from style to impact. Whether the bow and arrow or the gun provides the better experience is not at issue. The much-needed focus of debate is not what trickster style does for its adherents, but how it affects climbers preferring other styles. In the economist's jargon, tricks create an "externality," a negative public consequence from private action. Traditionalists are getting less information than they want or need to measure achievements. They are finding scarred rock or protection altered from the first ascent; they are getting fewer chances to try their style on first ascents. These important, concrete issues can and should spur intelligent debate.

From such debate, climbers can get down to the

business of mending old agreements or striking new ones. Everyone will be awake for the ensuing discussion. The tricksters will have their points:

—Who are traditionalists and why have they been so quiet if they perceive so much harm? How many are they?

—If traditionalists repeatedly fail to make a first ascent, shouldn't they agree to give us a chance?

—Will traditionalists agree that some climbs will *never* be done in their preferred style? If so, why should those walls be left alone forever?

And the traditionalists will have their points:

—How can we strike agreements with tricksters to ignore certain walls, areas, or established routes?

—If tricksters continue their ways, why don't they at least agree to report their style of ascent in articles and guidebooks?

—Should there be experiments with new bolting technology? Would climbers use the technology more to climb in traditional fashion or more to place aid ladders for protection? Or both?

Agreements among climbers about styles have changed and will continue to change. Although tricksters now dominate the scene in many climbing areas, they have not buried previous agreements favoring traditional styles. Agreements against tricks, for full reporting, and for preservation of established routes have a sound basis. They have protected the fundamental interests and experiences of climbers for many decades. Consequently, the agreements may have more proponents than tricksters know. At the very least, such agreements govern an older generation of climbers who still climb in the traditional style. Other proponents may be occasional visitors to climbing areas, who are numerous but not generally vocal about style. Also, a younger generation now beginning to climb will soon discover the reasons for agreements about traditional style. Many will be in a quandary about how new climbs are done. They will consequently find it hard to measure themselves against the challenge. And they will watch as beautiful, improbable walls succumb only to those who practice special tricks. It is likely that many in this generation will demand to know how first ascents were done, to try the "impossible" without resorting to tricks, and to experience the rock and protection of classic routes as they were originally. Perhaps it will not be long before demands for old and familiar agreements rise up like so many poltergeists. If so, what will the tricksters do? Agree or not? Abide or not?

Talbot Bielefeldt

ILLUSTRATIONS BY MARGARET BERRIER-PETRANOFF

A Matter of Character

FERNDECKER HAD BEEN WORKING ON the traverse for hours. His feet trembled on the rounded, weathered seam he was following across the cliff face. The tips of his fingers were sore from gripping small nubbins in the rock—although at the moment the nubbins had run out. The blue rope attached to Ferndecker's climbing harness ran sideways, limp, around a corner of rock. He could not hang on it for any support, and if he fell, he would drop some distance before the rope pulled tight.

"Traverses are tricky," Ferndecker noted. "Last man's in as much danger as the leader. Good thing I sent that Peters boy across first. Sometimes a guide can work best from the rear."

He shifted his feet on the seam and squinted at the sky and rock around him. He checked for storms, handholds, anything that might deserve his attention. His thin face was lined with a lifetime of squinting and checking. He tried to concentrate on the slab he had to cross to follow the rope around the corner. It was difficult; Ferndecker found his focus shifting to the airy drop below. Although the rock he was traversing sloped back enough for him to stand in balance, the cliff was dished in deeply beneath him. Beyond his heels the first thing he saw was the yellow talus, some two hundred feet below.

The boulders tumbled into a brown river that snaked around the base of the cliff. Across the river, the flat desert dotted with gray sage and juniper rolled away toward a vague blue line of mountains.

"The high peaks," Ferndecker said, squinting at the horizon. "That's where it really counts."

He made himself focus on the rock in front of him. A white crystal protruded at waist level about a yard to his left, just out of reach. The seam merged into the rock at Ferndecker's toes, but several feet down the face, below the crystal, was a large solution pocket.

"Dynamic move," Ferndecker decided. "Commitment. Rhythm. Good workout for the others. They must be getting the hang of it."

"Who's he talking to?" The shifting breezes off the desert carried the words up from below. Looking between his legs, the climber could see two figures sitting on a boulder by the river. "Hey, sir? Sir?" one of them called.

"God, can't they see I'm at the crux?" Ferndecker muttered.

"Sir? What route are you on?"

"Am I the guide for every idiot on the cliff?" Ferndecker wondered. "Hell if I know—use your judgment!" he shouted down. "Judgment! Route-finding!"

"Elephino? What page in the guide?"

"Guide!" snorted Ferndecker. "They couldn't recognize a guide if one walked up and shook their hands. Leadership isn't written in a book. It's a matter of character." He stood a little straighter on his holds. This caused a gentle tug on the rope, which resulted in a few inches of slack being fed from above. Ferndecker noticed the sag in the line.

"Sloppy," he said. "I should have worked longer with Peters. Attention to detail. Responsibility of the rope leader. Up rope!" The line tightened, forcing Ferndecker off balance, leaning left.

"Slack!" he called, and the rope resumed its lazy arc just as Ferndecker's left foot oozed off the seam. The right side of his body began to twist away from the rock. The slack that developed in the rope was immediately pulled in by the belayer, removing any possibility of Ferndecker regaining his balance.

Ferndecker saw the ground reeling below him, and he closed his eyes. As he toppled, his left hand slid down the rock and ran into the white crystal. The fingers reflexively clamped down, and Ferndecker pulled himself in. A button popped off the front of his chamois shirt as his chest scraped over the rough sandstone. He clung there for a moment, hugging the cliff, until his posture pried his other foot off the rock. Ferndecker felt the bottom drop out of his stance, and he was falling again. He waited for his fingers to be ripped from his last hold. Instead, his left foot skittered directly into the solution pocket. Ferndecker opened his eyes to find himself balanced neatly on one leg, left hand still gripping the crystal.

"Hey, nice move!" the climber on the trail called up.

"All in the balance," Ferndecker explained. "Keep the hands low. Climb with the eyes. Up rope!"

Ferndecker continued climbing left toward the corner on small nubbins and flakes. "Peters should have protected this pitch better," he noted. "It's all right for me, but what about the others?" He prepared to step around the corner, pausing for a moment to savor the exposure—he was only a foot above the edge of the overhang—and to see if the two climbers on the trail were watching. To his disappointment, they had walked on. He peered around the corner and looked up.

"Oh, no! Oh, God, no!" Ferndecker cried. Five feet above his head a piton protruded from a thin crack. The rope was connected to the anchor with a carabiner on a yellow webbing sling cinched around the eye of the pin. The flexible attachment between piton and carabiner allowed the rope to run past the anchor with minimum friction.

"A piton!" Ferndecker gasped. "I should have spent time with Peters on chocks in thin cracks. Never assume too much. No matter how much training you've done, when the leader's not around, the whole organization of the climb falls apart."

Ferndecker climbed quickly up to the pin. Just as he reached the anchor, he discovered that he had run out of holds on the face. The crack that contained the piton was smooth-sided and shallow, too thin to accept Ferndecker's fingers. Ferndecker noticed that the piton itself was hammered in only part way. It was a rusty piece of steel, obviously placed in the crack and left there years before.

"Purely psychological anchor," Ferndecker groaned. "Peters should have known better than to trust his life and those of the other clients to a relic like that. He should have placed a bolt." Ferndecker tried a tentative move past the anchor. As he gained an inch the rope was taken in. The snug belay almost pulled him off his stance. "Slack!" he shouted. "God, this is dangerous, climbing with these novices."

Ferndecker found that his right hand was now grasping the yellow nylon sling. His left hand brushed around on the rock for a moment, then also wrapped itself around the webbing. Ferndecker sagged a bit in the knees. As his weight came onto the sling, his fingers crushed against each other.

"Damn!" Ferndecker said. "Why didn't Peters clip directly into the pin?" He pulled one hand free and caught onto the piton itself. His feet churned against the rock until one of them caught on a small flake. Ferndecker stood up abruptly, snatched a large nubbin three feet above the anchor, and in a moment was standing with one foot on the head of the piton.

"Shouldn't blame Peters," he panted as he caught his breath. "My fault. Can't expect any more from someone that wet behind the ears."

"Who's he talking to?" a voice asked nearby. Ferndecker looked up and saw three heads peering around the edge of a jutting rock lip above him, about twenty feet to his left. Young heads—two men and a woman. One man with dark hair and sunglasses seemed to be handling the rope. "Mr. Ferndecker, you're almost up," he called. "The lip of the bulge is a pretty good hold. Just climb straight up where you are, and then you can scramble over to us."

Ferndecker did not acknowledge the advice but followed the directions anyway. The hold was indeed good, and he pulled up until he could see over the edge. The broad ledge had a sandy floor with a small manzanita growing against the back wall.

"Totally incompetent," Ferndecker muttered. "Should have belayed right here. Rope angle. Protection for the others. Take advantage of natural anchors. Too much dependence on his hardware."

"Oh, yeah—stay away from that bush on the ledge," the belayer called. "The other clients and I

loosened it. It'll probably pull right out, and this would be a bad place for a fall. Is your rope running okay? Feels like it might be hung up on something."

"You were going to use the bush? Oh, God— *never* use a vegetable hold. If only I'd been here to provide some. . . . *Up rope!*" Ferndecker's arms were beginning to burn, and he realized he would have to climb quickly onto the ledge or step back down to the piton to rest. For some reason, the rope did not give him the expected support when it pulled tight. It seemed to be actually pulling him back. "Slack!" he shouted.

"Look at his rope!" the woman cried. "He never unclipped it from the sling on the piton!"

"Oh, shit," the belayer murmured. Speaking up, he called, "Look, Mr. Ferndecker, can you go back down a step? It looks like your rope is still through the last carabiner."

Ferndecker tried to control his anger. "Can you believe this?" he muttered. "Peters wants to know if *I* can reverse a move. I wouldn't be the climber I am if I couldn't. On the other hand, I wouldn't have to if he hadn't messed up the protection." Ferndecker lowered himself on his arms again but could not find a foothold. His hands began to cramp.

"I don't think he can do it," the man next to the belayer said. "I think he was standing on the piton, and his foot's way off it now."

Ferndecker pulled up again, thrashing at the rock with his feet. He threw one elbow over the ledge, then the other; then he pushed up, supporting his body on the lip of the ledge with stiff arms.

"Great!" cried the belayer. "Now just throw your knee over! Throw your knee!"

Ferndecker paused where he was and fixed the other man with an icy stare. He tried to lift one foot onto the ledge, but he was not limber enough to make the high step. Breathing hard, he shifted his hands and tried again. This time his foot came within an inch of the lip. Ferndecker suddenly folded his torso over the ledge and with a deep grunt placed the very tip of his climbing shoe on the edge of the platform. He gave the three other climbers a tight smile and said, "We never, never use the knee." And then he fell off the ledge, slid feet first down the slab past the piton, and dropped over the edge of the overhang.

The shock when Ferndecker hit the end of the rope pulled the tied-off piton out of its crack. On the belay ledge Peters was yanked tight against the sling and carabiner that held him to an anchoring chock. Thirty feet below, Ferndecker struggled to right himself in his harness as he swung wildly back and forth under the overhang.

"Balance," he croaked. "Key to the whole thing."

The swinging gradually slowed and stopped. From above the overhang Ferndecker could hear muffled curses and the clanking of equipment. "That Peters," he whispered. "Disorganized. Can't cope. . . . Everyday emergencies." When they began to haul him, the rope twisted and Ferndecker started to spin. He fought back an urge to vomit. "Can't," he explained through clenched teeth. "Rattle the others. Morale. Key to it all."

"Who's he talking to?" the woman on the ledge asked.

Peters, straining to separate the tangled ropes of his jury-rigged block and tackle, was not sure. One thing he did know was that this was the last summer he was working for this company. Why did the office always send him clients like Ferndecker? While the others hauled in the line, Peters grabbed an anchored rope and leaned out from the rock. Here came Ferndecker now, turning round and round, squinting at his realm of stone and thin air, a crooked sprig of manzanita sprouting from one hand like a scepter.

Geoff Childs

ILLUSTRATIONS BY JAMICHAEL HENTERLY

Leviathan

KATHMANDU WAS COOL AND LUSH and muddy from the monsoon. The rail-thin Newar officials at the customs bench passed my bags along with an air of persecuted indifference and returned rapidly to their cold, white tile offices where they huddled in tight crowds around huge pots of tea on kerosene stoves. The odors of East and West mingled with the crowd in the airport lobby: leek and wool, deodorant and leather. The mistral wind gathered from the fields the oxymoronic scents of jet exhaust and ox dung. I hired a stern, hawk-nosed beggar standing near the gate to help me with my belongings and signaled for a taxi.

The city was crowded and surging, much the way I remembered Saigon. Instead of soldiers, though, there were Gurkha policemen wearing crisp khaki shorts, holding long, peeled switches, and sharing street corners with sniffling Dutch junkies. Instead of Montagnards, Tibetan refugees trotted to market in their red and black rags beneath enormous bundles of willow and alder twigs. Japanese taxis splashed the ooze and crap of the open sewers onto sidewalks and sacred cattle. Dogs lay dead and bloated in the streets. And I, Ishmael O'Brien (you can call me Izzy), found in the back pages of the *American Alpine Journal* by an English eccentric, was once more a pilgrim in someone else's cause. In the thirteen years since my last visit to the Orient, the only thing I'd learned was climbing.

I took a room in the older section of the city at a hotel named the Kathmandu Guest House. There was an enclosed cobblestone parking area out front with a small restaurant off to one side. A yard in the back was furnished with white, metal chairs and graced with parallel rows of neat Sussex gardening. The room had four beds and a large balcony overlooking the main entrance. The manager assured me that the beds were clean and that the water in the showers was always hot. A very attractive woman stood beside me speaking to one of the clerks in fluent Nepali as I paid a week's advance on the room. She wore a black leotard top with puffy, black silk trousers and Tibetan slippers. I thought her to be in her late twenties, possibly European, maybe American. We turned together toward the door.

"It's up there, just left," she told me in a strong Australian accent as we approached the stairs. Then she smiled. "And good luck with the showers."

She walked quickly away from any possibility of a conversation, and I hiked my three leaden rucksacks up the steps. I dumped out everything onto the floor of the room and spent an hour separating my own things from the expedition equipment I'd brought with me. The sun came out and the cement steamed. The humidity sat in my lungs like water. I put on a T-shirt and nylon running shorts and stood at the window for a time looking out on the haze of the Himalaya with my mind full of autumnal Colorado.

After a short nap I ate a light supper in the restaurant outside the hotel and walked through the city to Freak Street in the European Bazaar. The evening light was golden and coruscant. A small, wrinkled Hindu in dirty cotton pajamas stopped me as I passed under an enormous lattice of bamboo scaffolds leaning against the side of an ancient temple. He took my arm and pressed a small plug of black hashish into my hand.

"If you like," he grinned, as harmless and beatific as Timothy Leary, "you come back."

I walked through the booths and stalls until dark, then climbed stairs to a second-floor coffee and yogurt shop. The owner was a Frenchwoman with vermilion hair and eyes that hung in her head like broken bulbs. She brought me a bowl of sherbet with a mint leaf. With my spoon I crushed the hashish into powder against the table top and sprinkled it on the sherbet. All around me names and phrases were carved into the wood in a babel of tongues. When I went back outside, my head was dancing like a trout on April water. I shuffled brainless and awed down side streets where naked twenty-five-watt bulbs backlit alley scenes as if Vermeer had passed this way on Quaaludes. I walked aimlessly along labyrinthine passages that smelled of urine and dry rot, buzzing in pot-head amazement of everything. I followed some poor, pumpkin-faced child who seemed to me to be rich with omen, but I lost him in a web of side streets. Passing ghostly ruins and a huge, ornately carved stupa, I came to a wide, bustling courtyard filled with night hawkers and costermongers. Along the fence stood God's occasional mishaps, laughing and gossiping and swinging deformed arms or legs swollen with elephantiasis to calls of "Baksheesh, Sahb? Baksheesh?" One particularly capitalistic dwarf stepped directly in front of me, poking out his hand and forcing a perpendicular grin. His head was tilted sharply against his shoulder and the whole of his face and thorax—from skyward ear to his waist—was a single mass of featureless skin. No clavicle, no breast, no separated arm: just melted, homogenous flesh. An unfinished man; an act of staggering cosmic felicity and umbrage. I studied him for some time, then shook the outstretched hand, thinking to myself that, no, this was indeed not Boulder. I had come a long way on the strength of a voice over the phone and a ticket in the mail.

Two days later, on the eleventh of October, two of the others arrived. I met them at the airport and helped them pass through customs. They had met for the first time in Delhi but weren't able to sit together on the crowded flight to Kathmandu. I had no difficulty, however, in picking them out from among the other passengers.

Hamish Frazier was robust and heavyset, with a great, ginger-colored beard that flew loose at his temples and thinned to premature baldness atop his rosy, weathered head. His woolen shirt, tucked carelessly into baggy trousers, barely restrained his huge chest and shoulders. For a climber he had a surprisingly large paunch; for a Scots mountaineer he looked absolutely right. I liked him immediately.

Metilkja Martincz was a different sort altogether. A European hard man, he was taller, very dark, and somber. He seemed broodish: tender, angry, and contemplative. His hair hung in a tousled mop; his shoulders were enormously broad, and his hands were almost comically outsized. My hand seemed to disappear in his grasp when we met. Yet his clothes matched, and he was the only one of the three of us I would have called handsome.

Frazier and I loaded most of the gear and ourselves into two taxis while Metilkja went off to the Yugoslavian Embassy to straighten out his visa and visit some old acquaintances.

"Fookin' pigsty, this place, eh, Jimmy?" Hamish enthused as we sped toward town. "Third time I've been here and I'll be boogery if it smells any better. It's the fookin' cows, ye know, lad? Aye, ye can't have 'em muckin' about the fookin' kitchen without expectin' 'em ta draw flies now, can ye?" Then, turning back to me, "Where ye got us puttin' up ta doss, lad? The Kathmandu?"

I nodded, somewhat disappointed.

"Right as fookin' rain, then, Jimmy! I imagine there's the usual clutch of Aussie quim standin' by, right? It's a long good-bye on that, these voyages, in't it, laddie?" He laughed ironically for a moment and then turned to watch Kathmandu arrive. After a time he looked back at me, suddenly more serious. "When's the Major sneakin' inta town?" he asked, as we careened around a corner, scattering shoppers. "I'll bet a pint he dinna tell ye, now, did he? He's a bit queer for surprises, that one."

He paused, seeming to think that over, then started in again. "Fook, I'm hoongry. That wee spot next door still there? Bit dear, I thought, but the woggies cook a potato right. What sort of name did you say Ishmael O'Brien was, anyway, lad?" On and on like that, episodic monologues, almost all of them rhetorical, and less than half, I suspected, meant to be heard.

We hauled the gear upstairs and spent the rest of the afternoon dividing it into two dozen separate piles. "I've a wee taste, O'Brien," Hamish finally concluded. He looked tired from the long flight and the heat. We put on clean shirts and went downstairs to the Star Restaurant. The Nepali owner showed us to a table in the corner beside the woman I had met a few days earlier. " 'Ello, Sheila," Hamish muttered in a shammed Australian accent as we took our seats. She never lifted an eye, just kept to her book and tea. Frazier rolled his eyes and ordered six beers.

I had expected him to be more aggressive, louder as a drinker, but mostly we sat in silence. We both drank our first two bottles before he even spoke. He asked if I'd ever met the Major. I said, no; in fact, I knew very little about the man. Hamish looked at me doubtfully, almost angrily, for an instant, then switched his gaze to the room.

"Well, don't you be believin' everything you hear, O'Brien. He's all right. A bit odd, maybe, boot who isn't a bit queer comin' on these fookin' crusades, eh? Aye, you get caught up in somethin' like this, spendin' your money, dear as it is, to take a whack at killin' yerself for ten minutes o' standin' in the wind on some nameless mountaintop. Vicar's tits, mon, it'll make ye a bit funny, then, won't it?"

He was silent again for a moment, searching for the right words.

"You rich, O'Brien?"

I told him no.

"Major's rich as fookin' Croesus, I reckon," he said. "Probably crazier than a fookin' Cumbrian goose, too, for all I know about behavin' in public. But I kin tell ye this. He's a right hard man to have with you on a pissup, strong and steady as any I've ever seen touch axe to snow. Aye, game as they come and a straight man with ye, too. The type that'll see ye through a shitstorm without a word."

We sat quietly for a while. We each ordered another bottle of beer and Hamish got a sandwich. I asked him if he knew much about the mountain or the route. He said no, only that the Major had taken a close look at it the year before during his solo attempt. Some people, he added, were saying the usual thing about its being the hardest thing attempted at that altitude. The Major had spent two-and-a-half weeks on it by himself, he explained. No food at the end, bad weather, and, for a while, not much hope of getting down alive.

"Lost his mind up there, I suppose," Frazier said without emphasis or lifting his eyes from the remains of his sandwich. "Reckon he thinks he can find it again up on top. We'll bloody well find out about that when we get there, I guess."

He got up, winked, and threw a few rupee notes on the table. I watched him walk out and ordered some tea and a slice of pie. The food came after a while, and I picked at it, trying to sort through my thoughts. I hardly heard her voice.

"You going with them, then, Yank? Is that it?"

It took a moment before it occurred to me that she had spoken. The atmosphere around her had been so hard I didn't imagine it could be talked through. When I turned, she was facing me, smoking a small cigarette wrapped in brown paper. She was impossibly beautiful. I was stunned and a little drunk and desperately in love.

"Yeah," I stammered, trying to sound urbane and casual. "We're a mountaineering exped—"

"Right," she cut in, "the Kahli Gurkha bunch. I know. The southwest face, I believe?" I nodded and she went on. "The Leviathan—or something like that. Isn't that what you're calling it? Much better name than the Nepali one, I'm sure. Probably bloody hard to go about raising money to climb a mountain with a name the bankers in London can't pronounce. 'The last great problem,' " she mused cynically. "Get you laid back home, mate?"

I was shocked dumb. Titillated and overwhelmed.

"Look," she semi-apologized, "I work for the Sherpa Cooperative. I get all this shit across my desk season after season. Every year it's someone off to tame the hardest mountain, the worst route, the steepest face. Christ, our records are like obituaries of who's-been-who in the Himalaya for the last twenty years. The young and the starry-eyed off to get themselves killed for the greater glory of European alpinism and usually taking a few Sherpas with them. Hoo-fucking-rah, mate. I haven't seen a bloody Yank over here with his head on right yet, and you're just the same as the rest of them."

"Thanks," I grinned. I think I grinned. I tried to grin.

"Oh, look. . . . I've offended you; I'm sorry." She smiled and seemed to slow down for a moment. "Listen, I'm a bit off, I guess. I don't mean to come down like your bloody Mum or anything. It's just that I've seen this same act repeated so many times since I've been here I get the feeling that somebody ought to step in and say something, whether it changes anything or not!" She caught her rising frustration this time and sat back with it against the bench. She shook her head and smiled. I wondered if she could hear my heart beating.

" 'One climbs to know oneself,' " she recited, " 'and in so doing at last comes to know nothing. The being has been no more than the doing.' " She lit another cigarette, cupping her hand over the flame and letting the significance settle. "Does that mean anything to you at all?"

"Sure," I shrugged. "I guess it does."

"I knew it wouldn't," she replied after a pause. She smiled again and exhaled smoke. Westerners seem to glow with spiritual one-upsmanship when they have mastered the recitation of some enigmatic Zen parable.

"Do you know what a *chod* is?" she asked next. I shook my head no. "It's a tantric rite whereby the true believer commits himself to encountering his worst fears. A monk, for example, who finds he is frightened of the spirits he believes to inhabit a graveyard will spend a night meditating in the graveyard. Defeating fear: meeting the dragon and finding out that it is only air, the creation of his own imagination." I nodded my head, anticipating the lesson. "That is why you climb. Because you are afraid to. It is your *chod*."

"My mother will be crushed," I told her. "Quitting college was one thing, but if I turn into a monk, it's going to kill her." I smiled and she did not.

"The monk cleanses himself," she continued. "He goes expecting nothing and thus is prepared to accept everything. He empties himself of ambition. You, on the other hand, are not going to the mountain—you are going to the summit. Even if you succeed, you fail, because you never left New York or Iowa or wherever you're from. You just brought it all with you. You transpose instead of travel. There will be no understanding because there will be no humility. You do not come to find your God; you come to challenge Him. You long to stand upon the summit, not to be near God, but to slap His face. The mountain is just your method, your tool, and therefore it holds no revelation for you. There will be no truth of success, no conquest for you. The only God you will see will be Masta, the mountain god of horror." She stubbed out her smoke and leaned closer.

"Look, don't be daft, will you. Your Major. I've heard the Sherpas talk about him. None of them will work for him. You know that, don't you? They call him a *sennin*, a bloody mountain lunatic! That's why he's had to go ahead to Khandbari to find people. No one in Kathmandu will—"

"Look, lady," I cut her off, "I appreciate the introduction to Zen 101. I'm sure everything you say is absolutely true." She started to speak, but I held up my hand. "Honest to Buddha, I don't know what the hell you're talking about. You've got the wrong guy. I'm just good old, time-flogging Izzy O'Brien, and all I'm doing over here is going to climb a mountain. No spiritual mission, no ghosts or anything; just see the sights and do a little climbing. You can read whatever you want into that, I guess, but where I'm concerned, that's all there is to it."

She started to speak again.

"That's it," I almost shouted. "I'm sorry; I'm just not that complex. Christ, I thought *chod* was a frigging fish or something." She laughed over that one. She let her head fall back, and her wonderful breasts vibrated beneath her leotard. I grinned, feeling stupid again.

"Look, mate," she said finally, "I'm awfully sorry. Your pie is getting cold." We both laughed until the mood seemed better. "My name is Lucy," she added, sticking out her hand for me to shake. "Tell me, O'Brien, do you abuse drugs?"

We said goodnight on the steps below her door. She put her hand on the side of my face, but I made no effort to kiss her. I was beyond arousal, drug-sodden, bewildered, strangely mordant. I listened to her door close and went out onto the balcony. It was 3:00 A.M. and the city sighed. Its potpourri scent and amber lights lolled on breezes that rustled the palm fronds in the garden. Fred Astaire would have danced. I just weaved awkwardly toward our room and slipped quietly through the door, threading mounds of gear.

Hamish was in the far bed, snoring and gagging in perfect tranquility. I took off my shirt and trousers, Lucy still cartwheeling through my brain, and slipped under the sheets of my bunk. There was a grunt—distinct, sleepy, and very near—and an unexpected contact with skin. I dove out of bed yelping "Jesus!" and rolled sideways along the floor. Behind me the entire surface of the bed seemed to rise. I collided heavily with a rucksack and struggled wildly to get the ice axe off it.

"That'd be Metilkja, lad," Hamish explained sleepily. "Bonnie great booger he is. Aye." Then he drifted back into sleep. The Yugoslavian sat smiling as I circled warily to the next bunk, ice axe in hand, trying very hard to seem collected and poised.

"Goot day," he said pleasantly.

"Good day," I told him.

In the morning we went to work on the gear heaped on the porch, dividing, listing, and crating the food, tents, clothing, climbing equipment, and personal belongings into eighty-pound loads. We packed the loads into plastic garbage cans and covered them with burlap sacks. For two dollars a day a porter would carry one of the loads plus his own food and shelter. Lousy union, but they were still known to strike on occasion; so we were giving away sunglasses, tennis shoes, socks, and mittens. We also had cheap windshirts, with "Leviathan" emblazoned on the back, packed away for extra commercial leverage later on, should it become necessary. We worked steadily and without much conversation. The sky was clear, and the cement floor reflected the tropical heat at us. It was the first hard work of the trip. Our T-shirts darkened with sweat. Metilkja played depressing Croatian symphonies on his tape recorder. We dragooned a number of gleeful children into fetching pot after pot of tea for us. Hamish referred to the process as the British colonial touch.

By midafternoon we had tied off the last package. Twenty-six plastic garbage cans stood in a row, each with "International Kahli Gurkha Expedition" stenciled on the side in red letters. "Don't seem like much when you think about it," Hamish observed, as he clipped an inch off the mainspring of the scale we would carry to weigh out the loads.

"We must be fast on mountain," Metilkja explained, sounding like a Swiss guide with a mouth full of marbles. "Odervise. . . ." He grinned and patted his stomach. "Get very thin."

"Right, well, I reckon starvin' is probably goin' ta be our last fookin' worry on this whale hunt," Hamish laughed. "Puttin' up the route is goin' ta be the hard part."

"Alpine met-tod," Metilkja concluded. "Goot weather, we climb fast." That seemed to me to be about the beginning and the end of it. Get and go; what else could you say? Not enough food or rope to stick it out for long, anyway. "If you want to last, you got to go fast," was the expression we had used in Yosemite. No pain, no gain.

We all took cold showers—the hot water was mythical—got into our best clothes, and went out on the town for supper. The three of us and all our gear were scheduled to be flown out in the morning, and the atmosphere of celebration was dampened only by the question marks surrounding the Major's absence. Behind the laughter was the lingering sense that he was already on the expedition and we were holding him back, slowing him down. I think we all had the feeling of wanting to show him we were as committed and hungry as he was, which was probably just the way he wanted us to feel.

We walked back through the city in the last light. Kerosene stoves burned in the small shops and market stalls; rice and lentils and black tea boiled in tin pots. People were bustling past us on foot and pedaling bicycles. A water buffalo lay on its side in the street, legs bucking spasmodically as its freshly decapitated head was raised through a haze of flies to a butcher's bench. Rich, crimson blood pumped into the gutter. The same dull lights threw yellow halos around every act of love and antipathy. Turning to take the unpaved alley that led down to the guest house, we passed a beggar lurking in the shadows behind the wreck of a Datsun taxi. He crept out into the dirt behind us, crouched over slightly to one side, thin and tattered, a crude bamboo crutch held under his right arm. He was wearing the emaciated remains of what had once been a down parka. We

had never seen a beggar so close to the guest house, and his appearance caught us by surprise. Hamish took a threatening step toward him, and the beggar cringed back pathetically.

"No, Sahb! Please no, Sahbs," he pleaded, bending even lower to emphasize his terrible harmlessness. "Sahbs go Kahli Gurkha, please?" he asked.

We looked at each other. Hamish answered, "Aye."

"No go, Sahbs. Very bad, you go. Not good mountain. Masta go Kahli Gurkha. Avalokita Ishvara not go that mountain. Cannot see Sahbs. Masta live mountain. Sahbs go back America, please!" His voice broke with a sob. He paused and caught his breath. When he began again, his voice seemed to have changed, to have risen an octave. "Baksheesh, Sahbs? Baksheesh?" His shriveled, cupped hand stuck out at us from his rags.

"G'won, git, ye wee fookin' chough!" Hamish scowled and turned to join us. The beggar dodged off into the darkness, and the three of us walked back to the guest house in a profound and insulated silence.

We flew east. The valleys dropped away below us to isolate small hamlets on hogback ridges. No roads marred the landscape. I had been told in Kathmandu that atavistic Hindu sects still conducted human sacrifices in villages not forty miles from where commercial jets disgorged loads of camera-toting tourists on high-adventure tours of the world's most remote region. To the north, the Himalaya lay in the translucent shrouds of the monsoon season.

We landed on a grass runway with a miniature stucco terminal topped by an unattended bamboo control tower. A complement of police, militiamen, traders, and the curious stood watching. Our porters were waiting—thirty of them—under the direction of a rakish, good-looking sirdar named Ang Phu. We shook hands and left him to straighten out the load-carrying while we hiked the six miles into Khandbari, where, we had lately learned, the Major was awaiting our arrival.

The path was six feet wide, gentle, and well used. At the end of each uphill pitch, benches curled in the shade of walnut or plane trees. Everywhere, small Buddhist prayer walls and tiny stupas were decorated with brightly painted mandalas and symbols. It began to rain after we had walked an hour or so. We unfolded our umbrellas and stopped by a rickety tea shop for *chai* and cookies. A Nepali child watched us drink. Her mother brought us bananas, for which Metilkja arose and thanked her with a deep bow, sending her giggling uncontrollably back into a corner. Her husband, a withered and

tough-skinned old man, brought out his faded ledger. It showed that he had carried for several expeditions going into the Makalu area. We nodded. He smiled and came to attention, saluting. "Ed-mund Hil-lary," he pronounced carefully.

We arrived at the guest house in Khandbari around five. Ang Phu had caught up with us and showed us to a room with five or six straw pallets where we dropped our light trail sacks and went downstairs to join Major Abrams. He had arranged a side room for dinner and met us at the door.

A tall, lean, dark-haired man in his late forties or early fifties, the Major had sunken cheeks beneath a heavy beard, surprisingly narrow shoulders, and an awkward, almost feminine dimension to his posture. Much to my surprise, he walked with a marked limp, one leg being noticeably shorter than the other, though he was obviously not crippled. His squinted eyes threw out deeply weathered crow's feet around the most intense glare I have ever seen. His presence was commanding, whole and authoritative; there was a cool, almost military ferocity about him that made calling him Major far easier than using his Christian name.

He shook hands with all of us. A solid, measuring grip. "Ah, Mr. O'Brien! The American," he grinned. "Good, you've got long hair. Something to pluck you out of the crevasses by!" We all laughed. As we took our seats around the table, I thanked him for his help and for the photos he had sent me.

"I'm afraid I really haven't been much help at all," he apologized, "but you're welcome, and I thank you for the compliment. As you all know, things have been very difficult trying to put this trip together on short notice. Lost paperwork, troubles with permission, the usual Nepal muck-up. Didn't give me much time to help you lads at your end, I regret to say."

We all assured him that things had run very smoothly for us, largely owing to his efforts, and that we all were keen for the climb. He asked pointed, knowledgeable questions of each of us as we ate. Occasionally he would jot down a note or pause with his head back, studying a response. He seemed warmer and more accessible than I had dared imagine. I thought of Lucy's ersatz Buddhist hyperbole and nearly laughed out loud.

After we were done eating and everyone but me had produced a pipe, the Major ordered *chang*. It was served hot, in tall bamboo gourds. It smelled richly alcoholic and was the color of milk. Seeds and rice and bits of leaves floated in it innocently. "To Kahli Gurkha," the Major smiled, raising his gourd. "To the Leviathan. To us!"

We raised our *chang* after him. "To the Leviathan."

In the days that followed we hiked along the single spine of a long, fertile plateau. The Arun River lay to our left, gray and floury with the silt of unseen glaciers. On our right the terraced fields were black and ripe. We bought potatoes, carrots, and radishes along with an occasional chicken to supplement our trekking diet of rice and *tsampa*. The Nepalis we met on the trail were tolerant and friendly, although at night when we set up camp near their villages, the aggressive mobs of curious onlookers made us feel tense and militant.

Ang Phu had hired an assistant, a bull-shouldered comedian named Bahm, and two cooks, whom we called Sears and Roebuck. Ang Phu explained that he and Bahm owned a trading business and a small hostel together in the Khumbu-Everest area. Both of them had wives and children and were as glad as we were to be away on an expedition. They were intelligent, articulate, sophisticated men out to do a little work and have a little fun. Mornings, we could hear them laughing; always, as the first sun touched the tents, a cup of tea and a warm *chapati* came through the front flap at the end of a square, brown hand.

None of the rest of us were particularly gregarious men; perhaps the Major and I the least. Hamish could be loud and obscene, and he and Metilkja would walk together from time to time; but by and large we traveled alone on the trail. We carried simple lunches of candy and biscuits in our pockets. Sometime around midday I would stop at a tea shop, sit at one of the tables, and shout *"Namaste!"* to the porters as they came by under their huge loads.

The whole experience for me was an ongoing vision of incredible poignance and beauty, intensified by my solitude. Images of magnificent and seemingly untellable pulchritude were framed by even greater scenes of almost hallucinatory splendor. I stood in awe of every hut, every rhododendron, every detail. It was a walk like a dream, a fantastic trot. I watched huge leeches wavering at peristaltic attention from the ends of trailside leaves, with tropical wildflowers setting off their grotesque dance in a dazzling profusion of colors and shapes. The sun rose out of the high jungle above Darjeeling and set in the forbidding aridity of the Kampa Mustangh. I took my time and exposed roll after roll of film. I crouched underneath my umbrella during the afternoon showers and wrote long, jovial letters to Lucy and my family. I wrote about the mountain as if it were the Panama Canal: a place one sailed through, not one where people worked and died. I was very brave in print, of course, incapable of even alluding to the possibility of death. There, in the jungle, far away from the wind and snow, I was immortal.

We dropped down from the last Nepali villages, crossed the Arun on a primitive hemp-and-cable bridge, then hiked uphill for a day to the village of Sedua. For the Khumbu Sherpas it was like a voyage backward through time to what Namche Bazaar must have been like before it was "civilized." We called it Dodge City, guarded our baggage carefully, and moved on as soon as we could.

The days grew colder and clearer. We climbed steadily. At Shipton Col, I caught up with the Major; he was standing alone, above and to the right of the trail, his piercing eyes fixed on the northern horizon. We were at 14,000 feet and it was cloudless, perfect. Makalu, the fifth-highest mountain in the world, stood out spectacularly. Just to its east I saw Kahli Gurkha. It seemed small by comparison, but even at this great distance its awesome southwest face—the Leviathan—stood out in startling relief. Illuminated by the southern, postmonsoon light, it shone bronze- and sepia-colored with a blue-white fin of ice along its spiral summit ridge. As Abrams stepped down, his lips were moving wordlessly and his fists clenched so tight the knuckles seemed ready to burst his skin. He strode away from the crest and off toward the Leviathan in brusque, electric silence.

Supper was quiet that night. For the seventh consecutive night we shoved rice and *tsampa* around our plates without much enthusiasm and went to our tents early. Sometime after midnight I got up to urinate and stood for a long time in the moonlight looking down into the Arun Gorge. It was dark down there, as opaque as dirt. I could hear things bumping around: mysterious objects as basic as mud shoving each other about, shifting to the downbeat of eternity. The river, a black scratch on a torpid moonscape, gusted its Pleistocene melodies, life's earliest sonata. Sighs from the center of the earth hissed their valley song and stirred our nylon houses. I listened for a long time. Walking back in the metallic light, I heard the counterpoint: a dreamer in his guttural, midnight torment. I heard the lost soul of mankind, the private horror of such fragile limitation in such a hard and unlimited universe that it knew of no words. I knew, of course, that the dreamer was Abrams, and that his photos had told us far less about the mountain than his nightmares did now.

Early in the afternoon, two days later, we stood in a gentle snowfall outside the sturdy yak-herders' hut at Kahli La that was to be our base camp. After weighing out their loads, Ang Phu paid off our porters and sent them away with their socks, shoes, and Leviathan windshirts. Bahm and the two cooks built a kitchen out of field stones and our huge canvas tarpaulin. We sorted through the loads and heated water for tea. The mountain was veiled in dense clouds, and we neither spoke of it nor looked in its direction. It was there; that was enough to know.

We broke into our best food and had a superb dinner of beef stew with potatoes and barley. The Major produced a can of pears and a large gourd of a Nepali liquor called *rakshi*. For the first time in several days the conversation that night was animated and crude. The Europeans smoked their pipes and talked about climbing in the Alps. I went outside and dug into the small traveling stash Lucy had given me. I stood beside the river taking long draws and feeling the snow wet my face.

The snow fell steadily for a week. Avalanches sloughed off the peaks around us and roared unseen above the low-hanging clouds in the valley. We sat inside and waited. We killed time reading, writing letters, and playing with our equipment. I hung one of the single-anchor bivouac platforms in the branches of a poplar and watched the Europeans struggle with the notion of sleeping suspended in it. They, in turn, grinned at my lame enthusiasm for the cans of bacon and kippers they included in our climbing rations. We packed it all into our rucksacks along with rockclimbing gear, ice screws, pots, and stoves, then for a week we lifted, weighed, divided, and revised our loads. Hamish built a sauna out of willow wands and our tent flies. We would sit in it until the sweat exuded from the soles of our feet, then run and jump naked into the frigid Arun. The Sherpas loved it. They would always gather to watch the spectacle and laugh hysterically.

During the sixth day the snow came down heavily. By noon we were sitting in the hut, idle as monks, and listening to the almost constant rumble of the avalanches above us. We warmed our hands on teacups. The Major sat in a corner smoking his pipe and writing in his journal. An unusually loud, baritone roar drew all eyes to the ceiling. "That ought to clean the face," Hamish mumbled. The noise grew nearer and deeper. The ground shimmied. Our eyes came down to meet one another's. Outside we could hear Ang Phu's excited voice and the other Sherpas shouting. Pots and pans began falling.

"Ja-sus fookin' Christ!" Hamish suddenly bellowed. "It's comin' right fer home!"

We leaped simultaneously to our feet and pushed each other through the door, bounding miraculously through the kitchen without knocking over steaming pots, hitting the clearing on the run, and splitting in three separate directions. The ground quaked, and the shock wave blew snow horizontally at our backs, though by the time I had reached the trees at the riverbank the slide had lost its momentum in the talus breaks above the hut. I stood against a tree to catch my breath, watching the air clear. The main tongue of the avalanche had reached to within a hundred feet of the shack. A few small boulders were still rolling on the debris-strewn lower surface of the slide as Hamish approached.

"Christ's eyes, eh, laddie?" he laughed, wiping mud off his sweater. We walked back together. Metilkja and the Sherpas approached from the opposite direction. Metilkja explained with surprising seriousness that he took this to be a sign, that someday one of these was going to catch up with him. For all the noise of a few moments earlier, there was now an incredible stillness. Effort and release.

The Sherpas set to reconstructing the kitchen, and the three of us ducked back into the hut. The low door on the side of the building facing the mountain was open. Abrams was standing outside, some distance away, smoking his pipe, hands in pockets, and staring up at the Leviathan as it appeared in glimpses caught through the swirling clouds. Snow powdered the ground between where he stood and the hut, but I saw no trace of footprints. He had been there when the snow came. He had walked toward the avalanche, not away from it. It had stopped at his very feet.

The next morning dawned spectacularly clear—cloudless and sharp. We rapidly put the final touches to our gear and slipped into our windsuits. Ang Phu and Bahm served us a special breakfast of Sherpa horseradish on buffalo sausage with oatmeal, and fried potatoes covered with sweet syrup. Hamish honed his crampons and ice axe with a hand file. Metilkja painted his nose and cheeks with zinc oxide. It was going-up day. Abrams wrote a few notes, closed his journal, and placed it in a small plastic satchel hanging near the door. He tapped out his pipe and stuck it in his shirt. His face was set and hard. This was it, the point of it all, and I couldn't imagine any human being with whom I would rather have gone up on the mountain. Abrams had the power. You could feel it in everything he did that morning. His obsession was like a magnet, a beacon. I was amazed at my own fanaticism. The pointlessness, the triviality and expense, the whole dramatic absurdity that underlay our climb struck me at that moment as the most important purpose my life could ever have.

The Major stood and stretched. "Well, lads," he said, his quiet voice suggesting neither a question nor command. The three of us rose and he nodded.

"Major-Sahb!" Ang Phu called from the kitchen. "Mens coming Makalu. Four, maybe five. Come down valley very near now, Sahb!"

We followed Abrams through the door and saw the men emerging from the trailhead at a willow thicket. They looked grim, bent on a mission of importance and solemnity. The snow sparkled in the sunlight and crunched beneath their huge boots. The Leviathan, cut from the cobalt sky, stood massively indifferent to our meeting. Waiting.

We all shook hands. Their leader explained that they were Dutch, part of a team attempting the south face of Makalu. Tears welled suddenly in his eyes. One of their members, he said, his son, the expedition physician, was missing. He had gone out of one of the tents at high camp two nights earlier and simply disappeared. They wanted our help to search for him. It was two days' travel to their base camp; the search would last no more than a few days, then they would give up. We could be back in a week at the most.

Abrams never blinked. He never paused to search for words. "You are welcome to food and tea here," he said. "You may take our Sherpas to help you if they are willing to go with you. Ang Phu, there, is a fine mountaineer, as competent as any European, I assure you. But we did not travel this far to lose hold of our goal because you have lost yours, sir. I shouldn't ask that of you, gentlemen. I'm sorry. That's final. I hope it all comes out well for you. I wish you good luck and Godspeed. Good morning, gentlemen."

He turned and walked to his pack, brought it up onto his shoulders, and started toward the glacier. Less forcefully, the three of us fell in behind him.

"It is you I feel sorry for!" the leader of the Dutch party screamed after us. "I pray that you will find the same charity on your mountain that you have shown us, Abrams!"

The Major did not recoil or turn around upon hearing his name. It was hard to tell if he was even aware of its having been said.

We climbed steadily throughout the day. The going was not technically difficult, and we found the heat to be more of a problem than the crevasses or icefalls. At noon we stopped and took out the ropes. As the angle increased, the snow became wet and heavy. We sank in to our knees and ran short of breath beneath our monstrous loads. We dug a platform into the side of a crevasse and spent a comfortable night. The incline and mire increased all the next day. We reached the bergschrund where the lower glacier fractured at the base of an 1,800-foot ice face and carved out another small platform. We melted snow for tea and tried to make sense of what rose above us. The scale was out of proportion with anything I had ever experienced. The ice face led to a rock headwall, and that to the long, fin-shaped Whale's Tail. Then more snow and the summit. I stacked ropes and whistled with the stoves in joyful ignorance.

The following morning we set off at 3:00 A.M. to take advantage of the cold. We climbed by headlamps, pushing hard to reach the headwall before the sun touched the face and loosened the afternoon stone barrage. Two teams of two—slow-moving dots on a sixty-degree ocean of ice, lost and purposeful as gulls. Metilkja and Hamish, on separate ropes, took the leads. The Yugoslav seemed almost to float, one foot flat and the other front-pointing. He was economical and precise, making it all appear effortless. Hamish, on the other hand, brutalized the ice, kicking and hammering his way up, never pausing, never running down. He wore no cap in the dark, subzero cold. The Major and I came along pragmatically at the long ends of our ropes.

By one in the afternoon we stood at the base of the headwall. The mottled and broken skin of the Leviathan reached above us in a turbulent and darkening sky. Hamish and Metilkja dug a cave in the deep powder at the base of the wall while Abrams and I removed the rock gear from our packs.

The Major pointed me to a long, pencil-thin crack that cleaved a narrow buttress and seemed to widen to hand size after a hundred feet. I was the Yosemite wizard, the rock jock; that crack was the reason I was there. I reached high, placed a piton, and hammered it home.

Four hours later I was sitting on my foam pad talking about the wall with Hamish. Our cave glowed with the sparkling light of two stoves and a candle. Abrams and Metilkja cooked. The steam from our teacups hung in the warm, moist air, mixing with the smoke from Hamish's pipe. Life was as sweet and masculine as an after-shave ad. We talked about women and home the way sailors do. We ate cookies with yak butter and jam. Metilkja passed around a flask of Croatian *eau de vie*. Three hundred feet of rope was strung out on the rock above. My first contact with the Leviathan had left me ecstatic. It was more spectacular than I could have imagined: El Capitan at altitude, wide and weathered and old as infinity. Under a muted afternoon sun I had filled its cracks with my hands and feet, twisting and panting, moving quickly, charged by my own elation and energy. The clouds moved in time-lapse speed and snow began to fall—stellar, soft, collated flakes. My cheeks and hands were moist and hot. I drove a piton when the rope ran out and raised the haul sack before descending, breathless, back down to the cave, whispering, "In the morning," to myself.

The snow fell finer and harder the next day. The crack turned incipient and rotten, then disappeared altogether, leaving me swinging from sky hooks with the sweat stinging my eyes. I lost hours drilling holes for lousy bolts. Pitons I had hammered barely past their tips creaked and moved under my weight. I begged Jesus/Buddha, please, just ten more feet. My scrotum shrank in tingling cowardice. Scared to death of where I was and too frightened to go back down, I held my breath and swung on a rotten

flake lassoed from thirty feet away to reach for a huge, fragmented block. Around more corners the angle of the face dropped to less than vertical and the cracks were filled with ice. I climbed to a large ledge and secured the ropes. Less than 300 feet for the day. Abrams prusiked the fixed line to join me and we hauled the sacks. His face was contorted with impatience. He knew he couldn't have done it any faster, but he hated to depend on others, on me, to wait on the expertise and judgments of fools. It dawned on me that he did not climb out of love for the climbing. That had passed long ago. It was out of hate for the mountain, for its superiority, its naked power. And strangely, I admired that in him, wished that I could have his ruthlessness. I was his vehicle, I knew, and he could drive me faster. I would give him his snow ridge.

Early the next morning, our fourth on the mountain, we climbed the ropes to the ledges we were now calling the Hilton and pulled up our umbilical line. To get down now would mean getting up. It seemed like a significant moment; yet it passed without anyone giving it notice. The inclination of the rock continued to ease. I climbed quickly now, rope length after rope length, one boot on rock, one on snow, my mittened hands jammed between dank shelves of granite and rivulets of ice. The snow fell quietly, windlessly. Occasional breaks in the clouds let the sun through, and the rock steamed. We moved steadily up. When I leaned out to study the route, I could see the long, white tongue of snow above us: the Whale's Tail.

The day ended with the four of us suspended from a few shaky pegs without anything approximating a ledge in sight. We erected the bivouac platforms and crawled into them head to foot, the Major and Metilkja in one, Frazier and I sharing the other. The wind picked up during the night and dipped us gently. In the morning we all were eager to fold the platforms and get back to the solidity of climbing. We moved diagonally, gaining less than 200 feet of altitude in fifteen hours of work. The rock was not steep enough to hang our nylon platforms; so we chipped out whatever small grooves we could from the ice and spent the night there, suspended, with our feet stuffed into our rucksacks. We shivered silently in our individual tribulations, too far apart to pass food or drink. We popped Valium and stared into the storm-basted ribbon of sky that tacked the western horizon.

My feet were cold all night. They ached all day. I led up and left into a system of snow-clogged chimneys that left me, after several hundred feet of climbing, studying a conundrum. Above, the main chimney narrowed to a slot three feet wide and was blocked by an enormous chockstone. Both sides of the passage were coated with thick rime ice, white

and warted as the Elephant Man's keister. I dumped my pack and bridged out tenuously. My mind wandered intractably, taking me back to Boulder . . . the corner of Broadway and Pearl, to be exact. Hmmm. Bookstores and French bread, coeds and foreign cars, and—ah, yes—the "wall" at Macky crawling with punks carrying chalk bags, so close to the center of it all, dude, you could touch it. I thought of being warm again, and about dying. I looked down and saw myself tumbling tip over tail forever, the rope streaming like a purple and blue contrail, no longer flirting with space but flying at last, oh yeah.

For lack of anything else to do, I nudged up, shoulders and knees, to beneath the stone at the very back of the depression and thrust my axe up into the snow gathered behind it. Pressure, rest; effort, release. An hour later I was standing above the hole I'd chopped, fixing the ropes to a cluster of ice screws and runners. I shouted down to the others to come up. I thought I heard a voice, two shouts, perhaps more, then silence again. After a while the rope went taut with the weight of a climber. I touched the gray ice and wondered: how long? We were on the Whale's Tail, riding the very back of the beast.

The night was horrid and everlasting. I was utterly spent and passed the evening lapsing in and out of groggy soliloquies about how I had to rest, man, curl up in bed somewhere warm, turn on a tap and get water, rest these weary, cold, cold, arms. We sat huddled in our separate miseries and dreamed our lonely panaceas, hardly speaking, dressed in wool and nylon and feathers. My fingers pulsed, and each throb brought excruciating pains behind fingernails as white and hard as porcelain. We leaned off the edge of our sérac and shat hanging from a rope, our turds dropping soundlessly into the impossible abyss.

In the morning it was still snowing. Gentle waves of spindrift hissed down the face in filmy avalanches; so we stayed put and arranged the bivouac platforms. They lacked the gaiety of the cave—they were not so warm or nearly so bright—but they were an improvement on sitting out in the wind and cold with that dark space below and the distance above eating out our eyes.

We dined on freeze-dried shrimp creole and drank lukewarm, urine-colored tea that tasted like shrimp creole. Food and drink came, and I took it like communion. Abrams shared my platform, maintaining his complex, pontific silence. I heard Metilkja and Hamish talking quietly from time to time, but their words lacked animation or joy.

We were in deep. Very, very deep.

The snow continued and grew heavier. The spindrift slides came episodically, great waves of frigid surf breaking over us and surging into the void, where, a day earlier, and we might have joined it, hello below, tumbling and spinning earthward like paper. We packed without comment in the morning. We left behind the rockclimbing gear, a stove, the platforms, and some of the food. The hell with it: there was no going back down that way now, anyhow.

We divided into two teams again: Hamish and the Major, Metilkja and me. Hamish and the Major led off, and soon we were into the old stride, the pace of a thousand different climbs: tool, tool . . . step, step . . . rest and gasp for air, then more of the same, the brain as blank as oxygen. The scenery never varied from gray on white. The air temperature was warm, and occasionally, as the day wore on, we would hear the baseball *whoosh* of a stone. We would never see it and no one ever got hit. We were too tired to imagine any course of action other than what we were doing. Simply plod and hope. Storm-shrouded silhouettes, we climbed in egocentric removal from one another, companions in nothing more than the movement of the rope. We were shadows caught in random highlight against the whited-out sky. There was no sense of progress, no feeling of getting anywhere. Just the unabating impulse to go on.

In the murk of sunset we gathered on a small, uneven ledge and crouched leg to leg as Metilkja passed around sausage and cookies. We dug into our packs after headlamps and sweets. Without shelter it seemed pointless to try to bivouac in the open at such an altitude. So in our independent pools of light, we continued our long crawl, waiting and climbing, waiting and climbing.

The storm, of course, got worse. We were climbing upward into the nastiness of it. The wind came in violent gusts. The temperature dropped. The snow stung our cheeks and walrus snot-cicles hung from our mustaches. I went into long lapses of memory wherein I could not recall if I had been climbing or standing still. I huddled deeper within myself seeking warmth and coherence and would increasingly return to reality uncertain of what mountain I was on or with whom.

I began to hear Abrams.

At first I thought nothing of the voice. I have no idea how long I listened to it before it broke upon me that I was hearing an external sound. It was more the sporadic wail of the storm itself than of a man yelling. It was, I thought, some shrieking in my own mind. And then, clearly, I would hear it again. A shout, a sentence. I could never make out the words, but I became convinced that it *was* a voice. And in time it occurred to me that the voice was the Major's.

That it did not stop.

That he was crazy. Mad as the moon. A *sennin.*

And that I was on this mountain with him, being led by him, happy about it. Shit, I was laughing. It got so every time I heard that lunatic howl I'd grin as wide as a cat on crampons. The chaos of the storm reduced the revelation of our insanity to scale: who'd have been there but crazy people, anyway? Why go on peg-footing and stiff-lipping as if it all made sense in the first place? I loved it! I, too, felt like howling, but I couldn't find the air the Major could.

At the base of a sixty-foot runnel of water ice, the angle increased to near-vertical. I caught up with Metilkja standing roped in to a gathering of ice screws. Above us, Abrams was wailing and shouting, angry and laughing. Two hundred twenty volts of illuminated madness in that wind-bitten gloom. The stoic and dour Croat was grinning, too. We stood there smiling at each other until the screaming stopped and it was Metilkja's turn to climb. I flicked off my headlamp to save batteries and thought of Lucy. She was right, goddamnit. The Buddhists were right, too, and hell, so was the beggar in the alley for that matter. Only madmen and tantric Mansons up here, embracing their flaky *chods;* ice-men *sennins* and their mountain Masta. It was just the right place for them.

We reached the bottom of the summit ice flutings sometime after midnight. Maybe later. I remember finding Hamish hanging from all kinds of webbing and ice gear and plastered with rime.

"Major's gone up, laddies," he said slowly. " 'Fraid me hands 'ave aboot had it. Lost me fookin' mitts down there when we poot on the torches." He was trying to grin. He looked spent and sheepish, letting the rope run through hands jelled into rubbery spoons. He had his parka hood up now, but all the hours without a hat seemed to have had their effect. Metilkja took off his pack and dug into it for some spare socks to cover Hamish's hands. I took over the belay, watching Hamish as I let out the line. He seemed calm, happy, a little guilty, perhaps, but warm and unconcerned. Yet there was a blankness coming into his eyes and expression that carried the look of wistful martyrdom. When the line pulled tight to his waist, we unclipped him from the anchors and molded his hands around his ice axes. He started singing "The Hair of Her Dicky-Di-Do" and slammed in his tools.

The air seemed suddenly alive with voices. I could hear Abrams and Hamish, and soon Metilkja shouted and started climbing. We moved faster for a time. The snow stopped and the wind released us. I pulled hard, hand over hand, up the rope and turned a great, pillow-shaped cornice to reach the others clustered on the southwest ridge. The clouds below carpeted the valleys in every direction. The still-dark sky behind us shared its diamond stars with the pallid yellow blot of dawn. The Major stood in the saddle, ice axe in his hands, a serpentine black-and-beige rope hanging loose from his rucksack like the severed head of Hydra. His voice was as cracked and scratched as an old recording.

"This is it, boys!" he shouted. "Here you go! She's up there, not 500 feet, by God, and we're as good as there! Fancy foot you, O'Brien, eh? It's ours, all right, and no wind, no snow to stop us now! Not when we've come halfway around the world to put our footprints up there, I tell you. The hardest wall in the world?" He laughed, pointing the spike of his axe at the heavens. "Don't let me hear that talk again. Not in front of boys like these! Come along, then, Frazier! Another few hundred feet and you can spit in the face of the God that froze your hands, man, scuff your boots on His horrible face, if you've a mind to, eh?"

His wild hair sprang horizontally as a gust of wind carried off his woolen balaclava. The vapors danced up the wall like steam to reach for the mother-of-pearl clouds obscuring the sullen sky. The Major roared with laughter at the enormous, cosmic illusion of futility in which the mountain wished us to believe. Frazier was enraptured, his eyes glazed. Metilkja was harder to read: he went about his business neither awed nor annoyed. Myself, I grinned like a Mouseketeer for Abrams. His madness had fueled our upward determination, but getting down was going to take a different frame of mind, and I knew my best chance was with the Yugoslav. Frazier was weakening; Abrams was a whirlwind, vague as a chimera. Only Metilkja had the feel of substance.

Metilkja and I lifted Frazier to his feet and the four of us set out. The angle was easier, and we used our axes like canes. We hiked heads down into a burgeoning gale and rested on our knees. Again I fell behind the others and had only the comfort of their footprints and the Major's occasional shout until the mists parted and I saw them standing together twenty feet in front of me.

On the summit.

Abrams was hatless and howling. Frazier crouched with his frozen hands cupped in front of him as if he were holding snowballs. Metilkja stood beside him, looking away to the east. We danced staccato footsteps, buffeted by the suddenly ferocious wind. After only a few moments Metilkja looked over to me and shouted, "Down! Now!" He gestured with his ice axe in the opposite direction from which we'd come. He spoke as if we were the only ones there. Neither Frazier nor the Major paid him the least notice.

"There is no harder wall, no harder ice, no higher point upon this mountain, lads! Tea in hell, I tell you!" the Major shouted.

"Down! *Now!*" Metilkja screamed and began to stagger off into the full blast of the wind. I gave a sharp tug on the rope connecting us.

"What about them?" I yelled, pointing at Frazier and the Major. Frazier was staring straight up into heaven as the Major babbled his crazy sermon on the mount. Babes in Toyland.

Metilkja looked at me, his haggard, black eyes as hard as glass. His glance shifted for a moment to our teammates and then came back to mine. The message was clear and I understood. He turned and worked his way down, and I waited for the rope to run out before following him. I looked at the Major and Frazier as if they were apparitions. I felt nothing for them at all. In fact, I felt nothing about anything until the rope pulled tight and I took my first step down; then all I wanted to do was live. It was all lost now. Nothing was important. The climb, the summit, the entire expedition was without meaning to me. I just wanted down and Metilkja was headed that way. He did not need to pull me.

Descending into the storm was worse than climbing up to it. We had fought hard to get up, and now the mountain seemed to want to hold us there. The gale inflated our windsuits and pressed its hands against our chests. The cold was piercing and terrible. My face burned. Inside a thousand dollars worth of high-tech nylon, plastic, leather, and rubber, I felt the cold carve through me. I did not turn and look back for the others. I closed them out of my thoughts and concentrated instead on my own wooden steps. There were no voices now: the storm shrieked louder than Abrams's feeble hoots. It gave us back the proportion of our real achievement. We hadn't "conquered" the mountain any more than a rat conquers the ocean by hiding in a ship's bilge. We'd skittered across the summit and now crept wretchedly away from any protracted confrontation with the Himalaya's true adolescent savagery. We were running away on frozen feet, less victors than survivors.

The hours were fused with snow. We reached a sérac and stood in its lee to rest. My knees ached and my legs felt cold to the bone. I kept my mind off my feet. I had no idea whatsoever of where we were or where we were headed. We stood panting, our eyes interlocked. Metilkja looked withered and gaunt, awful. He motioned with his head to something behind me. Abrams came out of the storm, still hatless and striding confidently, crisp as a Yorkshire birder, Frazier staggering along after him.

"We'll be done with this in an hour, lads," the old man cheered. "We head down this ridge till we find the upper valley glacier. I looked this over last year. One man, by God! Happy me, boys, happy me! She'll not hold us off now, will she, eh? We're

too close to it now!" he barked, clenching one fist and holding it up to the sky. "By Judas, don't anyone talk to me about blasphemy! Why, I'd piss up the wind if I had a mind to. This mountain is *mine*, I tell you! Send down her storm and snow; I'll shove it up spout and stand this ice while I will!" Then, lowering his arm, his eyes on fire, he seemed to speak directly to me. "Heaven and hell by the short hairs! You'll tell them that for me, won't you? Tell them she was *mine!*"

Metilkja closed his eyes and for an instant dropped his head. When he looked back up, his face was full of the old sobriety and purposefulness. He raised his compass and studied it. I touched Hamish's arm and he looked at me. His cheeks were white, his eyes sunken back a thousand synapses from the horrible truths of the tactile world. I wanted to cry. Instead, I smiled and patted his shoulder.

"See you down there," I shouted, and he nodded his head. I walked away, knowing I would never see him again.

The rope drew me down into a well of storm. I thought about dying once more, about falling, about sitting down. I thought about heat and hallucinated a room full of stuffed chairs and couches with a stone fireplace and brandy glasses on a long table spread with a linen cloth and the dirty dishes of a sumptuous meal. Metilkja was standing in the corner of the room in his wretched, wind-torn, and rime-sheeted climbing suit. He was wiping away the ice from the headlamp he had been wearing since the night before. I turned on my own light and followed him down through the gloomy penumbra beyond the banquet and into the shelter of a crevasse wall. Just beyond, the ice fell away into an abysmal pit of hurricane updrafts and utter blackness.

Metilkja dropped his pack and pulled out a bandolier of ice screws. Nine in all. I had another six. I groped to fathom our behavior. The madman had said the ridge would bring us to the glacier and the glacier to the valley. But here? And how far down? And into this storm?

Metilkja suffered none of my neurotic ambivalence. He understood function much better than I. He knew that the doing was the important part and that the outcome would either reward or penalize our boldness. One acted out of strength without hesitation or consorting with hope. One suffered the consequences to the extent he was capable of influencing them. Everything else was either magic or religion. Metilkja threaded the rope through a carabiner and prepared to back off. The ends of the rope waved above us like tentacles, blown straight up into the night by the surging wind and illuminated by our headlamps. And again, for an instant, our eyes met. Then he was gone.

After several moments I felt the line go slack and then ran it through my braking device. I tilted backward and slipped down into the maw of the awful night.

Rappel followed rappel. The cold devoured us, and the wind snapped our sleeves and leggings so hard the material parted. My feet were lost, I knew that. I could feel nothing below my boot tops. I waited out my turns in an aura of torpor. No thought or feeling aroused me except to clip into the rope and slide down to where Metilkja would be waiting, his eyes always searching. During those silent, piercing, somber, shattering, wind-buffeted meetings, our faces were lit by the dim light of each other's headlamps like Welsh miners, and our silence was the only alternative to the storm.

I knew I was barely hanging on, slowing Metilkja down. I tried to meet his glances with my own strong gaze, but I knew he must be aware of my growing incapacity to think or move. I held tight to the ropes after he was down to keep him from pulling them through the anchor, stranding me.

And rappel followed rappel.

After so many that I had lost count, I found myself clipped to a set of ice screws, watching the flickering yellow light of Metilkja's headlamp disappear into the murk, when an enormous block of ice grazed the névé just above me and plunged on into the darkness, down the line of ropes. I was so frightened, so dazed, that I simply swung from my runner, cringing, my eyes closed for what seemed like fifteen minutes. The ropes were free when I lifted them; the stance below was empty when I arrived. Metilkja was not there. No screw protruded from the wall. No Croatian eyes. Just the night and the storm, the roaring black. I hung onto the ropes waiting for him. I poked around in the snow at my feet to see if I had missed a ledge. I swung left and right in small pendulums and called for him.

There was nothing but some crampon marks scraped in the ice.

I screamed his name, but my pathetic yap barely reached my own ears.

Perhaps he had begun downclimbing, I thought. Yes! That had to be it! The climbing was easy for him. We were going too slow by rappelling; so he had abandoned me and simply begun downclimbing. He had seen the same shadows in my eyes as I had seen in Frazier's: the confusion, the dependence I had on him.

I screamed until I couldn't breathe. I collapsed against the ropes, gasping and hyperventilating. Live, I told myself, live, you stupid fucker! You will *do* this thing. He's either dead or left you. They're all dead, but I will not die here, hanging on this wall, running away from this mountain. I slapped my arms to make the blood circulate and took an ice screw off my harness. I will do this thing and I will live. "I will live," I shouted, and pulled down on the ropes.

With two screws left I touched the glacier. I huddled in the protection of a small bergschrund and took off my pack. I crawled into my bivouac sack and sleeping bag. Among other things in my pack I found some sausage and two candy bars, along with an extra pair of mittens. My headlamp faded to dull orange. In its last light I found Metilkja's compass lying in the snow beside me.

I awoke at first light. It was overcast and snowing lightly, but the wind had stilled. I felt rested, weak but alert. I packed just the sleeping bag and a few odds and ends, then cut the rope in two and coiled half of it around my shoulders. Everything else I left to the haunting and oppressive silence.

I lost all concept of time. I followed the compass easterly with no notion of how far I'd come, how many crevasses I'd jumped or circled, no idea of how far I had to go. I found no footprints or discarded gear to suggest that Metilkja was ahead of me. The storm had consumed him as I was now being consumed. Everything was astonishingly white and featureless. I felt like Jonah, floating at peace in the saline bowels of the monster. My mind wandered out in front of me. I watched myself and laughed. I hallucinated fire and food. My body split into Metilkja's half and my half; his side was strong and elegant where mine stumbled pathetically, incompetently. I heard voices—singing, whispers, sighs—but saw nothing. No one. Just the enormous, hopeless white. I was exhausted by midmorning, traveling on slowly evolving sets of rules: walk two hundred paces and rest, two hundred paces and rest again. I lost count and rested. I lied and rested. I quit counting and rested. I came to a huge pressure ridge. Traversing around its south side, I found what looked like the trough a person might make in fresh snow. It was too blown over with spindrift to find bootprints, but I followed its vague, undulating course, squinting to pick out the subtle gradations of white.

I saw the Major from fifty feet away. I felt a remarkable absence of surprise. The color of his clothing against the blank canvas of snow and sky was sensational. He was sitting up against his pack. His skin was translucent. His eyes were open and his hands were tucked underneath the armpits of his open parka as if he had just stopped to warm himself. He was still hatless, his hair moving slightly in the ground-level breeze. The black-and-beige rope was crisscrossed over his chest and shoulders in a guide's coil. One end had been cut. I stopped in front of him. I knew he was dead; yet it would not have surprised me if his eyes had moved and his face had

turned up. Death had not taken him; he had simply exhausted life, worn it out.

Snow clung to the hairs of his face, and his trousers clapped in the wind. He continued staring back at the mountain, beckoning me to turn around, but there was nothing back there for me. Not anymore. There was nothing to say. I lifted Metilkja's compass and continued on my azimuth.

When it became dark, I used the adze of my axe to dig out a niche between two ice boulders. I emptied what little remained inside my pack onto the snow, crawled into my sleeping bag again, and pulled the pack over my feet and up to my waist. In a small stuff sack I found a tube of Chapstick. I tried to eat it and immediately threw it back up, speckling the snow with bright blood. After a time I dozed. During the night the snow changed to rain.

The air was warm and sodden when I awoke. My sleeping bag was drenched, but the rain had also washed away the snow around me, and for the first time I realized that I was no longer on the glacier. I was sitting between stones, not blocks of ice. I was on the moraine. Dirt and earth were below me. I left everything and started walking.

My feet were horrible. I began falling over everything, lying for a long time before I could rise. And then, finally, I simply couldn't get any higher than my knees. That was okay. I was prepared for that. It did not come as a shock or even a disappointment, just new rules for the game. I crawled for a while, the toes of my boots dragging in the gravel and leaving twin ruts behind me like those of a tiny ox cart. I struggled through a shallow stream of icy, fast-moving meltwater and reached a large boulder on the opposite side, where I lay back and rested. I tore off bits of my windsuit and used the strips to tie my mittens to my knees.

The rain was lighter, a fine Seattle mist. Through breaks in the clouds I could look up to splashes of green on the south-facing slopes of the valley. I noted this arrangement without elation or impatience. I was anticipating nothing. I felt no excitement.

I knew that I was off the mountain and that I would live—that, if necessary, I could crawl to the trail between Kahli La and the Dutch camp and from there crawl down to the yak-herders' hut. If the Sherpas had given up on us and left, then I knew, too, that I could keep crawling . . . over Shipton Col, past Sedua, to Khandbari, to Kathmandu, and all the way back to Boulder. It was no folly; I knew I could succeed in this *chod*.

So I progressed, staggering a few steps on dead feet and then collapsing to basic elbows and knees, shreds of my blue windsuit clinging to the ends of willow twigs. I left blood on the first grass that I

reached. I sat for long periods waiting for the energy to move, clinging always to my talisman, Metilkja's compass. I dragged myself on my stomach through thickets of willow and alder, occasionally stopping to listen for the sound of voices or feet.

It was raining slightly when I arrived at the trail. I crawled down into the rut of it—soggy with black mud and as empty as my memory—and lay there a long time, breathing slowly, letting the rain wash my face, and gazing up at the mountain through elliptical gaps in the clouds. It seemed as pristine and aloof to me as it had in Abrams's photographs.

Untouched. Unmoved. Unknowable.

Tears ran down my cheeks. I laughed. I laughed and I cried at the same time, gasping and falling over on my side, helium-headed and sick. Just me . . . of all the heartbeats and dreams, of all the struggle and obsession, I alone remained, more an abstraction than an alpinist, dumb as the last, great, silent *thump* at the end of the universe. I was all that was left. I cried and I laughed and I knew nothing. Only the mud and brush and pebbles.

And it was there that the Dutch expedition, returning with our Sherpas from the futile search for their lost son, found me, another soul orphaned by dreams.

About the Contributors

Talbot Bielefeldt has worked as a climbing guide, participated in expeditions to Canada and India, trekked in Nepal and New Zealand, and completed ski traverses across the Kashmir Himalaya and around Alaska's Mount Foraker. His stories and photographs have appeared in *Nordic Skiing, Mountain Gazette, Climbing, Northwest Magazine*, and other publications. He holds a degree in literature from Reed College and recently completed his first novel. He lives, writes, and teaches skiing in Eugene, Oregon.

Geoff Childs first climbed during U.S. Army Ranger School, an experience that temporarily eliminated any interest he might have had in mountaineering. At age twenty-seven, however, while living in Grenoble, he visited the Alps and since then has rarely been out of sight of mountains. A broken leg from a mountaineering accident in the summer of 1982 allowed him to work on "Leviathan," an idea that had been fermenting since he reread *Moby Dick* during another recuperation five years earlier. Childs is presently program director of the Pacific Crest Outward Bound School.

David Gancher isn't a mountaineer. Formerly senior editor of *Sierra* magazine, he is currently customer publications manager for Computerland Corporation, as well as a writer and a musician. He wrote "The Ascent of Typewriter Face" as a catharsis while in the midst of editing a recent Sierra Club book. He describes his effort as "an emergency rappel from the nauseous heights of some raw and rotting prose."

David Grimes has spent the last ten years living in Alaska, a long distance, in more ways than one, from his childhood home near the Ozarks. He began climbing at sixteen, in the Tetons and North Cascades, and kept heading north, both to climb and to search for "Ecotopia." Though he's ascended a few big mountains, including Denali, he prefers alpine-style rambles up the smaller and more intimate peaks that surround Prince William Sound, near his home in Cordova. When he's not climbing, Grimes can be found at sea: he is a commercial salmon and herring fisherman.

Tom Higgins is a California climber with two decades of experience clinging to rocks in various parts of the state, as well as on crags in England, Scotland, and Italy. His latest climbing achievements include two spectacular new routes on Chiquito Dome, a formation on the western slope of the Sierra Nevada. These climbs are protected by bolts placed in "agonizing, traditional style." Higgins has written about climbing for numerous publications; this is his fifth article for *Ascent*. In his other life, Higgins consults with cities, counties, states, and the federal government on transportation issues.

Charles Hood began climbing seven years ago in Sequoia National Park; since then, climbing urges have dragged him throughout the Southwest and to Alaska and England. His prose, poetry, and reviews have been published in journals ranging from *Off Belay* and *Climbing* to *Western American Literature* and *Poetry/L.A.* At present Hood is completing an M.F.A. in English at the University of

California at Irvine, with a thesis on John Wesley Powell. Living in Newport Beach, he commutes to the local boulders in an ocean kayak.

Joe Kelsey spends summers at his cabin in Jackson Hole, guiding in the Tetons and Wind Rivers. He winters in the San Francisco Bay Area, enjoying long lunches with members of the surprisingly large climber/writer community. In the spring and autumn Kelsey tires of lunching and guiding and heads for the Southwest with his collection of golden retrievers. This lifestyle doesn't allow much time for writing, but his articles have been published in *New West* and *Ascent*.

Bobby Knight migrated westward from Minnesota in search of adventure and a career after completing an undergraduate degree. An interest in skiing led him to work as a professional ski patrolman in Colorado for four years. During the past seven years he has lived in many of the western states, a victim of wanderlust. He is currently directing programs for the Colorado Outward Bound School, a vocation that keeps him close to the mountains.

Hank Levine is a photojournalist living in Bishop, California, on the east side of the Sierra Nevada. His photos have been published in *Climbing*. Levine is currently outdoor editor of a local publication, *Sierra Life*.

Jeff Long has written numerous articles for *Outside*, *Climbing*, and other publications. "Angels of Light" is his fourth and most ambitious piece for *Ascent*. Climbing is hardly his only interest: he has just completed a nonfiction account of the 1981 murders of two Idaho game wardens by "mountain man" Claude Dallas, to be published by William Morrow. Two future projects include a ghost story set during the Vietnam War (his collaborator on this will be fellow *Ascent* contributor Geoff Childs) and a biography of Robert McNamara.

Ron Matous, veteran of difficult ascents throughout North America, guides in the Tetons in the summers— when he's not bicycling around Jackson Hole or running up the Grand Teton for exercise. During the winter he teaches mountaineering in Colorado. In addition to traveling in the Karakoram, the subject of "Masherbrum, and Back Again," Matous also has climbed on Makalu, the world's fifth-highest mountain. His evocative account of climbing the notorious Eigerwand appeared in the 1980 *Ascent*.

Chris Noble is a writer and photographer whose work has appeared in *Geo, Powder, La Neige,* and *Outside.* He lives in Salt Lake City and is managing editor of the *Wasatch Sports Guide,* a magazine covering self-propelled sports throughout the Intermountain Region. Noble has climbed and guided on ice and rock across the continental United States and was a member of the expedition that made the second ascent of the Canadian Route on Denali's Wickersham Wall. "Slater's Tale" is part of a series of short fiction in progress.

David Roberts has, for the past three years, been doing the thing he most wanted to in life, next to playing shortstop for the Brooklyn Dodgers, a fantasy he gave up about the time the team gave up on Brooklyn. Roberts's second choice and current métier is writing for a living; he divides his efforts about equally between the arts and the outdoors. Among the magazines in which he has been published are *Geo, Audubon, Reader's Digest,* and *Outside.* Many of his essays, as well as a novella, have appeared in *Ascent.* He has also written several books, the latest of which is *Great Exploration Hoaxes* (Sierra Club Books).

Eric Sanford realized about eight years ago that he was spending undue time organizing and leading all the mountaineering trips he went on. So he cleverly decided to get paid for it, founding Liberty Bell Alpine Tours and guiding clients throughout his home range—the North Cascades—and various other climbing areas throughout the world. He has written about climbing for many outdoor publications, including *Ascent.* "I am currently working," he writes, "on about fifty ideas for books I will never write—but isn't everyone working on a book?"

Rick Slone, who lives in the countryside east of Pittsburgh with his wife, Joyce, spends his time climbing, skiing, surfing, or wishing he was. In addition to his climbing adventures with Norah Robertson in Scotland, Slone has climbed on Nanga Parbat, the so-called "killer mountain of the Himalaya." His account of this expedition, in which two men died, appeared in *Outside.*

Olaf Sööt began climbing and photographing in 1947 and has since traveled throughout the Western Hemisphere in pursuit of his avocation. His film "Alps of Wyoming" won the Mario Bello prize at the 1966 International Film Festival in Trento, Italy. Sööt is one of those rare individuals still practicing black-and-white mountain photography; most of the photos in this volume were taken with a Hasselblad.

Ed Webster, who directs a climbing school in Denver, is a talented and enthusiastic climber, equally adept on ice and rock. He has visited most of the country's major climbing areas, scaling the finest routes, talking with local old-timers, taking marvelous photographs, and writing about his adventures. Needless to say, Webster has an ambitious book in mind, one that will deal extensively with American climbing history, a consuming passion.

Paul Willis first tasted Alaska in 1973 as a geology student on the Juneau Icefield. For the next nine summers he led wilderness trips into the High Sierra and the Cascades. He returned to Alaska in 1976 as a member of the ill-fated National Crampoon Expedition, the experience evoked in "The Kahiltna Open." Besides Denali, Willis has many other incomplete ascents to his credit. He presently teaches writing at Whitworth College in Spokane while working on a Ph.D in English from Washington State University.

About the Editors

Allen Steck has taken part in landmark ascents of classic routes in Alaska and the Yukon, South America, and Asia; he was a member of the expedition that made the first ascent of China's Celestial Peak in 1983. He is the co-author of *Fifty Classic Climbs* and, with Lito Tejada-Flores, *Wilderness Skiing*. He and Roper are founding editors of *Ascent,* and both live in the San Francisco Bay Area of California.

Steve Roper is best known for his pioneering role in Yosemite Valley rockclimbing and for his ascents in the High Sierra. He is the author of three popular guidebooks: *Climber's Guide to Yosemite Valley, The Climber's Guide to the High Sierra,* and *Timberline Country: The Sierra High Route.* With Allen Steck he co-authored *Fifty Classic Climbs of North America.*